The Chinese Way

This volume seeks to develop new narratives on China's alternative policy and challenges policymakers on gender, regional, income and wage inequalities among rural migrant workers in China.

The book also looks at China's social, environmental, economic and governance policies aimed at implementing a sustainable financial and corporate system for a prosperous society. The argument that China follows 'capitalism or socialism with Chinese characteristics' emanates from the Eurocentric ideological narratives based on 'varieties of capitalism' and 'national socialism'. This book attempts to move away from the duality of ideological criticism and dichotomous defence of China based on the ideological prisms of capitalism or socialism. It rejects the flawed analysis of both sides of the ideological divide. For all its limitations within the world capitalist system, China's achievements can't be undermined. The attempt to undermine Chinese achievements is a process and a strategy to delegitimise the Chinese state, the Communist Party of China, the Chinese success story, and to hide the available alternatives from the experience of *The Chinese Way*.

The book will be a great read to students, researchers and scholars of Chinese studies, political economy, development studies and those interested in China's economic and public policies in general.

Bhabani Shankar Nayak is a political economist and works as Professor of Business Management and Programme Director of Strategic Business and Management at the University for the Creative Arts, UK. His research interests consist of closely interrelated and mutually guiding programmes surrounding political economy of religion, business and capitalism, along with faith and globalisation, and economic policies.

The Chinese Way
Alternative Policy Perspectives and Challenges

Edited by
Bhabani Shankar Nayak

Routledge
Taylor & Francis Group
LONDON AND NEW YORK

First published 2024
by Routledge
4 Park Square, Milton Park, Abingdon, Oxon OX14 4RN

and by Routledge
605 Third Avenue, New York, NY 10158

Routledge is an imprint of the Taylor & Francis Group, an informa business

British Library Cataloguing-in-Publication Data
A catalogue record for this book is available from the British Library

Library of Congress Cataloging-in-Publication Data
Names: Nayak, Bhabani Shankar, editor.
Title: The Chinese way : alternative policy perspectives and challenges / edited by Bhabani Shankar Nayak.
Description: Abingdon, Oxon ; New York, NY : Routledge, 2024. | Includes bibliographical references and index.
Identifiers: LCCN 2023018745 (print) | LCCN 2023018746(ebook) | ISBN 9781032568171 (hardback) | ISBN 9781032568195 (paperback) | ISBN 9781003437307 (ebook)
Subjects: LCSH: China—Economic policy | China—Social policy. | China—Cultural policy. | Income distribution—China. | China—Environmental conditions.
Classification: LCC HC427.95 .C48847 2024 (print) | LCC HC427.95 (ebook) | DDC 330.951—dc23/eng/20230620
LC record available at https://lccn.loc.gov/2023018745
LC ebook record available at https://lccn.loc.gov/2023018746

ISBN: 978-1-032-56817-1 (hbk)
ISBN: 978-1-032-56819-5 (pbk)
ISBN: 978-1-003-43730-7 (ebk)

DOI: 10.4324/9781003437307

Typeset in Times New Roman
by codeMantra

The book is dedicated to the hard working, creative and committed people of China.

Contents

List of contributors *ix*
Acknowledgements *xi*

Introduction: The Chinese Way 1
BHABANI SHANKAR NAYAK

1 **Regional differences in the gender wage differential of rural migrant workers in China** 5
GUO JINGGE AND BHABANI SHANKAR NAYAK

2 **Credit constraints for women-led micro and small enterprises in Beijing and Guangdong Province in China** 26
YIHAN LYU AND BHABANI SHANKAR NAYAK

3 **Critical reflections on the corporate social responsibility information disclosure: a case study of China Resources SANJIU from 2009 to 2020** 53
YITING ZHANG AND BHABANI SHANKAR NAYAK

4 **Impact of environmental and social governance (ESG) on the performance of Chinese companies** 83
CHENLEI WU AND BHABANI SHANKAR NAYAK

5 **Scientific research in universities and their impacts on regional economic development in China: a study of Zhejiang from 2009 to 2017** 97
JIE CHENG AND BHABANI SHANKAR NAYAK

6 **Impact of money laundering regulations on banks in China** 117
MINGCHI YANG AND BHABANI SHANKAR NAYAK

Index *145*

Contributors

Jie Cheng
Adam Smith Business School
University of Glasgow, UK

Guo Jingge
Adam Smith Business School
University of Glasgow, UK

Yihan Lyu
Adam Smith Business School
University of Glasgow, UK

Bhabani Shankar Nayak
Business School for the Creative Industries
University for the Creative Arts, UK

Chenlei Wu
Adam Smith Business School
University of Glasgow, UK

Mingchi Yang
Adam Smith Business School
University of Glasgow, UK

Yiting Zhang
Adam Smith Business School
University of Glasgow, UK

Acknowledgements

Knowledge production and dissemination is a collective endeavour to advance societies and individual lives in the path of peace, prosperity and equality. This volume is no different. I am thankful to all contributors in the making of this volume that integrates both essentialist and emancipatory ideals of knowledge traditions while critically challenging mindless criticisms of *The Chinese way* of economic development. It is a defence and comradely critique of Chinese way of the making of public policy. All inadvertent mistakes are mine.

Bhabani Shankar Nayak
London, 11 October 2022

Introduction

The Chinese Way

Bhabani Shankar Nayak

China and its path of development baffles and amuses the Eurocentric commentators and intellectuals of all varieties of ideological divide. The Chinese ability to learn, understand and expand skills, ideas and ideals in their own way led to the rise of the newfound confidence among the Chinese people. They trust their own development path and realised the limits of Eurocentric models of capitalist development. It is time to acknowledge Chinese perspectives. McGregor (2011) outlines five myths about the Chinese Communist Party while calling the Chinese path of economic development as 'Market Leninism'. Time is a great leveller against all kinds of rumours. The myths of McGregor were exposed by the forward march of China. Many such anti-Chinese propaganda have failed to stop Chinese economic growth. Mitter and Johnson (2021) have tried to outline the mistakes of West's understanding of China and its path of development. The development trajectory of China started changing its direction with the establishment of Chinese Communist Party (CCP) in July 1921 with 50 members. Most of the members were intellectuals, and a few were railway and mine workers. The party congress was held with 12 to 13 people only. After hundred years of its establishment, the CCP has 95 million parties with 4.8 million party branches in every nook and corner of China. The CCP membership is composed of 29% of female members, a quarter of members are under the age of 35, and more than 50% of members have a college degree in 2021.

From a backward and stagnant agrarian society to the industrial workshop of the world defines Chinese development, and it is a testament to the Chinese model of economic growth alternatives. The economic growth led to the rise of China from the tenth largest economy in 1979 to the second largest economy in 2022. The Chinese state under the leadership of the CCP has transformed Chinese society and lives of people in a positive and prosperous direction. As the capitalist economies and developed countries are suffering from a massive economic slump with rising public and private debt, China provides credit to the world. However, the CPC is concerned with the massive expansion of capitalist market. The Politburo of the CPC has promised to regulate and end 'disorderly expansion of capital' in its December 2020 meeting. Such expansion has accelerated risks in the field of banking, finance, housing, education and health sectors in China. It also widens different forms of inequalities and income disparities. The massive economic

DOI: 10.4324/9781003437307-1

growth and rising inequalities create contradictions in Chinese economy, which is a product of growing influence of capitalism in China. The capitalism in China is responsible for the declining of productivity, performance and profitability of Chinese economy. To face these challenges, China is building "a common prosperity demonstration zone" as part of its 2021–2025 national plan to reduce all forms of inequalities in Chinese society. It is a response to growing income inequalities in the country. The Chinese state and the CPC continue to be a party of the working-class people in China.

The Western intellectuals and their liberal distractors continue to characterise China as a capitalist state by looking at the rise of inequality, private property and commodity production with a vast network of worldwide supply chains in the country. Such arguments are emanating from both liberal and right-wing intellectuals to undermine the state-led development in China in the eyes of Chinese citizens. The idea is to delegitimise Chinese alternatives and weaken the Chinese state. In reality, the Chinese state continues to own all land and all-natural resources in the country. It continues to mobilise resources for the welfare of its masses. Despite special economic zones (SEZ), the labour power is not commoditised, and the state continues to dominate in all sectors of economy in China. Monopoly capitalism as experienced in the West is invisible in China. Some features of capitalism in collectivist Chinese form are visible in-service sectors and consumer markets which are products of Chinese engagement with worldwide capitalism. The rise of market-led depoliticised mass consumer society and its fictitious culture of consumerism is another challenge for China. It is a threat to social harmony, communitarian life, stability and culture in China.

The capitalism in Chinese form or socialism with Chinese character has failed to reverse the horrific environmental crisis. The water, air, farmlands, cities and its landscapes are polluted in a massive scale. Such a negative transformation in the age of climate crises put China and its people in a greater vulnerable position. This is a worldwide problem and not unique to China but still the CPC has failed to develop alternative policies for the protection of environment.

In March of 2005, while giving an interview to Der Spiegel magazine, Pan Yue, China's Vice-Minister of China's State Environmental Protection Agency (SEPA) said that "the Chinese miracle will end soon because the environment can no longer keep pace". He further argued that China is

> using too many raw materials to sustain [our] growth… Our raw materials are scarce, we don't have enough land, and our population is constantly growing. Currently there 1.3 billion people living in China, that's twice as many as 50 years ago. In 2020 there will be 1.5 billion… but desert areas are expanding at the same time; habitable and usable land has been halved over the past 50 years… Acid rain is falling on one third of Chinese territory, half of the water in our seven largest rivers is completely useless, while one fourth of our citizens do not have access to clean drinking water. One third of the urban population is breathing polluted air, and less than 20% of

> the trash in cities is treated and processed in an environmentally sustainable manner… Because air and water are polluted, we are losing between 8% and 15% of our gross domestic product. And that doesn't include the costs for health… In Beijing alone, 70%–80% of all deadly cancer cases are related to the environment.

He criticised the neoliberal capitalist model of development promoted by the Western countries and their economists. He argued that

> economic growth will give us the financial resources to cope with the crises surrounding the environment, raw materials, and population growth. [But] there won't be enough money, and we are simply running out of time. Developed countries with a per capita gross national product of $8,000 to $10,000 can afford that but we cannot. Before we reach $4,000 per person, different crises in all shapes and forms will hit us. Economically we won't be strong enough to overcome them.
>
> (as cited in Smith, 2015: 21)

It summarises the environmental challenges faced by China. The industrial bloom and the environmental gloom move together in China today. It questions sustainable economic growth and puts the future of China and Chinese people in jeopardy.

The Chinese banking system is dominated and owned by the state. There are private investors and private investment banks, but the Chinese government continues to be the major shareholders of these private banks. The four decades of market reforms in China did not allow markets to command the state and society in China. From banking to mining, manufacturing and all other sectors of economy continue to be under the control of Chinese state and government. The CPC plays a major role in shaping policy directions to keep the social visions of economic development where private capital always remains subservient to the Chinese needs. No doubt that there is bourgeoning of Chinese state and society but still China is not a purely capitalist state and society (Smith, 2020).

The unprecedented economic and social transformation in China during the last 50 years comes with different challenges. From environmental crisis to gender pay gap, uneven regional development and rising income inequalities are major challenges for China to overcome. The abilities of Chinese people, their state and the CPC to learn from their mistakes and adopt new strategies to overcome the crises, provide hope for continuous rise of alternatives from the resistance movements of people. The Chinese economy is growing five times higher than the capitalist American economy today. The growth trend shows that China will continue to grow faster than the capitalist G7 economies. Therefore, it is time to critically celebrate Chinese growth model while acknowledging its challenges. The state-led technologically driven economic model will address some of the major challenges China faces today.

References

Smith, R. (2020), *China's Engine of Environmental Collapse*, Pluto, London.

Smith, R. (2015), China's Communist-Capitalist Ecological Apocalypse, *Real-World Economics Review*, issue no. 71. http://www.paecon.net/PAEReview/issue71/Smith71.pdf (accessed on 6th June 2022).

McGregor, R. (2011), 5 Myths about the Chinese Communist Party, *Foreign Policy*, January 3, 2011. https://foreignpolicy.com/2011/01/03/5-myths-about-the-chinese-communist-party/ (accessed on 30th May 2021).

Mitter, R. & Johnson, E. (2021), What the West Gets Wrong about China, *Harvard Business Review*, May–June, 2021. https://hbr.org/2021/05/what-the-west-gets-wrong-about-china (accessed on 30th May 2022).

1 Regional differences in the gender wage differential of rural migrant workers in China

Guo Jingge and Bhabani Shankar Nayak

Introduction

In the post-reform era in China, the policies of the *hukou* system (household register system) have been less strict than before, which allowed massive rural migrant workers to move to prosperous urban areas to seek employment opportunities providing them with higher income than that from traditional agricultural industries. According to the *Monitoring Survey Report* of Migrant Workers in 2019 by the *National Bureau of Statistics of China*, the number of rural migrant workers reached 290.77 million, in which female rural migrant workers accounted for 35.1% (National Bureau of Statistics of China, 2020). There was a significant increase in the average monthly income of rural migrant workers from 1,417 Yuan in 2009 to 3,962 Yuan in 2019. In addition, their livelihood status, including the average floor space per person and the education level of their children, was generally improved compared with that of ten years ago.

However, despite the smaller gap of earnings between genders, general gender discrimination in earnings has still been reported in China, both in urban areas (Zhang et al., 2008) and rural areas (Dong et al., 2004), and female rural migrant workers are still suffering from serious gender discrimination (Liu et al., 2000). The importance of female rural migrant workers to the labor market is incontrovertible, however, little research has been conducted about the gender discrimination they suffer. A study on this issue may be helpful in legislation to reduce gender inequality and can support female workers to assert their lawful rights. Moreover, developed regions are often believed to have less gender inequality, which lacks empirical research result as an evidence. Research on that may be helpful to female workers in choosing the regions they work in China.

It is argued that the trend in global gender inequality has declined in varying degrees across diverse religious and cultural traditions (Zhang et al., 2008). Most countries try to prohibit gender discrimination, while some ultra-conservative countries still discriminate systematically against women. The problem is more serious in developing countries, which partially can be explained by the process of development and cultural norms (Jayachandran, 2015). Many research reports state that the Sex Ratio at Birth has increased in many Asian countries due to male bias and the spread of new technology of sex determination (Guilmoto et al., 2009). In

DOI: 10.4324/9781003437307-2

addition, discrimination against women in nearly all domains of society still has not been eradicated by anti-sexism efforts, though two hundred years have passed since the first-wave feminism rose in the Western world. Even in developed countries, the neglect of gender discrimination hides deeply in culture, such as sexist language, which concerns researchers (Douglas and Sutton, 2014). Gender inequality in health is discussed by Marmot, Friel, Bell, Houweling, and Taylor (2008). Mussida and Picchio (2014) argue larger penalties for low-educated women in the wage distribution.

Gender inequality in the workplace and gender wage differential

It is undeniable that obtaining women's right to work is a great achievement, however, gender discrimination against women in the workplace, including fewer employment opportunities, harder promotions, and lower salaries, is still a serious problem. Protsch (2021) studies the preference for male applicants by employers in male-dominated occupations based on a survey experiment conducted in Germany. As for promotion, De Paola and Scoppa (2015) state the evidence from Italian academia that proves that there is a slimmer chance of female candidates promotion with the evaluator committee composed exclusively of males.

To analyze the gender wage differential, a quantitative method was individually created by Blinder (1973) and Oaxaca (1973), which is called Blinder-Oaxaca decomposition and can divide the gender wage differential into two components. One of them is the part of differential that can be explained by measured factors, which are mostly characteristics related to productivity, such as relatively higher education level. It is positively related to wage and is observed among male workers. Another part of differential cannot be explained by these factors and is regarded as being caused by productivity-unrelated characteristics, such as discrimination against women in the workplace. Most literature analyzes the gender wage gap problem based on the Blinder-Oaxaca decomposition. Ismail, Farhadi, and Wye (2017) point out the gender wage differential is 27% in Malaysia, and 89.2% of the total wage differential is potentially attributed to discrimination against women in the workplace. Piazzalunga (2015) finds more than 60% of gender wage differential is unexplained by observable differences through analyzing data from a survey of female migrants in Italy. A similar result in Sweden is reported by Johansson, Katz, and Nyman (2005), and they argue that differences in the jobs' educational requirements significantly affect the equality of gender earnings.

The gender wage differential varies with privatization, degree of economic liberalization, and many other factors. Its cross-country differences are also noteworthy. Since reforms started in several former planned economies, state-owned enterprises, collective enterprises, and private enterprises have coexisted in these economies, and the gender wage differential in these economies has been compared and studied by researchers. Generally, discrimination against female workers in a highly competitive market usually leads to low profit, additionally, reduction of firm survival (Weber and Zulehner, 2014). Considering the earlier economic reform and deeper marketization in China than in Vietnam, it is probably the reason why Liu, Meng, and Zhang (2000) state that "overall gender wage differential declines substantially across ownership sectors from the state to the private" in research in China while the opposite result is found in Vietnam (Liu, 2004). Another research studies the difference in gender pay gap between for-profit hospitals and nonprofit hospitals in the US, which shows a higher gender pay gap in nonprofit hospitals, indicating the restraint of the competitive market on prejudice against women (Courey, 2020). Regarding cross-country differences of gender wage differential, researchers usually argue gender wage differential is negatively correlated to the degree of economic liberalization and collective bargaining (Blau and Kahn, 2001; Zweimüller et al., 2008). There is also lower gender wage differential in the economy with more egalitarian wage structures (Mandel and Semyonov, 2005).

Women are often discriminated against for their age and marital status, and they also face more serious age discrimination compared with men. Duncan and Loretto (2004) point out that discrimination may be reinforced when women face both gender discrimination and age discrimination. Married women also encounter gender discrimination for marriage. Luo (2018) studies the wages of the police, which reveals that men who are married or have kids have an income advantage, while wage premiums of women, who are married or have kids, are small and they even face wage penalties. The researcher further points out that "marriage penalty is partially explained by the stronger negative effect of motherhood on female police officers' income".

Different dimensions of gender inequality in China

Gender inequality in the workplace, including salaries, promotion, and employment opportunities, has been studied thoroughly in past literature (Isaacs, 1995). As an important aspect of it, gender wage differential has also been researched and emphasized by many scholars. Oaxaca (1973) and Blinder (1973) individually started to study the factors for the wage gap between men and women with the same productivity. The two literature and many other research papers generally show some objective characteristics, for example, relatively higher education level can explain men's advantages in wages, though they may suggest gender discrimination in other aspects (Agrawal, 2021). Some other studies measured characteristics that may indicate gender inequality in the workplace, which could also partially explain gender wage differential. For example, men's wages are less likely to be affected by local labor market conditions, which may show that women employees are expendable. The reasons for gender wage differential which have partially been explained are also called endowment part, while the rest of gender wage differential, which is unexplained, usually is deemed as the differential caused by gender discrimination (Courey, 2020).

There are many international studies on gender wage differential and sectoral differences that have been discussed in past literature, which reveal that the differences among the economies can affect gender wage gap. For example, Blau and Kahn (2001) state that gender wage gap is affected by labor market institutions, for the reason that female employees who are usually at relatively low points of wage distribution benefit more from collective bargaining. Zweimüller, Winter-Ebmer, and Weichselbaumer (2008) point out that there is a usually lower gender wage gap in economies with higher Economic Freedom Index. In addition, family-friendly policies are deemed to be negatively correlated to gender wage gap (Arulampalam et al., 2007), though Mandel and Semyonov (2005) hold an opposite opinion that cross-country differences in the wage structure are not controlled. The differences of gender wage differential in economic sectors have been researched. Liu, Meng, and Zhang (2000) point out that a higher degree of privatization of the economic sector usually leads to a relatively smaller share of discrimination in the overall gender wage differential based on a study in China. Similar research was done in Vietnam, and an opposite result was obtained (Liu, 2004). Nevertheless, the different results of the two research support the relationship between the gender wage gap and economic freedom, for the reason that Vietnam is in the earlier stages of marketization than China, so gender discrimination is more costly for the private sectors in China.

However, a common difficulty of international studies is hardly distinguishing the contribution of cultural factors to gender wage gap from the perspective of the influence of economic and political factors, which has not been faced by research at a regional level (Murillo Huertas et al., 2017). Most of the research about gender wage differential at the regional level discusses the difference between urban areas and rural areas. In addition, they generally argue the gender wage differential is larger in rural areas than in cities with the reason being assumed that the gender wage differential is reduced by relatively stiffer competition in urban areas (Phimister, 2005). The migrant workers that this study focuses on mostly work in urban areas, but few studies have been made on regional differences in the gender wage differential except urban-rural differences. Murillo Huertas, Ramos, and Simon (2017) study the regional difference of gender wage differential in Spain and point out the relative share of discrimination in the overall gender wage differential increases substantially across regions from the southwest to the northeast.

In China, gender discrimination has been reduced by two different forces (Ng, 2007), one of which is the socialist system, which existed before the Chinese economic reform and the other is market competition and feminism brought about by the Chinese economic reform. The Communist Party of China always encourages gender equality and is committed to eradicating gender discrimination, despite that its influence is shrinking after the Chinese economic reform and the effect is usually confined to state ownership now. Some researchers argue that the market competition faced by private enterprises which has emerged since the Chinese economic reform may reduce gender discrimination (Weber and Zulehner, 2014). The Chinese economic reform is also called "reform and opening up", whose impact on China is not limited to the economic field. Feminism has been welcomed in developed areas after the "reform and opening up", but its influence is very weak among people outside the middle class in big cities, such as rural migrant workers. Therefore, gender discrimination among them is rarely noticed by the public, but it has been studied by a number of researchers. Lu and Song (2006) state that no significantly lower wage is found among migrant workers based on a survey in a city, while Magnani and Zhu (2012) argue discrimination contributes largely to gender wage differential and it is more serious among low-income migrants, through a nationwide survey. Some literature about rural migrant workers also mentions the gender wage gap among them and suggests that double discrimination exists among those who are both female and migrant workers (Cook and Dong, 2011; Wang et al., 2015).

In general, gender wage differential has been discussed comprehensively in previous literature as a part of gender inequality in the workplace. Additionally, the differences of gender wage differential among different countries and sectors have been studied by many researchers. However, there is little research about regional differences which is what this research focuses on.

Chinese tradition and gender discrimination

Normatively speaking, one of the main reasons for gender wage differential is probably the strong bias of traditional culture against females (Xu et al., 2006). In Chinese traditional agricultural society, females are less productive than males in agricultural production due to physiological differences, which leads to a general underlying assumption that males usually earn more money and creates the Chinese traditional gender roles as "Men's work centers around outside, while women's work centers around the home" (Xu et al., 2006). Despite that the traditional gender roles were created based on agricultural society, they still deeply influence modern society and result in strong gender bias (Jayachandran, 2015). Female employees may be assumed to be less productive and be paid less due to the sex bias against them in the industrial society (Hansen et al., 2015). The societal pressure of traditional gender roles also forces females to do most of the housework, which makes them be even less focussed on career. Weakening of the competitiveness of women in the workplace can strengthen gender bias and create a vicious circle (Xiu and Gunderson, 2014).

It is difficult to speculate about the regional differences of traditional gender bias in China. The impact of this Chinese traditional culture has been softened by two different aspects, one of which is the efforts of the Chinese Communist Party for women's liberation (Loscocco and Bose, 1998). These efforts were usually made by the government, All-China Women's Federation, and state-owned enterprises, which were required to reduce their influence on the labor market after the Chinese economic reform (Cunningham, 2016). The flexible labor market has stimulated the national economy but it might also bring gender inequality. However, the economic reform was not committed simultaneously in all regions in China. Generally, the reform was implemented earlier and deeper in the east and south regions than in the west and north regions, thus the influence on the labor market of those official and semi-official institutions varies across the country (Song et al., 2019). In addition, not only the market economy but also Western feminism, which can also significantly affect the elimination of gender discrimination of traditional culture, was introduced in China by the reform, and the feminism has also shared the regional variations of the reform (Wu and Dong, 2019). Thus, these two aspects are the major factors that affect the regional differences of traditional gender bias in China.

The effect of the reform in the labor market on gender wage differential is also controversial. With the progress of the Chinese economic reform, state ownership has gradually abolished the permanent employment system, and the private sector has taken up an increasing proportion of the economy. A flexible and competitive labor market was deemed to be effective in eliminating gender inequality and gender wage gap, for the reason that enterprises with gender discrimination are less competitive and will finally exit (Black and Brainerd, 2004). However, the opposite opinion held by a number of researchers is that the inevitable psychological and physical differences are the disadvantages for women in the competitive labor market (Gneezy et al., 2003). Due to the preceding regional difference of deepening reform, the flexibility of the labor market varies across China, which additionally causes potential regional differences of gender wage differential.

Gender wage differential in China

According to the above review of literature, gender wage differential may be lower in China than in some developing countries, but it is probably more serious than in most developed economies. Liu, Meng, and Zhang (2000) find the existence of gender wage differential in three different ownership sectors based on data from two cities in China. An analysis of gender wage differential in China's urban labor market shows that female workers earn less, though they usually have higher level of education attainments (Heshmati and Su, 2017). It also points out a large proportion of gender wage differential cannot be explained, which means that it is assumed to be the discrimination against female workers. Another study on the urban labor market in China gives a similar result and compares the data in the 1990s and 2000s (Lee and Wie, 2017), the conclusion of which indicates that the differential is widened due to more severe discrimination in the 2000s than that in the 1900s, especially for low-skilled and middle-skilled female workers. However, similar research investigates a later survey and claims gender wage gap has been converging after 2007 in China's urban labor market (Zhao et al., 2019).

Wage differential of rural migrant workers in China

The urban labor market is not the only one that has received attention. Many researchers noticed the wage differential of rural migrant workers. Combes, Démurger, Li, and Wang (2020) evaluate the effect of internal migration and urbanization on the nominal earnings and argue the wage differential between rural migrant workers and urban residents or natives is one of the main factors that cause income inequality in China. This view is also shared by some other researchers (Cheng et al., 2020; Zhang et al., 2016). In addition, they point out that the ownership sectors that the workers work for, education level and work experience mainly contribute to the wage differential. Some literature also presents that there is discrimination against rural migrant workers.

Wage differential also exists among rural migrant workers. For example, married and young workers earn more than older workers and the wage of blue-collar workers is higher than that of white-collar workers (Zhang et al., 2016). In addition, the wage differential between male and female rural migrant workers has been studied. Most studies argue the existence of wage gender differential, while Lu and Song (2006) find no wage differential in their sample of migrant workers. A potential explanation of it is the evolution of gender wage differential of rural migrant workers in China. The data used by Lu and Song was obtained from a survey completed in 2003, which is earlier than most other research. Lu and Song's research has also been criticized for the limitation of its data collection, which was done in one city, which makes the research unrepresentative. The following three studies all use nationally representative data sets. Magnani and Zhu (2012) state male migrant workers' average wage is 30.2% higher than that of females. Another two research individually report a relatively small gender wage differential based on data collected in 2008, 2009, and 2010, which is regarded as a positive change in the labor market in China (Min et al., 2016; Wu et al., 2021).

Regional differences in gender wage differential

Only a little research is about the regional difference of wage gender differential except for the research comparing the difference between urban areas and rural areas, which argues that a more competitive market in the urban labor market probably constrains gender discrimination against women in the workplace, reduces the gender wage differential and leads to a smaller gender pay gap in urban than in rural (Phimister, 2005). Murillo Huertas, Ramos, and Simon (2017) study the regional difference of wage gender differential in Spain and the result of their research shows a substantially increasing trend of the unexplained share of the differential from the southwest to the northeast. Considering the northeast area of the Iberian Peninsula is relatively rich in Spain, this result indicates that the constraint of the competitive labor market on gender discrimination may be not always effective, though the authors state that not all unexplained share of gender differential comes from gender discrimination. The research investigates the wage differential between urban and rural migrant workers in China based on data from two different provinces and suggests a stronger discrimination against rural migrant workers in the relatively developed province, which also questions the effectiveness of the constraint (Cheng et al., 2020).

Methodological debates in gender wage differential

Generally speaking, Blinder-Oaxaca decomposition has still been widely used in studies on wage differential. The method used in this study, which consists of three steps, is also similar to the present studies. The first step is to analyze gender wage differential with OLS, followed by decomposition and discrimination index calculation, whose results are jointly analyzed to compare the wage gender differential in different regions (Guo et al., 2011).

Source of data

The data of this research comes from the *China Migrants Dynamic Survey (CMDS)* which is conducted by National Health Commission P.R. China and has provided data to many studies on migrant workers. It is a large-scale national sample survey, which surveys nearly 200 thousand families from the cities migrants mainly living in every year since 2009, covering basic information of migrants and their families, employment and social security, income, residence, etc.
Two models are built in this study.

Ordinary least squares (OLS)

What is needed to do first is to build the ordinary least squares model for analyzing the relationship between gender wage differential and relative variables. The OLS equation is:

$$\text{Ln}\, W = X_i \beta_i + \varepsilon$$

where Ln W is the logarithm of wage, ε is a residual error, X_i is several independent variables, and β_i is their coefficients. According to the previous research, the independent variables which are deemed relative include the level of education, age, work experience, marital status, the trade that the migrants work in, whether the enterprise is private or not, etc. The last two variables are dummy variables, and they are included in the model to represent part of wage differential that is accounted for by trade or corporate ownership. The OLS regression is conducted three times with male workers' data and female workers' data, respectively.

Blinder-Oaxaca decomposition

Blinder-Oaxaca decomposition is adopted based on the result of the OLS regression to decompose the impacts. Blinder (1973) and Oaxaca (1973) devised this method to decompose wage differential between two groups in the labor market. It can divide impact into two parts. The estimated equations of the two worker groups are:

$$\text{Ln}\, W_M = X_M \beta_M + \varepsilon$$

$$\text{Ln}\, W_F = X_F \beta_F + \varepsilon$$

where Ln W is the logarithm of equilibrium wage of each group, ε is a residual error, X is a matrix consisting of several variables that may affect wage excluding gender, and β is its coefficient matrix. M means male, and F means female. The wage differential can be represented as:

$$\text{Ln}\, W_M - \text{Ln}\, W_F = X_M \beta_M - X_F \beta_F$$

If the male wage is deemed as equilibrium wage in the labor market without discrimination, the equation can be decomposed as:

$$\text{Ln}\, W_{\text{M}} - \text{Ln}\, W_{\text{F}} = \left(X_{\text{M}} - X_{\text{F}}\right)\beta_{\text{M}} - X_{\text{F}}\left(\beta_{\text{M}} - \beta_{\text{F}}\right)$$

The explanation of the decomposition is the same as a previous study (Zhao et al., 2019). The first term on the right of the equation represents the wage differential that exists even though there is no discrimination, which means that the wage differential is caused by individual differential. The second term represents the wage differential caused by other factors which are unmeasurable.

According to the existing research on regional differences of gender wage differential, this decomposition can be done separately for each region (Murillo Huertas et al., 2017).

Through these two steps in the methodology of this research, two differential parts of gender wage differential can be obtained. One is the share of gender wage differential that can be explained by measurable factors and the other part is unexplained, which is usually deemed as appearing with discrimination. Therefore, this method can analyze gender wage differential better than that only uses OLS, which is why it has been widely applied in previous research (Magnani and Zhu, 2012).

In terms of the approach to examine gender wage differential in this study, Blinder-Oaxaca decomposition eradicates the impact of individual characters on wage differential and quantificationally calculates the effect of gender discrimination on wage. The first step to do the decomposition is the estimation of earning function by gender. As with most previous research on gender wage differential, the form of earning function of rural migrant workers in China is assumed as follows (Magnani and Zhu, 2012).

$$\text{Ln}\, W = \beta_{\text{i}} X_{\text{i}} + \varepsilon$$

where Ln W in the equation is the logarithm of hourly wage, ε is a residual error, X_{i} are the vectors of independent variables, and β_{i} are the corresponding vectors of estimated coefficients. The factors that are related to wage are chosen as the elements of the vectors of independent variables. According to previous studies, two types of factors are contained in the vectors, and one is personal characteristics including years of schooling, age, actual years of work experience, marital status, while the other is the factors related to enterprises that the migrants work in, such as sectors the enterprises belonged to, the type of enterprises' ownership, and enterprises' location (Magnani and Zhu, 2012; Zhao et al., 2019). Variables that belong to the second type of factors are mostly dummy variables. Gender is not included in independent variables because the OLS regression should be conducted two times with male migrant workers data and female migrant workers data, respectively.

The gender wage differential is $\overline{\text{Ln}\, W_{\text{m}}} - \overline{\text{Ln}\, W_{\text{f}}}$, where m represents male and f represents female, containing impacts of individual differences of those measured factors between male and female migrant workers. For example, it is understandable that generally longer years of schooling among male migrant workers lead to higher wages than female migrant workers. Thus, the part of gender wage differential caused by years of schooling is explainable. However, some parts of gender wage differential cannot be explained by those measured factors, such as gender discrimination. To distinguish the two parts of the gender wage differential, Blinder (1973) and Oaxaca (1973) devised a method, which is known as Blinder-Oaxaca decomposition, to decompose wage differential between two groups in the labor market. According to the estimation of earning function, the equation of gender wage differential is as follows:

$$\overline{\text{Ln}\,W_{\text{m}}} - \overline{\text{Ln}\,W_{\text{f}}} = \hat{\beta}_{\text{m}}\overline{X_{\text{m}}} - \hat{\beta}_{\text{f}}\overline{X_{\text{f}}}$$

Afterwards, the standard wage without gender discrimination needs to be set. Although Neumark (1988) demonstrates a method to use male-female mixed simple as the standard wage without discrimination, most previous studies set male migrant wage as the standard wage, which assumes that there is discrimination against females. On the contrary, the assumption is that males have an advantage in the workplace if female migrant wage is set as the standard wage.

Setting male migrant wage as standard wage without gender discrimination, the right-hand side of the equation of gender wage differential can be decomposed as follows:

$$\overline{\text{Ln}\,W_{\text{m}}} - \overline{\text{Ln}\,W_{\text{f}}} = \hat{\beta}_{\text{m}}\overline{X_{\text{m}}} - \hat{\beta}_{\text{f}}\overline{X_{\text{f}}} = \hat{\beta}_{\text{m}}\left(\overline{X_{\text{m}}} - \overline{X_{\text{f}}}\right) + \left(\hat{\beta}_{\text{m}} - \hat{\beta}_{\text{f}}\right)\overline{X_{\text{f}}}$$

The first term on the right-hand side of the equation represents the part of wage differential that exists even without discrimination, which means that the wage differential is caused by individual character difference between the two groups. The second term represents the unexplained part of wage differential caused by unmeasured factors, which is deemed as the impact of gender discrimination against female migrant workers. It is worth noting that no method can include every factor that affects wage, and the impact of these factors, which are not included in method, is contained in the unexplained part of wage differential. Moreover, measurement errors also contribute to it. Therefore, the unexplained part of wage differential is not actually the same as the impact of gender discrimination, however, previous studies generally agree this method is effective.

This decomposition can be done separately for each region in China (Murillo Huertas et al., 2017).

After that, the gender wage discrimination index, which is represented by *D*, should be defined as follows (Guo et al., 2011; Oaxaca, 1973):

$$D = \frac{\left(W_{\text{m}}/W_{\text{f}}\right) - \left(W_{\text{m}}/W_{\text{f}}\right)^{0}}{\left(W_{\text{m}}/W_{\text{f}}\right)^{0}}$$

where $W_{\text{m}}/W_{\text{f}}$ is the ratio of male wage to female wage that has been observed, and $\left(W_{\text{m}}/W_{\text{f}}\right)^{0}$ is the ratio of male wage to female wage without gender discrimination that cannot be observed. D can be calculated by the following steps (Yang and Wang, 2019):

The logarithm of this index is as follows:

$$\mathrm{Ln}(D+1) = \mathrm{Ln}\left(W_{\mathrm{m}}/W_{\mathrm{f}}\right) - \mathrm{Ln}\left(W_{\mathrm{m}}/W_{\mathrm{f}}\right)^{0}$$

According to OLS results, $\overline{\mathrm{Ln}\,W_{\mathrm{m}}} = \hat{\beta}_{\mathrm{m}}\overline{X_{\mathrm{m}}}$ and $\overline{\mathrm{Ln}\,W_{\mathrm{f}}} = \hat{\beta}_{\mathrm{f}}\overline{X_{\mathrm{f}}}$, define $\Delta\bar{X} = \overline{X_{\mathrm{m}}} - \overline{X_{\mathrm{f}}}$ and $\Delta\hat{\beta} = \hat{\beta}_{\mathrm{m}} - \hat{\beta}_{\mathrm{f}}$, male migrant workers wage is deemed as the standard wage without gender discrimination, the $\mathrm{Ln}\left(D+1\right)$ is:

$$\mathrm{Ln}\left(D+1\right) = \hat{\beta}_{\mathrm{m}}\overline{X_{\mathrm{f}}} - \hat{\beta}_{\mathrm{f}}\overline{X_{\mathrm{f}}} = \overline{X_{\mathrm{f}}}\Delta\hat{\beta}$$

Thus the gender wage discrimination index can be calculated.

As described above, despite that Blinder-Oaxaca decomposition is not the only method to study wage differential, it has significant advantages. OLS is a simple method for these research topics, but it cannot decompose the wage differential, thus it cannot measure the degree of discrimination, which, however, can be measured with the Blinder-Oaxaca decomposition, particularly in the case that Oaxaca raised the method to calculate the gender wage discrimination index based on Blinder-Oaxaca decomposition. Some researchers made improvement for Blinder-Oaxaca decomposition, such as Cotton (1988). The new method may be more accurate, but it is also more complex. Some others also discussed the choice of wage without discrimination by arguing that neither male wage nor female wage can be regarded as wage without discrimination and designed some methods to calculate the wage without discrimination based on both male and female wages (Cotton, 1988; Murillo Huertas et al., 2017; Neumark, 1988). However, the methods are complex and controversial (Guo et al., 2011). Therefore, male wage is still deemed as wage without discrimination in this study as it is in most previous research (Miaomiao et al., 2021; Yu et al., 2021; Yang and Wang, 2019).

Regional differences in the gender wage differential of Chinese rural migrant workers

The study is based on the data from the *China Migrants Dynamic Survey in 2011 and 2017*. The *CMDS* is an annual large-scale national sampling survey of the floating population that has been conducted by the National Health Commission since 2009, covering the areas, where the floating population is relatively concentrated, in 31 provinces (autonomous regions, municipalities) and Xinjiang Production and Construction Corps (National Health Commission P.R. China). This means the survey covers all the first-level administrative divisions in China mainland. Different regions are divided according to the criteria released on the webpage of the National Bureau of Statistics of China (National Bureau of Statistics of China, 2011). The eastern region includes Beijing, Tianjin, Hebei, Shanghai, Jiangsu, Zhejiang, Fujian, Shandong, Guangdong, and Hainan (ten provinces/municipalities). The central region includes Shanxi, Anhui, Jiangxi, Henan, Hubei, and Hunan (six provinces). The western region includes Inner Mongolia, Guangxi, Chongqing, Sichuan, Guizhou, Yunnan, Tibet, Shaanxi, Gansu, Qinghai, Ningxia, and Xinjiang (12 provinces/autonomous regions/municipalities). The northeast region includes Liaoning, Jilin, and Heilongjiang (three provinces). Xinjiang Production and Construction Corps is usually regarded as part of Xinjiang, thus it belongs to the western region.

CMDS is a household survey, and the original data are often from multiple family members. For the completeness and accuracy of the data, only the respondents' own data are selected for the research of this study. In addition, considering the research topic of this study, only data of floating population in rural areas are included. The criterion for selecting rural floating population samples from 2011 survey data is that the samples' hukou is registered as "agricultural household". The criterion for selecting rural floating population samples from 2017 survey data is the samples' hukou is "agricultural household" or "resident household" converted from an "agricultural household", as the household register system has been reformed since 2014. If a sample's hukou is "resident household" but no clear indication shows that which kind of hukou it was converted from, the sample is not selected. Moreover, all samples without wages, including seasonal closures and temporary shutdowns, are eliminated.

The proportion of female and wage difference of rural migrant workers is well documented in the works of Jingge (2021: 36). It provides detailed empirical analysis of the total number of samples and the number of samples in each region in 2011 and 2017. According to the documents of the National Health and Health Commission, the sampling method adopted by CMDS is Probability Proportionate to Size Sampling, which is proportional to the scale (National Health Commission P.R. China). Therefore, areas with large floating population, such as the eastern region, have larger sample sizes, and vice versa.

It also reports the number of samples by gender and the proportion of female samples. The proportion of women in the national and regional samples is less than 50%, the possible reasons for which are: first, women are more likely to do housework and take care of the elderly and children, thus they tend to stay in their hometowns compared with men; second, even if in a family, both husband and wife are migrants, the wife may do housework instead of work, and this type of sample has been eliminated; finally, all samples are respondents, who are more likely to be men who communicate with outsiders, such as survey researchers, on behalf of the family. These three reasons are all related to gender discrimination to a certain extent. In regions with relatively developed economies, such as the eastern region, female migrant workers account for a relatively large proportion, which means that the gender inequality is less serious in these regions.

The empirical analysis of Jingge (2021: 37) outlines wages of male and female migrant workers from rural China. The analysis clearly shows that the wage level in each region is basically in line with the level of economic development. For example, the eastern region that is most developed economically has the highest wages, while the fast-developing central region's wages increased rapidly in those years. Compared to 2011, the wages of male and female rural migrant workers in all regions increased significantly in 2017, which is consistent with the relevant report provided by the Chinese government (National Bureau of Statistics of China, 2018). The conclusion remains unchanged after the inflation adjustment. For jobs that include board and lodging, the cost of board and lodging is converted into income in 2011, but not included in the data of 2017. Therefore, due to changes in statistical method, the specific increase in the wages of migrant workers cannot be calculated. In theory, the income growth of migrant workers derived from this data is smaller than the actual value, thus the conclusion that the income of migrant workers has generally risen remains unchanged. Since the gender wage differential that this study focuses on is a relative value, the conclusion is not affected by the change in statistical method. The ratio of male and female wages is greater than one, which shows that wages of males are generally higher than that of females. However, the ratio of monthly wages is greater than the ratio of hourly wages, which indicates that males generally work longer hours than females (Jingge, 2021).

The OLS results and analysis

OLS regression is performed in this study on the wages of male and female migrant workers, respectively. As mentioned above, the explained variable is the logarithm of the hourly wage of migrant workers. Based on existing research, explanatory variables include years of education (eduy), age, the square of age, work experience (exp), the square of work experience, marital status (mar), mobility range, ownership of the company/organization he/she is working for, and the industry (Ng, 2007; Yang and Wang, 2019). The last four variables are dummy variables. Therefore, the regression equation is as follows:

$$\begin{aligned}\text{Ln}\, W = {} & \beta_0 + \beta_1 \text{eduy} + \beta_2 \text{age} + \beta_3 \text{age}^2 + \beta_4 \exp + \beta_5 \exp^2 + \beta_6 \text{mar} \\ & + \beta_{\text{m}} \text{mobility range} + \beta_{\text{o}} \text{ownership} + \beta_{\text{in}} \text{industry}\end{aligned}$$

where work experience is represented by the time period that the respondent has been working in that job, and only people who maintain a marriage in the legal sense are considered to be married.

The regression analysis of Jingge (2021: 40) shows that the last three variables, including mobility range, ownership of the company/organization he/she is working for, and the industry, have been controlled in the regression. The *F*-tests of all 16 regressions are statistically significant at least at 0.001 level. Jingge (2021: 40) presents that most variables are statistically significant in most regressions. It is worth noting that in all regressions on the wages of male migrant workers, the coefficient of marital status is positive, while in most regressions on the wages of female migrant workers, the coefficient of marital status is negative, and they are generally statistically significant, indicating that marriage has a positive impact on the wages of male migrant workers, while it has a negative impact on the wages of female migrant workers. The coefficients of other explanatory variables are basically consistent with expectations and existing theories (Yang and Wang, 2019).

The positive coefficient of age and the negative coefficient of its square value suggest that there may be an inverted U-shaped relationship between age and the wages. Similar coefficients of work experience and its squared value indicate that the impact of work experience on wages may be diminishing on the margins.

It is obvious that years of education have a positive effect on wages, and women mostly benefit more from it than men, except in the eastern region. One possible explanation for this phenomenon is that in areas where gender discrimination is serious, women's more years of education are a signal of high ability, thus the impact of gender discrimination can be reduced to a certain extent (Yang and Wang, 2019). The absence of this phenomenon in the eastern region indicates that gender discrimination there is less serious than in other regions.

It is clear that the proportion of the explained part and the unexplained part in the wage difference after the decomposition of the gender wage difference, and it also shows the gender wage discrimination index. Despite that there are certain conflicts in different empirical findings, the region with the highest gender equality, in general, is the western region, while in the eastern region genders are relatively equal, in the central region they are relatively unequal, and the northeast region has the lowest gender equality (Jingge, 2021: 47).

As mentioned earlier, gender discrimination in the Chinese labor market may be reduced for two forces (Ng, 2007), one of which is the socialist system, whose influence has weakened with the process of the Chinese economic reform, and the second is the market competition and feminism brought about by the Chinese economic reform, whose influence has strengthened with the process of the Chinese economic reform. The empirical results may indicate that they both affect gender discrimination. The western region is the region where the progress of economic reform is the slowest, on the contrary, the eastern region is the region that has the fastest progress of economic reform, which may indicate that gender discrimination in the western region has been reduced by the socialist system, while gender discrimination in the eastern region has been reduced by market competition and/or feminism (Jingge, 2021: 47).

The progress of economic reform in the northeast and central regions is somewhere in between the western region and the eastern region, which might suggest the existence of a time gap that the old socialist system has been reformed but market competition has not eliminated gender-discriminatory companies and/or feminism has not yet exerted an impact on gender discrimination. In other words, the change in gender discrimination can be divided into two stages. In the first stage, the influence of the socialist system on gender discrimination gradually declined, and gender inequality rose. At this stage, the market competition and feminism might not have exerted an impact on gender discrimination yet, or its influence might not be enough to offset the decline in the influence of the socialist system. At the end of the first stage, the degree of gender inequality reached its maximum. In the second stage, the growth of the influence of market competition and feminism exceeded the decline of the influence of the socialist system, or the influence of the socialist system ceased decreasing. At this stage, gender inequality gradually declined.

From 2011 to 2017, the conclusions on changes in gender discrimination in each region obtained through the decomposition results and the discrimination index are inconsistent. In this study, further discussion is based on the decomposition results (Jingge, 2021).

The decomposition results show that the unexplained part in all regions accounts for most of the gender wage differential. Except for the western region, the unexplained part accounts for more than 80% of the gender wage differential. The unexplained part in Northeast China accounts for more than 100% of the gender wage differential in 2017, which means that the explained part accounts for a negative percentage of the gender wage differential. This result reveals that the female rural migrant workers' characteristics are better than that of male rural migrant workers. If gender discrimination and the influence of the variables excluded in this study are removed, the female rural migrant workers' wages should be higher than that of male rural migrant workers (Jingge, 2021).

Although no consistent conclusions have been reached, according to the above analysis, with the process of the Chinese economic reform, gender inequality will fall in the eastern regions, and will first rise and then fall in the western region, which is also indicated by the decomposition results. Future changes in gender inequality in the central and north-eastern regions may depend on the stage of economic reform in these two regions. If the impact of the socialist system on the labor market is still significant, gender inequality may first rise and then fall, whereas if the market competition plays a role in reducing gender discrimination, gender inequality in these regions may gradually decline. The decomposition results indicate that the Chinese economic reform of the two regions may still be at the preliminary stage, which also suggests that the eastern region may be the only region in the second stage.

Nationally, years of education and work experience have a positive contribution to the explained part, while age and marital status have a negative contribution to it. Among them, work experience has the second largest contribution in 2011 and the largest contribution in 2017, which indicates that male migrant workers have an advantage over female migrant workers in terms of education and work experience. Additionally, the advantage of males in work experience is obvious. Age and marital status have a positive contribution to the unexplained part, and these two variables account for a large proportion of the unacceptable part. The contribution of work experience to the unexplained part is negative, whereas the contribution of education level to the unexplained part is negative in 2011 and positive in 2017, which is not significant, and the absolute value of its contribution is small, thus the effect of education level on gender discrimination may be small.

Comparing the decomposition results in 2011 and 2017, it can be noted that the contribution of years of education to the explained part decreases, while the contribution of work experience to the explained part increases, which probably means that the educational level of female migrant workers has improved and the advantages of male migrant workers in terms of work experience have been strengthened. For the unexplained part, the proportion of age contribution in 2017 increases significantly compared to that of 2011, indicating that age discrimination against women has rapidly deteriorated.

The contribution of years of education to the explained part is positive in the eastern region, and negative in the western, central, and north-eastern regions. A positive contribution generally means that men have a higher education level than women and therefore receive higher wages, and vice versa. Yang and Wang (2019) state that a high level of education reduces gender discrimination in workplaces by sending a signal to employers. As a result, female rural migrant workers with lower levels of education tend to work in eastern regions where gender discrimination is less serious compared with other regions, while male rural migrant workers and female rural migrant workers with high levels of education are not affected. The data comparison shows that the proportion of the contribution of education to the explained part in 2011 and 2017 declines in the eastern region. The proportion is always negative in the central and western regions, but it changes from statistically significant to insignificant in the central region, and from statistically insignificant to significant in the western region, which suggests that with the process of the Chinese economic reform, the influence of gender discrimination on the migration of female rural migrant workers has gradually weakened in the eastern and central regions, and has gradually increased in the western region. Although this proportion is positive in the Northeast region, the explained part in this region is negative, which suggests that the influence has increased in the Northeast region. This result is basically consistent with the changes in gender discrimination in each region from 2011 to 2017 shown above.

The result shows that from 2011 to 2017, the contribution of work experience to the explained part is positive in all regions, and the proportion of contribution in the explained part increases. However, the increase in the eastern region is small, which indicates that male rural migrant workers have an advantage over females in terms of work experience, implying that female workers' jobs are more unstable. One reason is that female migrant workers are more expected to take on housework, therefore, when someone in the family has to leave the job to housework and take care of the family, females, rather than males, may choose to give up their careers. Another possible reason is that this domestic division of labor is an economically rational choice. When male rural migrant workers have higher wages in regions where gender discrimination is serious, it is understandable that men are responsible for earnings, and women are responsible for housework. However, market competition may reduce the gender wage gap, and feminism is accepted by more people in the eastern region. Therefore, the effect of the two reasons above on female work experience becomes smaller in this region.

As shown in the results, the contribution of education in the unexplained part is positive in the eastern region, and is mostly negative in other regions, which is consistent with the above-mentioned result that the education reduces gender discrimination in the central, western, and north-eastern regions. In all regions, the contribution of work experience to the unexplained part is negative regardless of whether it is statistically significant or not. In addition, its proportion in the unexplained part increases in 2017 compared to that of 2011, which shows that work experience may reduce gender discrimination, though female rural migrant workers have disadvantages in work experience due to gender discrimination.

The contribution of age to the unexplained part is mostly positive in all regions, but it is not significant in 2011 except for the Northeast region. Nevertheless, it is significant in 2017 for all regions. This contribution of age in the Northeast region is statistically significant, and its proportion in the unexplained part increases significantly. Among these variables, the contribution of age accounts for the largest proportion of the unexplained part, and its rise may be one of the main reasons for the deterioration of gender discrimination. Moreover, in all regions, the contribution of marital status to the unexplained part is positive and statistically significant. In the eastern region, the proportion of marital status in the unexplained part increases from 2011 to 2017, while it declines in other regions. A possible explanation is that market competition is most intense in the eastern region, and married women may be discriminated against in the labor market for the negative impact of fertility on work.

The findings reveal that gender discrimination is higher in the central and northeast regions while less gender discrimination is shown in the eastern and western regions. It can be explained with the theory mentioned above, which suggests that a time gap exists between the two forces that reduce gender discrimination.

Conclusion

This study adopts CMDS data and Blinder-Oaxaca decomposition to decompose the gender wage differences of migrant workers in four different regions of mainland China and analyses the degree of gender discrimination in each region with the results of the decomposition and gender discrimination index.

The results of descriptive statistics show that men account for the majority of migrant workers, and the wages of male migrant workers are always higher than that of female migrant workers in all regions. The decomposition of gender wage differential shows that the wage differential caused by gender discrimination in all regions always accounts for most of the gender wage gap, but its proportion still varies with regions. In the northeast and central regions, the proportion of gender wage differential in the discrimination part is larger than that in the eastern and western regions. The gender discrimination index calculated based on the OLS results provides similar results. Therefore, gender discrimination in the northeast and central regions is considered to be more serious than that in the eastern and western regions, and the results also show that the degree of gender discrimination in regions did not change much from 2011 to 2017. However, it can be seen from the decomposition results of data in 2017 that gender inequality in the eastern region decreases, while gender discrimination in other regions becomes more serious compared with 2011.

The impact of several variables on gender discrimination is examined. In the eastern region, the years of education has a positive impact on the gender wage differential, while it exerts a negative impact in other regions. The contribution of work experience to the explained part is positive in all regions, whereas the contribution to the unexplained part is negative. The contribution of age and marital status accounts for a large proportion of the unexplained part in all regions, thus these two factors are also considered to be the major causes of gender wage differential.

There are two forces that reduce gender discrimination in mainland China, and their influence on gender discrimination has weakened or strengthened with the Chinese economic reform (Ng, 2007). The socialist system established before the Chinese economic reform may be the reason for the low degree of gender discrimination in the western region, which has a latest start of reform and a slowest process in mainland China. The market competition and feminism brought about by the Chinese economic reform may have reduced gender discrimination in the eastern region, in which the reform is firstly permitted and encouraged in China. The more serious gender discrimination in the central and north-eastern regions is resulted from the time gap between the weakening of the reducing effect of the socialist system and the not-yet-effective market competition or feminism. With the process of the Chinese economic reform, it is expected that gender inequality in the eastern region might decline in the future, while gender inequality in other regions may first rise and then decline.

References

Agrawal, T. 2021. Gender Segregation and Wage Differentials in India: The Role of Educational Attainment and Occupational Choices. *International Journal of Manpower*, 42, 1–20.

Arulampalam, W., Booth, A. L. & Bryan, M. L. 2007. Is There a Glass Ceiling over Europe? Exploring the Gender Pay Gap across the Wage Distribution. *Industrial & Labor Relations Review*, 60, 163–186.

Black, S. E. & Brainerd, E. 2004. Importing Equality? The Impact of Globalization on Gender Discrimination. *Industrial & Labor Relations Review*, 57, 540–559.

Blau, F. D. & Kahn, L. M. 2001. The Gender Pay Gap. *NBER Reporter*, 8.

Blinder, A. S. 1973. Wage Discrimination: Reduced Form and Structural Estimates. *The Journal of Human Resources*, 8, 436–455.

Cheng, H., Hu, D. & Li, H. 2020. Wage Differential between Rural Migrant and Urban Workers in the People's Republic of China. *Asian Development Review*, 37, 43–60.

Combes, P.-P., Démurger, S., Li, S. & Wang, J. 2020. Unequal Migration and Urbanisation Gains in China. *Journal of Development Economics*, 142, 102328.

Cook, S. & Dong, X.-Y. 2011. Harsh Choices: Chinese Women's Paid Work and Unpaid Care Responsibilities under Economic Reform. *Development and Change*, 42, 947–965.

Cotton, J. 1988. On the Decomposition of Wage Differentials. *The Review of Economics and Statistics*, 70, 236–243.

Courey, G. 2020. Gender and Racial Wage Differentials in Nonprofit Hospitals. *Labour (Rome, Italy)*, 34, 373–398.

Cunningham, M. E. 2016. Goods Girls Revolt: The Future of Feminism in China. *World Policy Journal*, 33, 18–22.

De Paola, M. & Scoppa, V. 2015. Gender Discrimination and Evaluators' Gender: Evidence from Italian Academia. *Economica (London)*, 82, 162–188.

Dong, X.-Y., Macphail, F., Bowles, P. & Ho, S. P. S. 2004. Gender Segmentation at Work in China's Privatized Rural Industry: Some Evidence from Shandong and Jiangsu. *World Development*, 32, 979–998.

Douglas, K. M. & Sutton, R. M. 2014. "A Giant Leap for Mankind" But What about Women? The Role of System-Justifying Ideologies in Predicting Attitudes toward Sexist Language. *Journal of Language and Social Psychology*, 33, 667–680.

Duncan, C. & Loretto, W. 2004. Never the Right Age? Gender and Age-Based Discrimination in Employment. *Gender, Work & Organization*, 11, 95–115.

Gneezy, U., Niederle, M. & Rustichini, A. 2003. Performance in Competitive Environments: Gender Differences. *The Quarterly Journal of Economics*, 118, 1049–1074.

Guilmoto, C. Z., Hoàng, X. & Van, T. N. 2009. Recent Increase in Sex Ratio at Birth in Viet Nam. *PloS One*, 4, e4624–e4624.

Guo, J., Li, J. & Lu, L. 2011. Decomposition Methods for Wage Differentials: A Survey. *China Economic Quarterly*, 2.

Hansen, C. W., Jensen, P. S. & Skovsgaard, C. V. 2015. Modern Gender Roles and Agricultural History: The Neolithic Inheritance. *Journal of Economic Growth (Boston, Mass.)*, 20, 365–404.

Heshmati, A. & Su, B. 2017. Analysis of Gender Wage Differential in China's Urban Labor Market. *Singapore Economic Review*, 62, 423–445.

Isaacs, E. 1995. Gender Discrimination in the Workplace: A Literature Review. *Communications of the ACM*, 38(1).

Ismail, R., Farhadi, M. & Wye, C.-K. 2017. Occupational Segregation and Gender Wage Differentials: Evidence from Malaysia: Occupational Segregation and Gender Wage Differentials. *Asian Economic Journal*, 31, 381–401.

Jayachandran, S. 2015. The Roots of Gender Inequality in Developing Countries. *Annual Review of Economics*, 7, 63–88.

Jingge, G. 2021. *Regional Differences in the Gender Wage Differential of Rural Migrant Workers in China: A Study Based on China Migrants Dynamic Survey (2011–2017)*. Adam Smith Business School, University of Glasgow, Glasgow.

Johansson, M., Katz, K., Nyman, H., Department of, E., Institutionen för Nationalekonomi Med, S., Handelshögskolan, Göteborgs, U., Gothenburg, U. & School of Business, E. A. L. 2005. Wage Differentials and Gender Discrimination: Changes in Sweden 1981–98. *Acta Sociologica*, 48, 341–364.

Lee, J.-W. & Wie, D. 2017. Wage Structure and Gender Earnings Differentials in China and India. *World Development*, 97, 313–329.

Liu, A. Y. C. 2004. Sectoral Gender Wage Gap in Vietnam. *Oxford Development Studies*, 32, 225–239.

Liu, P.-W., Meng, X. & Zhang, J. 2000. Sectoral Gender Wage Differentials and Discrimination in the Transitional Chinese Economy. *Journal of Population Economics*, 13, 331–352.

Loscocco, K. A. & Bose, C. E. 1998. Gender and Job Satisfaction in Urban China: The Early Post-Mao Period. *Social Science Quarterly*, 79, 91–109.

Lu, Z. & Song, S. 2006. Rural–Urban Migration and Wage Determination: The Case of Tianjin, China. *China Economic Review*, 17, 337–345.

Luo, X. 2018. *Is There a Marriage Or Parenthood Income Penalty among Police?: A Case Study of Occupational Gender Inequality in the Public Sector*. Norman, OK: University of Oklahoma.

Magnani, E. & Zhu, R. 2012. Gender Wage Differentials among Rural–Urban Migrants in China. *Regional Science and Urban Economics*, 42, 779–793.

Mandel, H. & Semyonov, M. 2005. Family Policies, Wage Structures, and Gender Gaps: Sources of Earnings Inequality in 20 Countries. *American Sociological Review*, 70, 949–967.

Marmot, M., Friel, S., Bell, R., Houweling, T. A. J. & Taylor, S. 2008. Closing the Gap in a Generation: Health Equity through Action on the Social Determinants of Health. *The Lancet*, 372, 1661–1669.

Miaomiao, Y., Xianwei, L. & Yonghong, M. 2021. The Characteristics and Influencing Factors of Gender Difference in the Starting Salary of Master Graduates in China. *Heilongjiang Researches on Higher Education*, Issue 2.

Min, Q., Brown, J., Padmadas, S., Bohua, L., Jianan, Q. & Falkingham, J. 2016. Gender Inequalities in Employment and Wage-earning among Economic Migrants in Chinese Cities. *Demographic Research*, 34, 175–202.

Murillo Huertas, I. P., Ramos, R. & Simon, H. 2017. Regional Differences in the Gender Wage Gap in Spain. *Social Indicators Research*, 134, 981–1008.

Mussida, C. & Picchio, M. 2014. The Gender Wage Gap by Education in Italy. *The Journal of Economic Inequality*, 12, 117–147.

National Bureau of Statistics of China. 2011. *Method of Dividing East, West, Central and Northeast Regions* [Online]. Available: http://www.stats.gov.cn/ztjc/zthd/sjtjr/dejtjkfr/tjkp/201106/t20110613_71947.htm [Accessed].

National Bureau of Statistics of China. 2018. *2017 Monitoring Survey Report of Migrant Workers*. PRC, Beijing: The State Council of China.

National Bureau of Statistics of China. 2020. *2019 Monitoring Survey Report of Migrant Workers* [Online]. Available: http://www.stats.gov.cn/tjsj/zxfb/202004/t20200430_1742724.html [Accessed].

National Health Commission P.R. China. *Migrant Population Service Center* [Online]. Available: https://chinaldrk.org.cn/wjw/#/home [Accessed 12/08/2022].

Neumark, D. 1988. Employers' Discriminatory Behavior and the Estimation of Wage Discrimination. *The Journal of Human Resources*, 23, 279–295.

Ng, Y. C. 2007. Gender Earnings Differentials and Regional Economic Development in Urban China, 1988–97. *Review of Income and Wealth*, 53, 148–166.

Oaxaca, R. 1973. Male-Female Wage Differentials in Urban Labor Markets. *International Economic Review (Philadelphia)*, 14, 693–709.

Phimister, E. 2005. Urban Effects on Participation and Wages: Are There Gender Differences? *Journal of Urban Economics*, 58, 513–536.

Piazzalunga, D. 2015. Is There a Double-Negative Effect? Gender and Ethnic Wage Differentials in Italy. *Labour (Rome, Italy)*, 29, 243–269.

Protsch, P. 2021. Employers' Recruitment Contexts and Hiring Preferences in the German Youth Labor Market. *Research in Social Stratification and Mobility*, 73, 100608.

Song, X., Wu, S., Xu, X. & Springerlink. 2019. *The Great Change in the Regional Economy of China under the New Normal*. Singapore: Springer Singapore.

Wang, H., Guo, F. & Cheng, Z. 2015. A Distributional Analysis of Wage Discrimination against Migrant Workers in China's Urban Labour Market. *Urban Studies (Edinburgh, Scotland)*, 52, 2383–2403.

Weber, A. & Zulehner, C. 2014. Competition and Gender Prejudice: Are Discriminatory Employers Doomed to Fail? *Journal of the European Economic Association*, 12, 492–521.

Wu, A. X. & Dong, Y. 2019. What Is Made-in-China Feminism(s)? Gender Discontent and Class Friction in Post-socialist China. *Critical Asian Studies*, 51, 471–492.

Wu, Y., Pieters, J. & Heerink, N. 2021. The Gender Wage Gap among China's Rural–Urban Migrants. *Review of Development Economics*, 25, 23–47.

Xiu, L. & Gunderson, M. 2014. Glass Ceiling Or Sticky Floor? Quantile Regression Decomposition of the Gender Pay Gap in China. *International Journal of Manpower*, 35, 306–326.

Xu, W., Tan, K.-C. & Wang, G. 2006. Segmented Local Labor Markets in Postreform China: Gender Earnings Inequality in the Case of Two Towns in Zhejiang Province. *Environment and Planning A: Economy and Space*, 38, 85–109.

Yu, M., Liu, X. & Ma, Y. 2021. The Characteristics and Influencing Factors of Gender Difference in the Starting Salary of Master Graduates in China. *Heilongjiang Researches on Higher Education*, Issue 2.

Zhang, J., Han, J., Liu, P.-W. & Zhao, Y. 2008. Trends in the Gender Earnings Differential in Urban China, 1988–2004. *Industrial & Labor Relations Review*, 61, 224–243.
Zhang, L., Sharpe, R. V., Li, S. & Darity, W. A. 2016. Wage Differentials between Urban and Rural-Urban Migrant Workers in China. *China Economic Review*, 41, 222–233.
Zhao, X.-Z., Zhao, Y.-B., Chou, L.-C. & Leivang, B. H. 2019. Changes in Gender Wage Differentials in China: A Regression and Decomposition Based on the Data of CHIPS1995–2013. *Economic Research-Ekonomska Istraživanja*, 32, 3168–3188.
Zweimüller, M., Winter-Ebmer, R. & Weichselbaumer, D. 2008. Market Orientation and Gender Wage Gaps: An International Study: Market Orientation and Gender Wage Gaps. *Kyklos (Basel)*, 61, 615–635.

2 Credit constraints for women-led micro and small enterprises in Beijing and Guangdong Province in China

Yihan Lyu and Bhabani Shankar Nayak

Introduction

Today, women's entrepreneurship is one of the main contributors to prosperity in the general world economy. However, it is still significantly less common for women to own and manage businesses compared to men (Radović-Marković and Achakpa, 2018). As early as 1987, Neider (1987) pointed out that women face more challenges than men when starting and operating businesses. That is, there is a lack of equality between the genders when comparing job opportunities, wages, ownership, decision-making positions and other economic variables (Radović-Marković et al., 2010: 23). Empirical evidence reveals that women entrepreneurs receive less support from financial institutions than do their male counterparts (Demirguc-Kunt et al., 2018). Over the past decades, the issue of whether this fact means that there are tighter credit constraints for women entrepreneurs has been extensively studied.

Since the 1990s, an increasing number of studies have explored how gender influences women's entrepreneurial behaviour (Marlow and Martinez Dy, 2018). Whether banks impose credit constraints on women entrepreneurs is a widely discussed issue. Information asymmetry leads to credit constraints as lenders cannot determine borrowers' risk levels (Stiglitz and Weiss, 1981). It is important for lenders to obtain more information to identify the moral hazard and adverse selection risks of small businesses requesting loans (Berger and Udell, 2002). Rich information on borrowers can help financial institutions find the most appropriate borrowers so as to maximise benefits for the institution. However, according to the theory originated by Becker (1971), lenders who are biased would likely be willing to pay the price of rejecting some loan applicants belonging to the specific groups against which the lender is biased. Therefore, if banks are biased against women entrepreneurs, they might refuse to lend to women, even at the expense of profit. Many scholars have examined whether access to credit differs according to gender at various times and in many countries around the world.

Whether or not gender influences access to credit has been debated for several years, but scholars have not reached a consensus. Blanchflower et al. (2003), Wellalage and Locke (2017), Moro et al. (2017) and Galli et al. (2020) find that financial institutions are not biased against women when deciding whether to approve loan applications, based on data from the United States, South Asia and Europe.

DOI: 10.4324/9781003437307-3

Specifically, Pham and Talavera (2018) document that a woman-led enterprise is more likely to apply for a loan successfully and pays lower interest rates than a male-led enterprise. Women's risk aversion is more likely to lead to successful bank loan applications during periods of financial uncertainty because banks need more conservative lenders to hedge risks in such times (Cowling et al., 2020). A similar conclusion is obtained by Galli et al. (2020), who observe that gender bias is likely to only appear during periods of economic growth.

On the contrary, several studies show that women-owned firms face tighter credit constraints than men-owned firms (Bellucci et al., 2010; Chaudhuri et al., 2020; Wellalage and Thrikawala, 2021). Moreover, on the condition of having obtained loans, women also face significantly higher interest rates than men (Aristei and Gallo, 2021), although there is no evidence that women present with higher risk levels (Alesina et al., 2013). To evaluate the claim that women entrepreneurs are more likely than men entrepreneurs to experience adverse pricing conditions for bank lending, Mascia and Rossi (2017) analysed firms whose leaders changed from female to male, and they found a decrease in interest rates. In addition, studies suggest that the reason for the gender gap is the different behaviours of female borrowers. Galli et al. (2020) show that women entrepreneurs are more likely to refrain from applying for loans than males because they have a higher risk aversion (Croson and Gneezy, 2009) or expect to be rejected (Moro et al., 2017).

In different countries and regions, gender influences access to credit differently. In China, using the data from The Seventh National Sample Survey of Private Enterprises, Yan (2011) finds that, after controlling other related information, the number of women who successfully applied for loans was 42% lower than the number of men. After analysing the data from 826 small and micro enterprises in China, Hu (2015) also concludes that female business owners face more serious credit constraints than male business owners. She finds that fewer female CEOs choose to apply for loans due to their lower probability of getting a loan and the higher interest rates they would face. Chen and Gao (2013) also demonstrate that gender has a negative effect on applying for loans. Female entrepreneurs' higher risk aversion leads them to make prudent decisions about applying for loans (Sun and Zhou, 2016). Similarly, this study examines the relationship between gender and credit constraints in the context of China. Furthermore, this study will innovatively examine and compare women-led micro and small enterprises' credit constraints and entrepreneurs' reluctance to apply for bank loans in the more developed Beijing and the less developed Guangdong Province, as well as discuss the reasons for such constraints and reluctance.

Most of the literature on gender and credit constraints in China is based on national data. However, although economies vary by region within China, few studies are based on regional data and compare the differences within specific provinces. China is a developing country, having the largest population and third-largest total area in the world (Worldometer, 2021). This study will focus on Beijing and Guangdong Province. According to statistics released by China's National Bureau of Statistics (2020), the GDP per capita of Beijing was around 24,000 USD, ranking it first in GDP per capita among all Chinese provinces and showing that the economic development of Beijing has reached the level of a developed economy. Although Guangdong Province ranks first in China in terms of GDP, it ranks seventh in terms of GDP per capita, coming in at approximately 13,000 USD (Lin, 2021). These metrics indicate that the economic development of Guangdong is more similar to that of a developing economy. This chapter compares access to credit for women entrepreneurs of micro and small enterprises (MSEs) in Beijing and Guangdong to determine whether gender discrimination exists. The study of women entrepreneurs of MSEs and credit access in Beijing and Guangdong could, to some extent, reflect gender issues and inequities in China's credit markets.

Therefore, this study has three interrelated objectives. The first objective of this chapter is to research whether women-led MSEs face tighter credit constraints than men-led MSEs in Beijing and Guangdong Province, China. The second objective is to examine whether women entrepreneurs of MSEs are more likely to refrain from opting for loan financing than men entrepreneurs in these locations. The third objective is to compare the access to credit of women entrepreneurs of MSEs in Beijing and Guangdong Province to examine whether women-led MSEs in more developed regions are less likely to face tighter credit constraints than men-led MSEs.

Gender and entrepreneurship

According to the World Economic Forum (2021), the gender gap in Economic Participation and Opportunity is the second-largest gap measured by the Global Gender Gap Index. It is estimated that it will take 267.6 years to close this gap at the current rate. Historically, and even today, the gender gap can be explained by the perception and treatment of women as inferior and, arguably, by gender discrimination.

Over the past few decades, theories on the economics of discrimination have matured, and they can be divided into two main categories: taste-based discrimination and statistical discrimination (Guryan and Charles, 2013). Becker (1971) introduced the theory of discrimination based on taste, which is caused by cultural and institutional factors. People who have a discriminatory preference for a particular group, such as men, are willing to avoid working with or associating with women, even at a cost they would not otherwise have to pay. Statistical discrimination usually results from information asymmetry. Stereotyping, caused by a lack of information, is the belief of discriminators that group characteristics are equivalent to those of individuals who belong to the group (Arrow, 2015). As a result, due to statistical discrimination, women may receive different treatment than men depending on the social group to which they belong. In this chapter, the focus is on gender differences in entrepreneurship.

In the context of entrepreneurship, entrepreneurial firms have been dominated by men historically. For many years, women have been struggling to break the 'glass ceiling'. However, the gap in favour of men when it comes to entrepreneurship still exists (Ughetto et al., 2020). According to the World Bank (2018), only about 30% of businesses are owned by women globally. There has historically been a perception that entrepreneurial traits, such as competitiveness, aggression and risk-taking, are male characteristics (Jennings and Brush, 2013), which puts men in a privileged position and women at a disadvantage in entrepreneurship. It has been pointed out by Marlow and Martinez Dy (2018) that such gendered depictions limit women's accumulation of entrepreneurial capital and legitimacy, abilities to succeed as entrepreneurs and evaluations of their capabilities. As a result, the number of female entrepreneurs is lower than that of male entrepreneurs.

Meanwhile, women leaders are often undervalued (Wolfers, 2006). Burgess and Tharenou (2002) argue that women leaders can bring innovative ideas to the table. Similarly, Cunningham et al. (2017) find a significant positive effect of female leadership on the innovation environments and survival prospects of firms. Therefore, the diversity of gender in decision-making positions is a strength for companies (Weber and Zulehner, 2010). To be specific, in the United States, Srinidhi et al. (2011) show that increasing female involvement on boards implies higher earnings quality. Carter et al. (2003) and Lückerath-Rovers (2013) suggest that the financial performance of companies with female directors is better than that of those without them in the Netherlands and in the United States. Additionally, Abbott et al. (2012) suggest that gender diversity on boards means that a business will be less likely to issue financial restatements. Based on their research, Gul et al. (2011) conclude that stock prices of companies with women on their boards reflect more specific information about companies. Furthermore, Bear et al. (2010) observe that gender diversity on boards has a positive influence on the corporate social responsibility ratings of companies. Nielsen and Huse (2010) found that gender diversity on boards positively influenced board development activities in Norway.

Credit constraints faced by women-led enterprises in China

In China, several decades ago, the leader Mao Zedong said that 'women hold up half the sky', an important declaration for the promotion of gender equality. With the development of the economy, the number of women entrepreneurs in China has increased rapidly over the past 20 years, with women entrepreneurs accounting for approximately a quarter of all Chinese entrepreneurs today (China Development Research Foundation, 2017). For example, the establishment of a number of government support programs has had a positive effect on female entrepreneurial activity (Zhu et al., 2009). Compared to men, women entrepreneurs have a number of advantages. For example, firms with women CEOs are more inclined to establish collaborative work environments (Liu and Liu, 2013). Li and Huang (2014) also observe that, compared to men, female CEOs are more prudent in making investments and in facilitating mergers and acquisitions (M&As). Similarly, Zhu et al. (2012) observe that in the face of uncertainty, the risk aversion associated with female leaders is beneficial in reducing over-investment and in helping companies overcome the negative effects of the financial crisis. Li and Huang (2014) additionally find that both the proportion of female executives and their part-time employment in other organisations are positively associated with improved M&A performance. Regarding firm performance, Hu and Zhou (2016) and Zhang (2013) show that the participation of women directors significantly improves firm performance and that the improvement increases with the level of education of the women directors.

Nevertheless, a number of issues and constraints exist for Chinese women entrepreneurs. Liu et al. (2013) find that women are less likely than men to start a business due to factors such as discrimination. Even when women start businesses, they usually do not make much use of government resources in the entrepreneurial process (Ju and Mei, 2014). Moreover, Liu and Liu (2013) show that female CEOs are paid significantly less in total than male CEOs, with this trend increasing each year, while there is no significant difference in the financial performance of companies led by women versus those led by men. Their research suggests that female CEOs also receive relatively fewer salary incentives. It is thus clear that even after women have overcome many constraints such as gender discrimination to start a business, they may still encounter further obstacles.

Financing is one of the most significant parts of running an enterprise. Because SMEs have difficulty accessing credit from the stock market, they usually rely on bank loans (Caglayan and Xu, 2016). Notably, SMEs also have more difficulty receiving bank loans than do larger enterprises (Wang, 2016). Such credit constraints are mainly due to information asymmetry, which makes it difficult for lenders to analyse the risk levels of borrowers (Stiglitz and Weiss, 1981; Canton et al., 2013). The reason for the credit constraints of SMEs is that banks tend to make decisions in terms of factors such as the experience, size and turnover of the business (Canton et al., 2013). SMEs have no advantages in these areas when compared against larger enterprises. Additionally, some financial institutions prefer to gather as much information about borrowers as this information can help them in identifying the moral hazards and adverse selection risks of enterprises (Berger and Udell, 2002). This information can help financial institutions find the most appropriate borrowers so as to maximise the benefits to themselves. Risk factors that commonly influence banks' lending decisions and loan prices are the age and size of the venture, the availability of collateral, and the length of the venture's relationship with the bank (Cowling et al., 2020). Theoretically, the ability of firms owned by female and male entrepreneurs to obtain bank loans should be no different if firms are similar in characteristics. However, according to the theory originated by Becker (1971), if lenders are biased, they would likely reject some loan applicants from the specific groups against which they are biased, even if it meant paying a higher price. This can lead to credit constraints for specific groups, such as women.

Since the 1990s, a growing number of studies have focused on the influence of gender on women's entrepreneurial activities (Marlow and Martinez Dy, 2018). Klapper and Parker (2011) find there are apparent gender differences in business entries, with men-led businesses predominating over women-led companies in many parts of the world. In general, businesses managed by men are more likely to have access to financing than those run by women entrepreneurs (Kalleberg and Leicht, 1991). Many scholars have studied this topic across different types of companies and different regions. Whether or not gender influences access to credit has been debated for several years, but scholars have failed to reach a consensus. In the following sections, this chapter analyses gender-based discrimination in credit markets in developed and developing countries.

There are numerous studies on discrimination against women in the credit markets of developed countries. For example, Blanchflower et al. (2003) observe that female managers of small businesses do not face discrimination based on data from the United States. Moro et al. (2017) and Galli et al. (2020) analysed the data of European SMEs and found that banks do not discriminate against women when deciding whether to approve loan applications. Interestingly, women were found to be more likely to apply successfully during periods of financial uncertainty because their risk aversion leads to conservative loan applications that are more readily approved by banks in these times (Cowling et al., 2020). A similar conclusion is obtained by Galli et al. (2020), who observe that, in European countries, gender bias is likely to appear only during periods of economic growth.

On the contrary, many studies show that women-owned firms face tighter access to credit than do men-owned ones. Bellucci et al. (2010) show that women-owned companies are at a disadvantage in the credit market in Italy. Furthermore, after analysing the data from several countries in Europe and eastern Asia, controlling for creditworthiness and performance, Muravyev, Talavera and Schäfer (2009) conclude that, beyond the difficulties of applying, women face higher interest rates than men. Similarly, Aristei and Gallo (2021) observe that women also face significantly higher interest rates than men under the condition of having obtained loans in European countries. There is no evidence that shows that women have higher risk levels (Alesina et al., 2013), though female entrepreneurs are more likely to experience adverse pricing conditions for bank lending compared to their male counterparts. Mascia and Rossi (2017) analysed the firms whose leaders changed from female to male and found a decrease in interest rates in European countries. This evidence strongly supports the existence of gender inequity in the credit markets of developed countries.

The influence of gender on access to credit varies across different countries or regions. In developing countries, banks are more likely to lend loans to state-owned or larger firms due to insufficient information and risk aversion (Wang, 2016). As a result, not taking other factors into account, SMEs in developing countries have some difficulties in accessing credit. In addition, women entrepreneurs in some developing countries might face more difficulties than their male counterparts because of pervasive social and cultural gender bias (Bui et al., 2019). That is, it can be seen that women-led SMEs may have extra difficulty in accessing bank loans in developing countries. However, in academia, scholarly research on this issue has produced mixed results similar to those found in developed countries.

In South Asia, Wellalage and Locke (2017) find that women-owned SMEs are on average 3% less likely than male entrepreneurs to be subject to credit constraints. Similarly, Pham and Talavera (2018) and Bui et al. (2019) document that women-led enterprises have a higher probability of being successful when applying for bank loans, based on data from Vietnam. Pham and Talavera (2018) also observe that female entrepreneurs face lower interest rate costs than male entrepreneurs.

However, the results obtained by Le and Stefańczyk (2018) indicate that there is a 34% greater chance of loan denials for women-led businesses than men-led businesses in Vietnam. Wellalage and Thrikawala (2021) find evidence of discrimination against women-led companies after analysing the dataset from unlisted firms in 22 developing countries. They also advise that the government should encourage female leaders to apply for bank loans to promote gender equity. In the study of Bui et al. (2019), they find that women CEOs are less likely to apply for loans than males. The conclusion they reach is that this may be because most women who get loans own larger size enterprises. The same conclusion is obtained by Chaudhuri et al. (2020) with the SMEs data in India.

Also, as a developing country, the relationship between entrepreneurs' gender and credit constraints has been studied by a number of scholars in China. Since this chapter is focused on the Chinese context, a review of the literature on Chinese women entrepreneurs will be presented in detail in the next section.

This study examines gender discrimination in the credit market in China, a developing country with the largest population and third-largest total area in the world (Worldometer, 2021). In China, women entrepreneurs face greater difficulties than men entrepreneurs when seeking capital, so women entrepreneurs usually rely on their own capital and support from friends in the early stages of their businesses (Hu and Zhu, 2007). Wang and Li (2008) find that the gender bias in traditional culture limits the participation of women in indirect access to entrepreneurial finance. In agriculture, Bai and Ma (2010) asked farmers directly about the difficulty of accessing loans in their questionnaire and used this as a measure of credit constraints, finding that rural microcredit recipients were predominantly male. Using the SMEs data from The Seventh National Sample Survey of Private Enterprises in China, Yan (2011) finds that, after controlling other related information, the number of women who have successfully applied for loans is 42% lower than that of men. These gender differences in financing are significant. After analysing the data from 826 SMEs in China, Hu (2015) demonstrates that firms with female CEOs face more severe credit constraints in their lower use of debt financing. Gender discrimination in the lending process makes it more difficult for women-led firms to obtain bank loans, which cost more in terms of interest rates and require more collateral. This credit constraint is more serious in regions of high social trust than others. Chen and Gao (2013) also demonstrate that gender has a negative effect on applying for loans, as female entrepreneurs have higher risk aversion and make more prudent decisions when applying for loans (Sun and Zhou, 2016).

After the above review of previous literature on whether women entrepreneurs in developed and developing countries face financing constraints in the credit market, no clear distinction was found on this issue between developed and developing countries. Mixed results have been obtained in studies of women facing credit constraints in both developed and developing countries. However, utilising a cross-country sample while observing gender discrimination in the credit market, Muravyev et al. (2009) observe that women-owned firms in developed economies have a greater likelihood of obtaining loans and have lower collateral requirements than those in less developed economies. In this chapter, Beijing, which is a developed economy, and Guangdong Province, which is a developing economy, are selected to test this point by means of a comparison of the presence and extent of gender discrimination existing in their credit markets.

In addition, some studies suggest that the reason for the gender gap is the different behaviour of female borrowers. Women-led companies tend not to apply for bank credit because they usually have less confidence in their bargaining power than men do when dealing with lenders (Galli et al., 2020). Moro et al. (2017) and Galli et al. (2020) show that women entrepreneurs are more likely to refrain from applying for loans than men and behave as discouraged borrowers. Coleman and Robb (2009) find that women entrepreneurs largely rely on personal rather than external sources, because they have a higher risk aversion than men (Croson and Gneezy, 2009; Huang and Kisgen, 2013) or expect to be rejected (Moro et al., 2017). The prudent behaviour of female leaders makes it difficult for scholars to identify gender discrimination in the credit market. For example, Moro et al. (2017) do not find evidence of the existence of gender discrimination in borrowing from banks.

Existing literature on the relationship between gender and credit constraints is based on national data. However, few studies are based on regional data and compare the differences within specific regions in a country. The number of studies specifically investigating gender and credit constraints in China is also limited. This study will examine gender differences in access to bank loans in a comparison of Beijing and Guangdong Province, which have different levels of economic development, to see if more developed regions have fewer credit constraints. Specifically, this chapter contributes to the field in three ways. First, it provides evidence on the relationship between gender and credit access in China. Second, it investigates whether women-led companies tend not to apply for bank credit. Third, this chapter examines whether more developed regions have fewer credit constraints. The findings of this study can provide suggestions for scholars to perform follow-up studies as well as for regulators to consider potential factors affecting access to credit for women-led businesses.

Although women entrepreneurs have done their best to break the 'glass ceiling', and although research has shown that women have equal advantages as leaders, there are still differences between men and women in entrepreneurship. In general, however, women appear to be more likely to face credit constraints, and this is more pronounced in developing countries than in developed countries. Studies have also shown that women are more reluctant to apply for bank loans than are men.

Methods and methodological debates to study gender-based credit constraints

This study uses secondary data from the China Micro and Small Enterprise Survey (CMES), run by the Survey and Research Centre for China Household Finance of Southwest University of Finance and Economics. The survey is a nationwide survey on MSEs with a sample of 5,601 MSEs across 28 provinces (autonomous regions and municipalities directly under the central government), 80 counties (districts and county-level cities) and 240 subdistricts (townships) in China (Gan et al., 2019). Data relevant to the objectives are selected for use in this research.

This study is a comparative case study that uses mixed methods that integrate both quantitative and qualitative research. In general, mixed methods can enhance the study of causal processes, as quantitative studies can assess regularities while qualitative methods identify and describe contexts and mechanisms (Bazeley, 2018). Therefore, the integration of qualitative and quantitative data produces information that goes beyond that provided by either quantitative or qualitative data alone (Creswell, 2017). This study will employ a quantitative approach to examine whether women-led MSEs face credit constraints and are not inclined to apply for bank loans in Beijing and Guangdong Province. Qualitative methods will be employed in a comparison of the credit constraints faced by women-led MSEs in Beijing and Guangdong Province, taking into account the economic context of each location, other related data from the survey and the regression results, to investigate whether women-led MSEs in more economically developed regions face fewer credit constraints than those in less developed regions.

This chapter has focused on Beijing and Guangdong Province as its research subjects because, in 2020, the GDP per capita of Beijing was around 24,000 USD, which ranked first in GDP per capita among Chinese provinces, meaning that the economic development of Beijing has reached the level of a developed economy. Although Guangdong Province ranks first in China in terms of GDP (National Bureau of Statistics, 2020), it ranks seventh in terms of GDP per capita, at around 13,000 USD, which indicates that the economic development of Guangdong is similar to the level of a developing economy (Lin, 2021). The previous literature review showed that women entrepreneurs would face tighter credit constraints and be less likely to apply for loans than men. Further, women-owned firms in more developed economies are more likely to face tighter credit constraints than women-owned firms in less developed economies (Muravyev et al., 2009). This chapter evaluates these arguments by means of a comparison of the credit constraints faced by women-led MSEs in the more developed Beijing and the less developed Guangdong Province.

To achieve the objectives of this study, this chapter uses secondary data on MSEs' basic information, borrowing activities, gender of the majority owners and other factors, all of which are taken from the China Micro and Small Enterprise Survey (CMES). In 2015, the Survey and Research Centre for China Household Finance of Southwest University of Finance and Economics conducted a nationwide survey on MSEs. The survey aimed to collect relevant information about MSEs to allow for the construction of a basic database that could be used to support academic research and government decision-making (Gan et al., 2019).

To ensure the representativeness and randomness of the sample, a three-stage probability proportional to size sampling method was adopted for the survey. In the first stage, a systematic sampling of 2,585 counties (including districts and cities), excluding Xinjiang, Tibet, Hong Kong, Macao and Taiwan, was carried out in order of GDP per capita, and 80 counties were selected. In the second stage, three subdistricts (towns and townships) or industrial parks were selected within each county.

In the third stage, the names, addresses, sizes and geographical information of enterprises were collected in the subdistricts or industrial parks on the basis of the lists of MSEs from the industrial and commercial bureaus and streets, and a sampling list was made for systematic sampling. Finally, the survey was conducted on MSEs with independent legal personalities, with a sample of 5,601 MSEs in 28 provinces (autonomous regions and municipalities directly under the central government), 80 counties (districts and county-level cities) and 240 subdistricts (townships) in China (Gan et al., 2019).

Quantitative research is used to examine whether female MSE entrepreneurs in Beijing and Guangdong face more credit constraints or are more reluctant to apply for bank loans than male entrepreneurs. As both dependent variables in the study are binary, this chapter uses a logit regression model. The equations are as follows:

$$\text{Logit}(\text{CREDC}) = \alpha + \beta * \text{GENDER} + \gamma * X_{\text{i}} + \varepsilon \tag{2.1}$$

and

$$\text{Logit}(\text{NO\_APPLY}) = \alpha + \beta * \text{GENDER} + \gamma * X_{\text{i}} + \varepsilon, \tag{2.2}$$

where CREDC indicates whether the MSE faces credit constraints. CREDC = 1 means that the company is facing financing constraints, and CREDC = 0 means that it is not. In the China Micro and Small Enterprises survey, entrepreneurs of MSEs were asked if they needed a loan, and those who selected 'yes, but did not apply' and 'yes, but applications were rejected' are defined as credit-constrained enterprises (Leon, 2015). Similarly, NO_APPLY = 1 indicates that the MSE entrepreneur chose 'yes, but did not apply', and NO_APPLY = 0 indicates that they did not. GENDER = 1 means that the main owner of the MSE is female, and GENDER = 0 means that the owner is male. The X_{i} term indicates controlled variables, including the MSE entrepreneur's age (AGE), education level (EDUCATION) and whether the entrepreneur has another business (OTHER), as well as the type of business structure (TYPE), industry (INDUSTRY) and whether it is profitable (PROFITABLE). In particular, the regression on Guangdong Province also includes CITY_LAB, which indicates the city in which the MSE is located (Lyu, 2021).

To compare the access to credit of female MSE entrepreneurs in Beijing and Guangdong, the chapter uses qualitative approach. In this study, Beijing and Guangdong will be compared and contrasted in the context of the city and province in terms of the conclusions drawn from the quantitative analysis and other relevant study data. In addition, the reasons for the conclusions obtained will be explained.

Most studies that investigate the relationship between gender and credit constraints use binary dependent variables. Therefore, reviewing the existing literature, most empirical studies have used logit or probit regression models to examine the likelihood of either successfully obtaining a loan or being denied a loan. For example, Cowling et al. (2020) and Wellalage and Thrikawala (2021) use a probit model with sample selection. Similarly, Bellucci et al. (2010), Bui et al. (2019) and

Wellalage and Locke (2017) employ the probit model in their studies about gender and financial constraints. Also, Bui et al. (2019) use an industry-specific effect specification to mitigate the endogeneity problem, as the gender of entrepreneurs could be endogenous. Further, Chaudhuri et al. (2020) estimate a logit regression model to research gender and financial constraints. The dependent variables of Mascia and Rossi (2017) were qualitative and ordinal, so they employed an ordered logit model. Similarly, Moro et al. (2017) analysed the relationship between gender and credit constraints using a pooled logit regression model (Hosmer et al., 2000).

Cai et al. (2018) used a linear probability model since it is easier to transform than the logit and probit models and offers similar results to them in the case of a large sample size. Moreover, Creswell (2017) and Galli et al. (2020) used multinomial logistic regression models in which multiple binary logistic regressions are run at the same time to compare the different outcome categories in the model. Further, Le and Stefańczyk (2018) employ zero-inflated negative binomial regression, which also considers the frequency of applying for loans and the frequency of rejection, in contrast to the logit and probit models.

After reviewing the literature, one can find that the quantitative methods used in most studies to analyse the relationship between gender and credit constraints are logit and probit regression models or special cases thereof. However, some studies use other models to meet their specific research needs.

In addition, the measurement of credit constraints is an issue that has been discussed. Identifying credit constraints through direct observation is difficult, and there are a variety of measures of credit constraints discussed in prior work. Hayashi (1985) compared the regression coefficients of consumption to income for both the overall sample and the constrained subsample to identify household credit constraints, which were concluded to exist if the coefficients were significantly different between groups. Leon (2015) finds that existing studies measure credit constraints by estimating how a firm perceives its financial situation as an obstacle to growth, by measuring the mix of internal and external financing, or by the use of credit. However, these measures of credit constraints are not applicable to all types of firms. Therefore, Leon (2015) has proposed a solution to this problem by classifying firms into those whose loan applications have been rejected and those credit-constrained firms who have been discouraged from applying. This approach to measuring credit constraints is applicable to studies using data from social surveys. Therefore, this chapter will use this established measure of credit constraints to examine whether female entrepreneurs face credit constraints.

While most studies only use quantitative methods to analyse the relationship between gender and credit constraints, this chapter uses mixed methods. This is because, in general, mixed methods enhance the study of causal processes. The use of mixed methods can be used to obtain regularities through quantitative analysis and to identify and describe contexts and mechanisms through qualitative means (Bazeley, 2018). This chapter investigates the existence of credit constraints among female entrepreneurs in Beijing and Guangdong while also comparing and analysing the similarities, differences and reasons behind credit constraints in relation to the regional economic context and other related information taken from the survey.

Women entrepreneurs of MSEs in China

According to the China Micro and Small Enterprise Survey, after removing data that lacked information on gender, 4,926 observations were obtained. The study by Lyu (2021) shows that the number of female entrepreneurs of MSEs accounts for 17.6% of the total sample. That is, it can be seen that the gender of entrepreneurs of MSEs in China is highly unbalanced, with the number of female entrepreneurs being only one-fourth of the number of male entrepreneurs. However, in China, women entrepreneurs account for about a quarter of the total number of entrepreneurs of all business sizes (China Development Research Foundation, 2017). This shows that the proportion of female entrepreneurs in MSEs is less than average (Lyu, 2021).

The analysis of the China Micro and Small Enterprise Survey (CMES) by Lyu (2021: 24) shows the unequal gender distribution of Chinese MSE entrepreneurs during 2015 due to credit constraints. Lyu (2021) has further argued that there is a serious credit constraint problem faced by entrepreneurs.

Age and credit constraints

In the works of Lyu (2021: 24), it is argued that the age distribution is generally consistent between female and male MSE entrepreneurs. Most female and male MSE entrepreneurs are between the ages of 25 and 60, accounting for approximately 94% and 92% of MSE entrepreneurs, respectively. The largest proportion of female and male entrepreneurs are aged 31–50, representing about 37% each of the total. The overall age distribution of female MSE entrepreneurs skews younger than males, with around 5% more female entrepreneurs being under the age of 40 than males. In China, around 60% of female entrepreneurs are aged 45 and above (China Development Research Foundation, 2017). Lyu (2021: 24) has argued that only about 56% of female MSE entrepreneurs are over 41 years old, indicating that the average age of female MSE entrepreneurs is younger than the overall level. This may be because it is easier to start an MSE than to start a medium or large enterprise.

With regard to credit constraints, the age range is divided into those aged 30 and under, 31–40, 41–50 and 50 and over, within which the number of MSEs facing credit constraints is counted according to gender. As shown in Lyu (2021: 24), the share of female and male MSE entrepreneurs facing credit constraints decreases roughly with age, presumably because banks perceive that older entrepreneurs are more solvent (Blanchflower et al., 2003), irrespective of other factors. The exception to this is that female entrepreneurs aged 31–40 also have a smaller share of credit constraints than those aged 41–50, perhaps due to some gender bias that makes banks believe that female MSE entrepreneurs aged 41–50 are the least capable of paying back their loans. Horizontally, male MSE entrepreneurs in all age groups face tighter credit constraints than do female entrepreneurs, except for the case of female MSE entrepreneurs younger than 30. There may also be a gender bias here, as banks may believe that women under 30 are not as capable of managing businesses as are men in the same age group.

The analysis of China Micro and Small Enterprise Survey (CMES) by Lyu (2021: 26) shows that the younger MSE entrepreneurs generally face tighter credit constraints, except for women aged 41–50, who face tighter credit constraints than women aged 31–40. When classified according to age, no significant evidence was found that female MSE entrepreneurs face tighter credit constraints than do male ones, with the exception of female MSE entrepreneurs younger than 30 years old, who faced the tightest credit constraints of all.

Education and credit constraints

Lyu (2021: 24)'s work shows that the distribution of education levels is also generally consistent among female and male MSE entrepreneurs. Approximately 91% of all female and male entrepreneurs have an education level between a junior high school degree and a bachelor's degree. The largest proportion of female and male MSE entrepreneurs have bachelor's degrees, at approximately 27% and 25%, respectively. The overall education level distribution of female MSE entrepreneurs is higher than that of males, with 2% more female entrepreneurs having bachelor's degrees or higher. In China, 87.3% of the female entrepreneurs surveyed had a university degree or above (China Development Research Foundation, 2017). In contrast, about 32% of female MSE entrepreneurs have a bachelor's degree or higher, roughly 55% less than the overall education level of female entrepreneurs. This is probably because it is easier to start an MSE than to start a medium or large enterprise, thereby providing more opportunities for those with relatively low levels of education.

As seen in the works of Lyu (2021), vertically, the proportion of female and male MSE entrepreneurs facing credit constraints decreases broadly with educational level, possibly because banks perceive higher educational attainment to signal higher business management capability, and thus more solvent borrowers, regardless of other factors. An exception to this is that female MSE entrepreneurs with education levels higher than junior high school and lower than bachelor's degree also face a greater share of credit constraints than do female MSE entrepreneurs with a junior high school education or below. Banks may have a gender bias towards women with medium education levels when compared to the relationship between education level and credit constraints for males in the same age group. Horizontally, male MSE owners of all education levels face tighter credit constraints than do females, and no evidence of gender bias against women is found. The analysis of the China Micro and Small Enterprise Survey (CMES) by Lyu (2021) shows that MSE owners with lower levels of education face tighter credit constraints, except for women with a medium level of education, who face tighter credit constraints than others. When grouped by education level, no evidence was found that women-led MSEs face tighter credit constraints than men-led MSEs.

Industry and credit constraints

Lyu (2021: 24)'s work shows that the industry distribution of female and male MSE entrepreneurs is roughly the same. Although the majority of both female and male MSE entrepreneurs are in the manufacturing and retail trade sectors, there are approximately 10% fewer women than men in manufacturing and 7% more women than men in retail trade. More women MSE entrepreneurs work in leasing and business services and other industries, including education, services, advertising, consulting and beauty. Compared to men, fewer women MSE entrepreneurs work in the more industrial industries. Lyu (2021) has argued that the largest shares of credit constraints faced by female and male MSE entrepreneurs are in the agriculture, forestry, animal husbandry and fishing sectors, while the rest of the sectors do not differ substantially. This may be due to banks' biases against those involved in agriculture-related industries. In general, incomes in agriculture-related industries are closely related to the climatic environment, and there is a social stereotype that those working in agriculture-related industries have low levels of education and insufficient management skills. Horizontally, the proportion of women-led MSEs facing credit constraints is generally less than that of men-led MSEs, with the exception of women-led MSEs in the retail sector. This disparity reflects the gender bias of banks against women-led MSEs in the retail sector.

Overall, MSEs engaged in agriculture-related businesses face tighter credit constraints. From the perspective of the gender of the entrepreneur, women-led MSEs in the retail sector face tighter credit constraints than men-led MSEs in the retail sector. This phenomenon is not found in other sectors (Lyu, 2021).

Region and credit constraints

The majority of women-led and men-led MSEs are concentrated in the eastern region of China at approximately 51% and 60%, respectively. This is mainly due to the fact that most developed provinces and cities are clustered in eastern China and that the eastern part of the country has a unique geographical and natural environment. The proportion of women-led MSEs concentrated in the east of China is about 9% less than that of men-led MSEs, while the proportion of women-led MSEs concentrated in the western region is around 8% more than men-led MSEs. In China, on the whole, the majority of women-owned businesses are located in the eastern region, accounting for 61.2% of all women-led businesses (China Development Research Foundation, 2017) and being 10% greater than the number of women-led MSEs in the eastern region. This fact is also presumably due to the fact that MSEs, which are easier to start than are medium or large enterprises, give women in the less developed western and middle regions more opportunities to start their own businesses (Lyu, 2021).

The regional analysis shows that the levels of economic development in China are, in descending order, eastern, central and western. As shown in the works of Lyu (2021), the share of MSE entrepreneurs facing credit constraints largely increases from east to west, which supports the point mentioned in the previous chapters that MSE entrepreneurs in economically developed regions face fewer credit constraints than do those in less economically developed regions. The one exception is that male MSE entrepreneurs in the central region face the largest share of credit constraints, due in part to the fact that more male MSE entrepreneurs in the central region are engaged in agriculture-related industries. The central region is an important food production base in China (Xu, 2018), and, as was shown above, MSEs engaged in agriculture-related industries face the greatest credit constraints, while the majority of MSE owners engaged in agriculture-related industries in the central region are male. Horizontally, when grouped by region, women MSE entrepreneurs in each region face fewer credit constraints than do their male counterparts (Lyu, 2021).

In conclusion, after dividing by region, it is found that the less economically developed the region, the tighter the credit constraints faced by MSEs. Furthermore, no evidence was found that women-led MSEs face tighter credit constraints than do men-led MSEs. The preliminary analysis of the total sample in the previous section on the ages and education levels of MSE entrepreneurs, as well as the industries and regions in which the MSEs are located, did not provide significant evidence that women-led MSEs face tighter credit constraints than do men-led MSEs.

Comparative study of women-led MSEs and credit constraints in Beijing and Guangdong Province

The proportion of MSEs facing credit constraints is generally smaller in Beijing than in Guangdong by approximately 6% when other factors are not taken into account. Specifically, vertically, the percentage of women-led MSEs facing credit constraints is about 1% smaller than that of men-led MSEs in Beijing, while in Guangdong, the percentage of women-led MSEs facing credit constraints is about 3% larger than that of men-led MSEs. This reflects the fact that women-led MSEs in Beijing do not face tighter credit constraints compared to men-led ones, while women-led MSEs in Guangdong may face gender discrimination in regard to credit. Horizontally, the share of women-led MSEs in Beijing facing credit constraints is approximately half of that measured in Guangdong, which indicates that women-led MSEs in Guangdong face tighter credit constraints than do women-led MSEs in Beijing (Lyu, 2021).

The empirical analysis by Lyu (2021) shows that there is no statistically significant evidence that women-led MSEs in Beijing face tighter credit constraints than men-led MSEs. Lyu (2021) further argued that the empirical evidence suggests that the credit constraints faced by MSEs in Guangdong are positively correlated with the gender of entrepreneurs, implying that women-led MSEs face tighter credit constraints than men-led MSEs, holding other factors fixed. Additionally, the regression results show a significant negative relationship between credit constraints and the education level of MSE owners, as well as a significant positive relationship between credit constraints and whether MSEs are profitable, and their business structure types (Lyu, 2021). In practice, however, these control variables are somewhat related to whether or not MSEs face credit constraints. This may be due to the presence of other relevant variables that were not considered, such as the personal wealth of the entrepreneur, political affiliation of the entrepreneur, firm-specific financial data, among other factors (Yan, 2011). Thus, women-led MSEs in

Beijing do not face tighter credit constraints than do men-led MSEs, while women-led MSEs in Guangdong do face tighter credit constraints, with roughly twice as many women-led MSEs facing credit constraints in Guangdong than in Beijing (Lyu, 2021).

Women entrepreneurs and banks in Beijing and Guangdong

Lyu (2021) has argued that the MSE entrepreneurs in Beijing who do not want to apply for bank loans is less than that measured in Guangdong by about 3%. Vertically, the percentage of women MSE entrepreneurs in Beijing who do not want to apply for bank loans is about 1% less than that of men, while in Guangdong, the percentage of women MSE entrepreneurs who do not want to apply for bank loans is about 4% more than that of men. This reflects the fact that women MSE entrepreneurs are not less likely to apply for bank loans in Beijing, while the opposite is true in Guangdong. Horizontally, women MSE entrepreneurs in Beijing account for nearly half of those in Guangdong who are reluctant to apply for bank loans, reflecting the fact that women entrepreneurs in Guangdong are more likely to be reluctant to apply for bank loans (Lyu, 2021). There is no significant evidence that female MSE entrepreneurs in Beijing are less willing to apply for bank loans than their male counterparts. In addition, the regression results show that the choice not to apply for a bank loan is significantly negatively related to the education level of MSE entrepreneurs, holding other factors fixed (Lyu, 2021).

In Guangdong Province, the empirical evidence suggests that a Guangdong MSE entrepreneur's choice not to apply for a bank loan is positively correlated with gender, implying that female MSE entrepreneurs are less likely to apply for bank loans than are their male counterparts, holding other factors fixed. In addition, the regression results show that MSE entrepreneurs choosing not to apply for bank loans is significantly negatively related to the entrepreneur's age, the entrepreneur's education level and the city where the entrepreneur's business is located, while it is significantly positively related to whether or not the entrepreneur's business is profitable (Lyu, 2021). A limitation of this study is that there are other control variables not considered, such as the personal wealth of the entrepreneur, the political affiliation of the entrepreneur and firm-specific financial data, among other factors (Yan, 2011).

In summary, no statistically significant evidence suggests that women-led MSEs in Beijing are less likely to apply for bank loans than are men-led MSEs, while statistically significant evidence does suggest that women-led MSEs in Guangdong are less likely to apply for bank loans than are men-led MSEs, and their share is twice as high as that measured in Beijing.

Women-led MSEs in Beijing and Guangdong

In the previous two sections, a comparison of data on credit constraints and whether female MSE entrepreneurs chose to apply for bank loans in Beijing and Guangdong was made. It was found that women-led MSEs in Beijing neither face tighter credit constraints nor are less likely to apply for bank loans compared to men-led MSEs. Women-led MSEs in Guangdong, however, face tighter credit constraints and are more reluctant to apply for bank loans than men-led MSEs.

Beijing is one of the most urbanised cities in China, with a GDP per capita already at the level of that of developed countries. Guangdong is the number one economic province in China, with the highest total GDP in the country, but its GDP per capita is only the seventh highest in China (2021). On the one hand, this is because Guangdong has a large migrant population and a large population base. On the other hand, this is because there is a large regional development gap in Guangdong, with the Pearl River Delta (PRD) being developed, but the gap between the east, west and north of Guangdong and the PRD being large. There is a popular saying that 'The richest place in the country is in Guangdong, and the poorest place is also in Guangdong' (Lin, 2021). Therefore, Beijing can be regarded as one of the more developed regions of China, while Guangdong Province is regarded as one of the less developed regions of China. The women MSE entrepreneurs in more developed regions face fewer credit constraints than do women MSE entrepreneurs in less developed regions (Muravyev et al., 2009).

It is clear that there is no evidence that women-led MSEs in Beijing are less likely to apply for bank loans than are men-led MSEs, while there is significant evidence of this occurring in Guangdong. There are approximately twice as many MSE entrepreneurs in Guangdong who are reluctant to apply for bank loans than in Beijing, especially among female MSE entrepreneurs. It follows that women-led MSEs in more economically developed areas are also less likely to refuse to apply for bank loans than are those in less economically developed areas (Lyu, 2021).

The empirical analysis by Lyu (2021) shows that the reasons women-led MSEs in Beijing do not apply for loans are the excessively high interest rates, lack of knowledge of how to apply, fears of not being approved or not being able to repay and a troublesome application process. In Guangdong, female MSE entrepreneurs do not apply for bank loans due to excessively high interest rates, a fear that they will not be approved, the troublesome application process, a lack of collateral or guarantors and other reasons, including age restrictions and temporary non-requirement. Comparing the reasons female MSE entrepreneurs in Beijing and Guangdong do not apply for loans, it can be found that in Beijing, female entrepreneurs are more worried about high interest rates, while in Guangdong, no obvious main reason was found.

In Beijing, no factors were found to significantly influence the credit constraints faced by MSEs. In Guangdong Province, empirical results show a significant negative relationship between credit constraints and the education levels of MSE owners, as well as a significant positive relationship with whether the MSE is profitable and the type of business structure.

The works of Lyu (2021) shows that the choice not to apply for a bank loan is significantly negatively related to the education level of MSE entrepreneurs.

Meanwhile, in Guangdong Province, the choice of MSE entrepreneurs not to apply for bank loans is significantly negatively related to age, education level and the city in which the business is located, while it is significantly positively related to whether or not the business is profitable. This means that, all other factors being equal, the lower the education level of MSE entrepreneurs in Beijing and Guangdong, the more likely they are to choose not to apply for bank loans. In Guangdong, the younger the MSE entrepreneur is, the less likely the entrepreneur is to apply for a bank loan. Also, MSEs that are not profitable are more likely to choose not to apply for bank loans. In addition, whether or not a business applies for a bank loan is also related to the city in Guangdong Province in which the business is located. It is not possible to tell in which city businesses are operating from the dataset used in this study. However, based on the previous findings, it is not unreasonable to suggest that the less economically developed the city in which an MSE is located, the less inclined the MSE is to apply for a bank loan (Lyu, 2021).

In conclusion, by comparing women-led MSEs in Beijing and in Guangdong, it can be concluded that women-led MSEs in the more developed regions do not face tighter credit constraints and are not less likely to apply for bank loans compared to men-led ones. In contrast, both phenomena are present in the less developed regions of Guangdong Province. Regarding the causes of these two phenomena, no representative conclusions can be drawn from the data in the survey questionnaire, as the response rate was too low. However, some conclusions can be drawn from the previous regression results. In Beijing, no influencing factors were found for MSEs facing credit constraints, while the choice of MSEs not to apply for bank loans was found to be negatively related to the education levels of the entrepreneurs. In Guangdong, the credit constraints faced by an MSE were found to be negatively related to the level of education the entrepreneur and profitability and business structure type of the MSE. The choice of Guangdong MSEs not to apply for bank loans is negatively related to the education level and age of the entrepreneurs, the profitability of the businesses, as well as related to the cities in which the MSEs are located.

The preliminary analysis of the relationship between credit constraints faced by MSE entrepreneurs and gender was conducted based on the age and education level of MSE entrepreneurs as well as the industry and region in which the MSEs were located. In the end, a general pattern was obtained in which tighter credit constraints were associated with younger MSE entrepreneurs, lower education levels, agriculture-related businesses and businesses located in less developed regions. First, the empirical analysis finds that female MSE entrepreneurs in Beijing do not face tighter credit constraints and are not less likely to apply for bank loans than male entrepreneurs, while in Guangdong, both phenomena are observed. With regard to the reasons for these two phenomena, in Beijing, no influencing factors were found for MSEs facing credit constraints, while the choice of MSEs not to apply for bank loans was negatively related to the education level of the entrepreneurs. In Guangdong, the credit constraints faced by MSEs were negatively related to the education level of the entrepreneur as well as the profitability and business structure types of the MSE. The choice of Guangdong MSEs not to apply for bank loans is negatively related to the education levels and ages of the entrepreneurs, the profitability of the business, as well as related to the city in which the MSEs are located.

Conclusion

Using data from the 2015 China Micro and Small Enterprise Survey, this study examines and compares the credit constraints and reluctance to apply for bank loans among women-led MSEs in Beijing and Guangdong Province through a mixed quantitative and qualitative approach. The following conclusions can be drawn from this research. A preliminary analysis of the data does not suggest that, in general, women-led MSEs face tighter credit constraints than do men-led MSEs in China. In terms of the ages of MSE entrepreneurs, in general, the younger they are, the tighter the credit constraints they face. In particular, female MSE entrepreneurs below the age of 30 face the tightest credit constraints of all entrepreneurs. Regarding the education level of MSE entrepreneurs, the lower their education levels, the tighter the credit constraints they face, generally. In particular, women with a medium level of education (more than junior high school and less than a bachelor's degree) face the tightest credit constraints of anyone. Concerning MSEs' industries, MSEs in agriculture-related industries face tighter credit constraints than do those in other industries. Also, women-led MSEs in the retail trade sector face even tighter credit constraints than do men-led MSEs. In terms of the location of an MSE, the less developed the region, the tighter the credit constraint faced by an MSE.

The first objective of this chapter was to research whether women-led MSEs face tighter credit constraints than men-led MSEs in Beijing and Guangdong Province, China. Regression analysis showed that women-led MSEs in Beijing are not facing tighter credit constraints than are men-led MSEs, while women-led MSEs in Guangdong are facing tighter credit constraints, with the number of women-led MSEs facing credit constraints in Guangdong being approximately twice that measured in Beijing. The second objective was to examine whether female entrepreneurs of MSEs were less likely to apply for bank loans than were male MSE entrepreneurs in Beijing and Guangdong Province, China. Similarly to the last objective, the method used to address this objective was regression analysis. It is concluded that there is no significant evidence that women-led MSEs in Beijing are less likely to apply for bank loans than are men-led MSEs, while there is significant evidence that women-led MSEs in Guangdong are less likely to apply for bank loans than are men-led MSEs, with twice as many women-led MSEs choosing not to apply for bank loans in Guangdong Province as measured in Beijing. The third objective was to compare the access to credit of women entrepreneurs of MSEs in Beijing and Guangdong Province. Women-led MSEs in economically developed Beijing are less likely to face tighter credit constraints and are less likely to be reluctant to apply for bank loans than are men-led MSEs, while women-led MSEs in the less economically developed Guangdong Province are more likely to face tighter credit constraints and are less likely to apply for bank loans. This finding is consistent with the argument of Muravyev et al. (2009) that women-owned businesses in economically developed economies have a greater probability of obtaining loans. The regression results from this study on Beijing and Guangdong reveal the factors that lead MSEs to face tighter credit constraints and be more reluctant to apply for loans. In Beijing, no factors were found to significantly influence the credit constraints faced by MSEs, while the choice of MSEs not to apply for bank loans was negatively related to the education levels of the entrepreneurs. In Guangdong Province, the credit constraints faced by MSEs were negatively related to the education levels of the entrepreneurs as well as the profitability and business structure types of the MSEs. The choice of Guangdong MSEs not to apply for bank loans was negatively related to the education level and age of the entrepreneur, the profitability of the MSE, as well as related to the city in which the MSE was located.

Finally, despite the statistical significance of the findings of this study, there are limitations to the use of this survey-based dataset. The dataset used in this study does not include some entrepreneur-specific information, such as personal wealth, political affiliation, or marital status, among other factors, nor does it include financial statement information of the MSE. If these specific data were available, more solid conclusions could be drawn. Another limitation of the dataset used in this study is its relatively small sample size. If a larger sample size were obtained, then the conclusions obtained would be more reliable.

References

Abbott, L.J., Parker, S. and Presley, T.J. 2012. Female board presence and the likelihood of financial restatement. *Accounting Horizons*. **26**(4), pp. 607–629.

Alesina, A.F., Lotti, F. and Mistrulli, P.E. 2013. Do women pay more for credit? Evidence from Italy. *Journal of the European Economic Association*. **11**, pp. 45–66.

Aristei, D. and Gallo, M. 2021. Are female-led firms disadvantaged in accessing bank credit? Evidence from transition economies. *International Journal of Emerging Markets*. **17**(6), pp. 1484–1521.

Arrow, K.J. 2015. *The Theory of Discrimination*. Princeton: Princeton University Press.

Bai, Y. and Ma, X. 2010. Nonghu Geti Tezheng Dui Xindai Yunshu de Yingxiang: Laizi Shaanxi de Jingyan Zhengju 农户个体特征对信贷约束的影响:来自陕西的经验证据 [Influence of farmers' individual characters upon credit constraint: an experiential evidence from Shaanxi]. *Zhongguo Ruan Kexue* 中国软科学 *[China Soft Science]*. (09), pp. 148–155.

Bazeley, P. 2018. *Integrating Analyses in Mixed Methods Research*. [Online]. London: SAGE Publications Ltd. [Accessed 17 August 2021]. Available from: http://methods.sagepub.com/book/integrating-analyses-in-mixed-methods-research.

Bear, S., Rahman, N. and Post, C. 2010. The impact of board diversity and gender composition on corporate social responsibility and firm reputation. *Journal of Business Ethics*. **97**(2), pp. 207–221.

Becker, G.S. 1971. *The Economics of Discrimination*. Chicago, IL: University of Chicago Press.

Bellucci, A., Borisov, A. and Zazzaro, A. 2010. Does gender matter in bank–firm relationships? Evidence from small business lending. *Journal of Banking & Finance*. **34**(12), pp. 2968–2984.

Berger, A.N. and Udell, G.F. 2002. Small business credit availability and relationship lending: the importance of bank organisational structure. *The Economic Journal*. **112**(477), pp. F32–F53.

Bialek-Jaworska, A. and Matusiewicz, A. 2015. Determinants of the level of information disclosure in financial statements prepared in accordance with IFRS. *Journal of Accounting and Management Information Systems*, Faculty of Accounting and Management Information Systems, The Bucharest University of Economic Studies. **14**(3), pp. 453–482.

Blanchflower, D.G., Levine, P.B. and Zimmerman, D.J. 2003. Discrimination in the small-business credit market. *Review of Economics and Statistics*. **85**(4), pp. 930–943.

Bowen, H.R. 1953. *Social Responsibilities of the Businessman*. New York: Harper & Row.

Bui, A.T., Nguyen, C.V., Pham, T.P. and Phung, D.T. 2022. Female leadership and borrowing constraints: evidence from an emerging economy, *International Review of Financial Analysis*. **81**.

Burgess, Z. and Tharenou, P. 2002. Women board directors: characteristics of the few. *Journal of Business Ethics*. **37**(1), pp. 39–49.

Caglayan, M. and Xu, B. 2016. Inflation volatility effects on the allocation of bank loans. *Journal of Financial Stability*. **24**, pp. 27–39.

Cai, D., Song, Q., Ma, S., Dong, Y. and Xu, Q. 2018. The relationship between credit constraints and household entrepreneurship in China. *International Review of Economics & Finance*. **58**, pp. 246–258.

Campbell, D., Craven, B. and Shrives, P. 2003. Voluntary social reporting in three FTSE sectors: a comment on perception and legitimacy. *Accounting, Auditing & Accountability Journal*. **16**(4), pp. 558–581.

Canton, E., Grilo, I., Monteagudo, J. and van der Zwan, P. 2013. Perceived credit constraints in the European Union. *Small Business Economics*. **41**(3), pp. 701–715.

Carter, D.A., Simkins, B.J. and Simpson, W.G. 2003. Corporate governance, board diversity, and firm value. *Financial Review*. **38**(1), pp. 33–53.

Cao, Q., Zhou, Y., Du, H., Ren, M. and Zhen, W. 2022. Carbon information disclosure quality, greenwashing behavior, and enterprise value. *Frontiers in Psychology*. **13**, p. 892415.

Chaudhuri, K., Sasidharan, S. and Raj, R.S.N. 2020. Gender, small firm ownership, and credit access: some insights from India. *Small Business Economics*. **54**(4), pp. 1165–1181.

Chen, X. and Gao, Y. 2013. Qiyejia Renkou Tongji Tezheng Dui Zhong Xiao Qiye Rongzi Yunshu de Yingxiang Jizhi Yanjiu 企业家人口统计特征对中小企业融资约束的影响机制研究 [Influencing mechanism of demographic traits of entrepreneurs on financing constraints of SMEs]. *Ke Yan Guanli* 科研管理 *[Science Research Management]*. **34**(12), pp. 110–119.

China Development Research Foundation 2017. *Zhongguo Nvxing Chuangye: Shifang Zengzhang Xin Jiyu* 中国女性创业：释放增长新机遇 *[Female Entrepreneurship in China: Unlocking New Opportunities for Growth]*. Beijing: China Development Research Foundation.

Chunhui, L. and Yuetang, W. 2018. Research on the relationship between CSR information and stakeholders' behavioral intention. *Journal of Audit & Economics*. **33**(3), pp. 73–82.

Colaço, R. and Simão, J. 2018. Disclosure of corporate social responsibility in the forestry sector of the Congo Basin. *Forest Policy and Economics*. **92**, pp. 136–147.

Coleman, S. and Robb, A. 2009. A comparison of new firm financing by gender: evidence from the Kauffman Firm Survey data. *Small Business Economics*. **33**(4), p. 397.

Cong, F.E.N.G. and Xinyan, P.E.N.G. 2015. An empirical study on identification of corporate life cycle phases. *Canadian Social Science*. **11**(5), pp. 48–52.

Cowling, M., Marlow, S. and Liu, W. 2020. Gender and bank lending after the global financial crisis: are women entrepreneurs safer bets? *Small Business Economics*. **55**(4), pp. 853–880.

Creswell, J.W. 2017. *Research Design: Qualitative, Quantitative, and Mixed Methods Approaches* (5th international student edition). London: SAGE Publications.

Croson, R. and Gneezy, U. 2009. Gender differences in preferences. *Journal of Economic Literature*. **47**(2), pp. 448–474.

Cunningham, J.A., O'Reilly, P., Dolan, B., O'Kane, C. and Mangematin, V. 2017. Gender differences and academic entrepreneurship: a study of scientists in the 27 principal investigator role. In *Gender and Entrepreneurial Activity*. Cheltenham: Edward Elgar Publishing.

Davis, K. 1960. Can business afford to ignore social responsibilities? *California Management Review*. **2**(3), pp. 70–76.

Demirguc-Kunt, A., Klapper, L., Singer, D. and Ansar, S. 2018. *The Global Findex Database 2017: Measuring Financial Inclusion and the Fintech Revolution*. Washington, DC: World Bank Publications.

Edmans, A. (2011). Does the stock market fully value in tangibles? Employee satisfaction and equity prices. *Journal of Financial Economics*. **101**, pp. 621–626.

Feng, L., Lin, F. and Xu, J. 2011. Property rights, ownership concentration and corporate social responsibility performance. *Journal of Shanxi University of Finance and Economics*. **33**, pp. 100–107.

Feng, M., & Chen, K. (2016). Exploring variations of corporate social responsibility across business sectors and geographic scope. *Journal of Applied Business and Economics*, Vol–*18*(7).

Galli, E., Mascia, D.V. and Rossi, S.P.S. 2020. Bank credit constraints for women-led SMEs: self-restraint or lender bias? *European Financial Management*. **26**(4), pp. 1147–1188.

Gan, L., Qin, F. and Wu, Y. 2019. Xiao Wei Qiye Zengzhishui Qizhengdian Tigao Shishi Xiaoguo Pinggu-Laizi Zhongguo Xiao Wei Qiye Diaocha (CMES) Shuju de Fenxi 小微企业增值税起征点提高实施效果评估——来自中国小微企业调查（CMES）数据的分析 [Effects of increasing VAT threshold on small and micro enterprises: an estimation based on the date of China Micro-and-Small Enterprises Survey]. *Guanli Shijie* 管理世界 *[Management World]*. **35**(11), pp. 80–88+231–232.

Gong, N. and Duan, M. 2021.The motivation and influencing factors of corporate carbon information disclosure: an analysis of the constituent enterprises of SSE social responsibility index. *Journal of Environmental Economics*. **6**, pp. 31–52.

Gul, F.A., Srinidhi, B. and Ng, A.C. 2011. Does board gender diversity improve the informativeness of stock prices? *Journal of Accounting and Economics*. **51**(3), pp. 314–338.

Guo, H. and Lu, W. 2021. The inverse U-shaped relationship between corporate social responsibility and competitiveness: evidence from Chinese international construction companies. *Journal of Cleaner Production*. **95**, pp. 126–374.

Guryan, J. and Charles, K.K. 2013. Taste-based or statistical discrimination: the economics of discrimination returns to its roots. *The Economic Journal*. **123**(572), pp. F417–F432.

Haixia, W. and LIsi, C .2018. Analysis on the influencing factors of food safety information disclosure. *Journal of Northwest Agricultural and Forestry University of Science and Technology* (SOCIAL SCIENCE EDITION), **18**(4), pp. 152–160.

Haniffa, R.M. and Cooke, T.E. 2005. The impact of culture and governance on corporate social reporting. *Journal of Accounting and Public Policy*. **24**, pp. 391–430.

Hengwang, N., Changqing, L. and Zhihua, W. 2015. Media attention, corporate voluntary social responsibility information disclosure and financing constraints. *Journal of Shanxi University of Finance and Economics*. **37**(11), pp. 77–88.

Hayashi, F. 1985. The effect of liquidity constraints on consumption: a cross-sectional analysis. *The Quarterly Journal of Economics*. **100**(1), pp. 183–206.

Hosmer, D.W., Lemeshow, S. and Sturdivant, R.X. 2000. *Applied Logistic Regression*. New York: Wiley.

Hu, H. and Zhu, X. 2007. Chuangye Dongju, Shehui Ziben yu Nvxing Chuangye 创业动机、社会资本与女性创业 [Motivation, social capital and the female in pioneering work]. *Beijing Gongye Daxue Xuebao (Shehui Kexue Ban)* 北京工业大学学报（社会科学版） *[Journal of Beijing University of Technology (Social Sciences Edition)]*. **7**(4), pp. 18–22.

Hu, Q. and Zhou, D. 2016. Nvxing Dongshi dui Qiye Jixiao Yingxiang de Shizheng Yanjiu-Jiyu Guquan Xingzhi Huafen de Zhongguo Shangshi Gongsi Jingyan Shuju 女性董事对企业绩效影响的实证研究——基于股权性质划分的中国上市公司经验数据 [Effects of female board members on firm performance]. *Caijing Lilun Yanjiu* 财经理论研究 *[Journal of Finance and Economics Theory]*. **3**, pp. 78–87.

Hu, Z. 2015. Nvxing CEO Shehui Xinren he Gongsi Rongzi Yunshu 女性CEO、社会信任和公司融资约束 [Female CEO, social trust and financial constraints]. *Jinji Guanli* 经济管理 *[Economic Management Journal]*. **37**(08), pp. 88–98.

Huang, S.Y., Lin, C.C., Chiu, A.A. and Yen, D.C. 2017. Fraud detection using fraud triangle risk factors. *Information Systems Frontiers*. **19**, pp. 1343–1356.

Huang, J., Xu, N. and Yuan, Q. 2013, September 27. Divergence of shareholder rights and corporate risk-taking. Available at SSRN: https://ssrn.com/abstract=1786581; https://dx.doi.org/10.2139/ssrn.1786581

Huang, J. and Kisgen, D.J. 2013. Gender and corporate finance: are male executives overconfident relative to female executives? *Journal of Financial Economics*. **108**(3), pp. 822–839.

Huang, R. and Chen, D. 2015. Does environmental information disclosure benefit waste discharge reduction? Evidence from China. *Journal of Business Ethics*. **129**, pp. 535–552.

Hung, M., Shi, J. and Wang, Y. 2015. Mandatory CSR disclosure and information asymmetry: evidence from a quasi-natural experiment in China. Hong Kong University of Science and Technology Working Paper.

Jennings, J.E. and Brush, C.G. 2013. Research on women entrepreneurs: challenges to (and from) the broader entrepreneurship literature? *Academy of Management Annals*. **7**(1), pp. 663–715.

Jones, P., Comfort, D. and Hillier, D. 2012. Corporate social responsibility on the catwalk. *Journal of Business and Retail Management Research*. **7**(1).

Jiang X. and Yuan Q. 2018. Institutional investors' corporate site visits and corporate innovation. *Journal of Corporate Finance*. **48**, pp.148–168.

Ju, L. and Mei, Q. 2014. Nvxing Chuangye de Xianzhuang yu Xuqiu Fenxi 女性创业的现状与需求分析 [Analysis of the female entrepreneurial actuality and demand]. *Ruan Kexue* 软科学 *[Soft Science]*. **28**(4), pp. 78–82.

Kalleberg, A.L. and Leicht, K.T. 1991. Gender and organizational performance: determinants of small business survival and success. *The Academy of Management Journal*. **34**(1), pp. 136–161.

Klapper, L.F. and Parker, S.C. 2011. Gender and the business environment for new firm creation. *The World Bank Research Observer*. **26**(2), pp. 237–257.

Le, L.H. and Stefańczyk, J.K. 2018. Gender discrimination in access to credit: are women-led SMEs rejected more than men-led? *Gender, Technology and Development*. **22**(2), pp. 145–163.

Leon, F. 2015. Does bank competition alleviate credit constraints in developing countries? *Journal of Banking & Finance*. **57**, pp. 130–142.

Li, W. and Huang, X. 2014. Woguo Shangshi Gongsi Nvxing Gaoguan dui Qiye Binggou Jixiao de Yingxiang Yanjiu 我国上市公司女性高管对企业并购绩效的影响研究 [Research on the impact of women top managers in China listed companies on the performance of M&A]. *Guanli Gongcheng Xuebao* 管理工程学报 *[Journal of Industrial Engineering and Engineering Managemen]*. **28**(3), pp. 18–25.

Lin, B., Cai, S. and Wang, W. 2017. The definition of variables in the study of CSR evaluationis analyzed. *Finance and Accounting Monthly*, Issue 8.

Lin, X. 2021. *31 Shengfen Renjun GDP Bipin: Jing Hu Chao 15 Wan Yuan, Chongqing Hubei Chao Shandong 31省份人均GDP比拼：京沪超15万元，重庆湖北超山东 [GDP per Capita in 31 Provinces: Beijing and Shanghai Exceed 150,000 Yuan, Chongqing and Hubei Exceed Shandong]*. [Online]. [Accessed 29 September 2021]. Available from: https://www.yicai.com/news/101048478.html.

Liu, P., Li, L. and Wang, X. 2013. Qiyejia Jingshen de Xingbie Chayi - Jiyu Chuangye Dongji Shijiao de Yanjiu 企业家精神的性别差异——基于创业动机视角的研究 [Gender differences in entrepreneurship - a study based on the perspective of entrepreneurial motivation]. *Guanli Shijie* 管理世界 *[Management World]*. **8**, pp. 126–135.

Liu, Y. and Liu, X. 2013. Zhongguo Minying Shangshi Gongsi Gaoguan Xingbie yu Xinchou Chaju Yanjiu 中国民营上市公司高管性别与薪酬差距研究 [Research on managers' gender and compensation gap for China's private listed companies]. *Funv Yanjiu Luncong* 妇女研究论丛 *[Collection of Women's Studies]*. **4**, pp. 49–53.

Lückerath-Rovers, M. 2013. Women on boards and firm performance. *Journal of Management & Governance*. **17**(2), pp. 491–509.

Luo, X. and Zheng, Q. 2013. Reciprocity in corporate social responsibility and channel performance: do birds of a feather flock together? *Journal of Business Ethics*. **118**, pp. 203–213.

Lys, T., Naughton, J.P. and Wang, C. 2015. Signaling through corporate accountability reporting. *Journal of Accounting and Economics*. **60**(1), pp. 56–72.

Lyu, Y. 2021. *Credit Constraints for Women-led Micro and Small Enterprises in China: A Comparative Study of Beijing and Guangdong Province*. Glasgow: Adam Smith Business School, University of Glasgow.

Marlow, S. and Martinez Dy, A. 2018. Annual review article: is it time to rethink the gender agenda in entrepreneurship research? *International Small Business Journal*. **36**(1), pp. 3–22.

Mascia, D.V. and Rossi, S.P.S. 2017. Is there a gender effect on the cost of bank financing? *Journal of Financial Stability*. **31**, pp. 136–153.

McWilliams, A. and Siegel, D. (2000). Corporate social responsibility and financial performance: correlation or misspecification? *Strategic Management Journal*. **21**(5), pp. 603–609.

Maignan, I., & Ferrell, O. C. (2004). Corporate social Responsibility and Marketing: An Integrative Framework. *Journal of the Academy of Marketing Science,* **32**, Issue-1, pp. 3–19.

Mellahi, K., Frynas, J. G., Sun, P., & Siegel, D. (2016). A Review of the Nonmarket Strategy Literature: Toward a Multi-Theoretical Integration. *Journal of Management*, **42**(1), 143–173.

Maloni, M.J. and Brown, M.E. 2006. Corporate social responsibility in the supply chain: an application in the food industry. *Journal of Business Ethics*. **68**(1), pp. 35–52.

Maignan, I., Ralston, D. (2002) Corporate Social Responsibility in Europe and the U.S.: Insights from Businesses' Self-presentations. *Journal of International Business Studies,* **33**, pp. 497–514.

Moro, A., Wisniewski, T.P. and Mantovani, G.M. 2017. Does a manager's gender matter when accessing credit? Evidence from European data. *Journal of Banking & Finance*. **80**, pp. 119–134.

Mukherjee, A., Bird, R. and Duppati, G. 2018. Mandatory corporate social responsibility: the Indian experience. *Journal of Contemporary Accounting & Economics*. **14**(3), pp. 254–265.

Muravyev, A., Talavera, O. and Schäfer, D. 2009. Entrepreneurs' gender and financial constraints: evidence from international data. *Journal of Comparative Economics*. **37**(2), pp. 270–286.

National Bureau of Statistics 2020. *Regional GDP*. [Online]. [Accessed 29 September 2021]. Available from: https://data.stats.gov.cn/easyquery.htm?cn=E0103.

Neider, L. 1987. A preliminary investigation of female entrepreneurs in Florida. *Journal of Small Business Management*. **25**(3), pp. 22–29.

Nielsen, S. and Huse, M. 2010. The contribution of women on boards of directors: going beyond the surface. *Corporate Governance: An International Review*. **18**(2), pp. 136–148.

Pham, T. and Talavera, O. 2018. Discrimination, social capital, and financial constraints: the case of Viet Nam. *World Development*. **102**, pp. 228–242.

Polo-Redondo, Y., Bordonaba-Juste, V. and Lucia Palacios, L. 2011. Determinants of firm size in the franchise distribution system: empirical evidence from the Spanish market. *European Journal of Marketing*. **45**(1/2), pp. 170–190.

Radović-Marković, M. and Achakpa, P. 2018. Employment women through entrepreneurship development and education in developing countries. *Journal of Women's Entrepreneurship and Education*, No. 1–2, pp. 17–30.

Radović-Marković, M., Beraha, I. and Jaško, A. 2010. Female employment in formal and informal sectors of the Serbian economy. *Journal of Women's Entrepreneurship and Education*. No. 3–4, pp. 18–27.

Rupley, K. H., Brown, D. and Marshall, S. 2017. Evolution of corporate reporting: from stand-alone corporate social responsibility reporting to integrated reporting. *Research in Accounting Regulation*. **29**(2), pp. 172–176.

Sheldon, O. 1924. *The Philosophy of Management*. London: Pitman Publishing Corp.

Shamsuddeen, A. M., and Muhammad Aminu Isa. "Firms attributes and corporate social responsibility disclosure: A literature review." *International Journal of Academic Research in Business and Social Sciences* 8.4 (2018): 312–325.

Srinidhi, B., Gul, F.A. and Tsui, J. 2011. Female directors and earnings quality*. *Contemporary Accounting Research*. **28**(5), pp. 1610–1644.

Stiglitz, J.E. and Weiss, A. 1981. Credit rationing in markets with imperfect information. *The American Economic Review*. **71**(3), pp. 393–410.

Sun, L. and Zhou, L. 2016. Nvxing Dongshi Guodu Touzi yu Jixiao Bodong: Jiyu Jinshenxing Shijiao de Yanjiu 女性董事、过度投资与绩效波动——基于谨慎性视角的研究 [Female directors, overinvestment and variability of corporate performance: from the perspective of prudency]. *Guanli Pinglun* 管理评论 *[Management Review]*. **28**(07), pp. 165–178.

Ughetto, E., Rossi, M., Audretsch, D. and Lehmann, E.E. 2020. Female entrepreneurship in the digital era. *Small Business Economics*. **55**(2), pp. 305–312.

Wang, H. and Li, S. 2008. Touxi Nvxing Chenggong Chuangye de Beihou 透析女性成功创业的背后 [A perspective behind successful female entrepreneurship]. *Zhejiang Jingji* 浙江经济 *[Zhejiang Economy]*. **2**, pp. 44–45.

Wang, W. and Wang, S. 2014. A study on the correlation between social responsibility and corporate performance of state-owned enterprises in China. *China Soft Science*. No. 8, pp. 131–137.

Wang, Y. 2016. What are the biggest obstacles to growth of SMEs in developing countries? – An empirical evidence from an enterprise survey. *Borsa Istanbul Review*. **16**(3), pp. 167–176.

Weber, A. and Zulehner, C. 2010. Female hires and the success of start-up firms. *American Economic Review*. **100**(2), pp. 358–361.

Wellalage, N. and Locke, S. 2017. Access to credit by SMEs in South Asia: do women entrepreneurs face discrimination. *Research in International Business and Finance*. **41**, pp. 336–346.

Wellalage, N.H. and Thrikawala, S. 2021. Bank credit, microfinance and female ownership: are women more disadvantaged than men? *Finance Research Letters*. **42**, p. 101929.

Wolfers, J. 2006. Diagnosing discrimination: stock returns and CEO gender. *Journal of the European Economic Association*. **4**(2–3), pp. 531–541.

World Bank 2018. *The World Bank Gender Data Portal*. [Online]. [Accessed 20 August 2021]. Available from: https://www.worldbank.org/en/data/datatopics/gender.

World Economic Forum 2021. *Global Gender Gap Report* [Online]. [Accessed 20 August 2021]. Available from: https://www.weforum.org/reports/ab6795a1-960c-42b2-b3d5-587eccda6023/in-full/.

Worldometer 2021. *China Population (2021) - Worldometer*. [Online]. [Accessed 12 July 2021]. Available from: https://www.worldometers.info/world-population/china-population/.

Wu, X. and Hąbek, P. 2021. Trends in corporate social responsibility reporting. The case of Chinese listed companies. *Sustainability*. **3**(15), p. 8640.

Xu, S. and Yang, R. 2010. Indigenous characteristics of Chinese corporate social responsibility conceptual paradigm. *Journal of Business Ethics*. **93**, pp. 321–333.

Xu, P. 2018. *Guojia Tongji Ju Fabu Gaige Kaifang Sishi Nian Lai Quyu Fazhan Baogao - Dong Zhong Xibu, Fazhan Chaju Xiao le* 国家统计局发布改革开放四十年来区域发展报告—— 东中西部，发展差距小了 *[National Bureau of Statistics Releases Report on Regional Development in the Past 40 Years of Reform and Opening Up - East, Central and West, the Development Gap Is Smaller]*. [Online]. [Accessed 30 September 2021]. Available from: http://finance.people.com.cn/n1/2018/0919/c1004-30301569.html.

Yan, J. 2011. Siying Zhong Xiao Qiyezhu Xingbie yu Rongzi Yueshu de Shizheng Yanjiu 私营中小企业主性别与融资约束的实证研究 [An empirical study on the relationship between entrepreneurs' gender and financing constraints in SMES]. *Shangye Jingji yu Guanli* 商业经济与管理 *[Journal of Business Economics]*. **5**, pp. 50–57.

Yang, H. and Wu, D. 2015. Motivation and path selection of corporate social responsibility information disclosure: an analytical framework based on "Institutional Identity". *Journal of Zhongnan University of Economics and Law*. No. 1, pp. 55–62+159.

Yin, K., Liu, X. and Chen, H. 2014. Study on the relationship between corporate social responsibility and financial performance from the endogenous perspective-evidence from Chinese listed companies. *China Soft Science*. No. 6, pp. 98–108.

Zhang, N. 2013. Nvxing Dongshi dui Qiye Jixiao Yingxiang de Shizheng Yanjiu-Laizi Zhongguo 973 Jia Shangshi Gongsi de Zhengju 女性董事对企业绩效影响的实证研究——来自中国973家上市公司的证据 [Effects of female board members on corporate performance: evidence from 973 listed companies in China]. *Funv Yanjiu Luncong* 妇女研究论丛 *[Collection of Women's Studies]*. **4**, pp. 38–48.

Zhang, C., Lou, Z. and Jan, D. 2014. Political connection, financial performance and corporate social responsibility—management review from the listed companies of China's chemical industry. *Business Review*. **26**, 130–139.

Zhu, J., Ye, K. and Yan, D. 2012. Nvxing Dongshi de Fengxian Guibi yu Qiye Touzi Xingwei Yanjiu - Jiyu Jinrong Weiji Shijiao 女性董事的风险规避与企业投资行为研究——基于金融危机的视角 [Risk-avoidance of women directors and firm investment——from the perspective of financial crisis]. *Caimao Jingji* 财贸经济 *[Finance & Trade Economics]*. **4**, pp. 50–58.

Zhu, Y., Liu, J. and Chen, Z. 2009. Chuangye Huanjing dui Nvxing Chuangye de Yingxiang- yi Anhui Sheng wei Li 创业环境对女性创业的影响——以安徽省为例 [Influence of entrepreneurial environment on female entrepreneurship: taking Anhui province as an example. *Science-Technology and Management*. **4**, pp. 29–32.

3 Critical reflections on the corporate social responsibility information disclosure

A case study of China Resources SANJIU from 2009 to 2020

Yiting Zhang and Bhabani Shankar Nayak

Introduction

The advancement of science and technology has led to the growth of the industrial economy in China. However, in recent years, the social responsibility problems arising from rapid economic and social development have become increasingly prominent, with many irresponsible enterprises being exposed by the press (Jia et al., 2016). According to research by Maignan and Ferrell (2004), there is potential conflict of interest between different stakeholders of the same enterprise, which could lead to contradictions and conflicts. Companies may be required by investors to develop environmentally unfriendly products for financial benefits, despite the expectation of consumers and communities for green and sustainable products, as reflected in the case of Ningbo Municipal Hai District opposing the PX project in 2012.

Many countries, especially developed ones, have enforced laws and regulations aimed at protecting the environment and shifted toward sustainable development. Currently, China is at a critical stage of building a prosperous society for all. In the fifth plenary session of the Communist Party of China, it was proposed to "strengthen the legislation of corporate social responsibility." The decision to "strengthen the consciousness of social responsibility" reflects the government's shift of focus toward the social responsibility placed on firms. In this circumstance, disclosing Corporate Social Responsibility (CSR) reports has become essential for Chinese companies to be supervised by society and build a positive corporate image among the public.

Corporate Social Responsibility (CSR)

The current research on CSR disclosure indicates that there are various differences among studies due to factors such as countries, cultures, economics, and resources. Additionally, policy differences across countries also result in variations in the content of CSR disclosure. Many scholars have conducted in-depth studies on the contents of corporate social responsibility information disclosure in various

DOI: 10.4324/9781003437307-4

countries and industries. Regarding foreign regulations on the disclosure of CSR information, there are four mainstream viewpoints. The first is based on the "pyramid model" of corporate social responsibility, which includes four levels. The second viewpoint suggests that social responsibility information disclosure should focus on issues related to ecological and environmental protection.

The basic framework adopted for corporate social responsibility is determined by its content. According to Isabelle Maignan and David A. Ralston (2002), socially responsible disclosure should include five elements: investor interests, social contributions, employee interests, consumer interests, and suppliers. Campbell (2003) assessed the content of CSR reports by selecting publicly available social responsibility reports for research and analysis, and developing scoring criteria and evaluation indicators. Based on this, preliminary evaluation criteria were established. Maloni and Brown (**2006**) proposed eight components of environmental protection, with community stability, technological progress, nutrition and health, and workers' rights being regarded as the main directions of social responsibility content.

As the economy and society continue to develop at a fast pace, people have higher expectations for corporate social responsibility. Polo (2011) conducted research on the US food industry, as the US government places great importance on high levels of corporate social responsibility in the food sector. In this context, many associations and non-governmental organizations impose requirements on social responsibility information disclosure for food industry enterprises, including regulations on enterprise economic performance, employees' rights and interests, information security, and environmental protection. Focusing on UK food companies, Peter Jones, Daphne Comfort, and David Hillier (2012) analyzed their publicly disclosed social responsibility and found that companies can communicate social responsibility information through product packaging and customer groups. According to Isabelle Maignan and others (2019), corporate disclosure should involve social activities, employee protection, ecological protection, and other elements.

As noted by Rupley (2017), global pressure initially led to independent CSR reporting, but later shifted to more comprehensive reporting. The Integrated Report (IR) combines financial, economic, governance, and social information into a single report. While reporting is voluntary in the United States, only a few companies have published IRs. The most of French companies disclosed social responsibility information related to employees, environment, customers, and shareholders in that order of importance. However, there was limited disclosure about the community. Shamsuddeen and Muhammad (2018) argued from both theoretical and practical perspectives that companies need to engage in activities that improve the welfare of their communities and society and report on such activities for society to better understand the extent and level of CSR activities. Colaço and Simão (2018) found through a study of forestry corporate social responsibility information disclosure that the company pays close attention to wood certification and tends to focus on disclosing information about the environment related to its business. Additionally, there is a clear relationship between the content of disclosure and geographical location, with Western companies disclosing more information than Asian and African companies.

With the growth of emerging economies, CSR disclosure has garnered more attention. The content of corporate social responsibility information disclosure in rapidly developing countries such as Bangladesh differs significantly from that in developed countries. Issues such as corruption, child labor, and poverty, which are prevalent in many developing countries, are not prioritized in information disclosure in developed countries. However, Bangladeshi businesses generally feel a growing responsibility in various areas, including human rights, the environment, customers, healthcare, sports, and the community.

Growth of social responsibility system in China

There are four stages in the growth of CSR in China. The first stage (2002–2006) was the start-up stage of the social responsibility system developed in China. In 2002, the China Securities Regulatory Commission and State Economic and Trade Commission jointly published the Code on the Governance of Listed Companies, bringing the concept of CSR to China for the first time and requesting that enterprises assume their social responsibility. Subsequently, the overhauled Company Law of China, which included CSR, was published in 2004. The second stage (2006–2008) saw companies displaying a willingness to voluntarily disclose their CSR reports. First, the 2006 Company Law made it mandatory for Chinese enterprises to assume social responsibility from a legislative perspective. Second, the Shenzhen Stock Exchange made relevant provisions in September 2006 on the details to be disclosed in the Guidelines on Social Responsibility of Listed Companies. As a result, companies started to release their CSR reports, with a total of 33 companies voluntarily releasing their reports in 2006. Therefore, 2006 is considered the first year for companies to disclose CSR in China.

The third stage (2008–2018) was the compulsory and voluntary disclosure phase. On December 30th, 2008, the Shanghai Stock Exchange required all companies engaged in the "Shanghai governance sector," as well as domestic and foreign-listed companies and financial companies, to publish their social responsibility reports along with their annual reports. The Shenzhen Stock Exchange followed suit by releasing a mandatory document on the 31st, requiring "Shenzhen 100 Index" enterprises to disclose their social responsibility reports. As a result, two modes of mandatory and voluntary social responsibility disclosure were adopted in China. The fourth stage (2018–now) is the voluntary disclosure stage. On September 30, 2018, the CSRC published the revised Code of Governance for Listed Companies, which requires listed companies to enhance their leading role in assuming environmental protection and social responsibility. In 2018, the number of listed companies voluntarily disclosing their social responsibility reports surpassed that of listed companies mandated to disclose their social responsibility reports for the first time.

In recent years, scholars have integrated research on the content of CSR disclosure with industry standards to conduct detailed studies on the content of corporate social responsibility information across various industries. Wu and Hąbek (2021) revealed that the number of CSR reports disclosed by Chinese listed companies surged from 2008 to 2019. Moreover, on September 25, 2006, the Shenzhen Stock Exchange issued the "Guidelines on Social Responsibility of Listed Companies," with Article 2 defining the social responsibility of listed companies as the responsibility they assume for the overall development of the state and society, resources, and the natural environment, as well as shareholders, creditors, employees, consumers, customers, suppliers, communities, and other stakeholders. This guideline provides Chinese companies with a framework for the content of CSR. Both government institutions and the public expect accounting personnel of enterprises to disclose more information about corporate social responsibility, such as the company's investment and contribution to environmental protection, healthcare, employee training, and community relations maintenance. There are six types of information that represent categories of corporate social responsibility information. These include environment, staff, community, social issues, consumers, and others. Environmental information pertains to energy conservation and environmental protection, while employee information relates to the protection of employees' rights and interests, placement of unemployed employees, and more. Other information, including community and social issues, are also classified in detail.

Based on the classification of accounting, The content of social responsibility from four perspectives: assets, liabilities, income, and cost. Combining international standards of social responsibility reporting with the national conditions of China, Xiaoqian Fu, and Wenli Zhu (2011) proposed categorizing the details of the social responsibility report into four categories: environment, employee, society, and others, corresponding to different stakeholder groups such as employees, consumers, and creditors of enterprises, respectively. The social responsibility information can be studies from five different perspectives, including the economy, security, environment, social welfare, and voluntary responsibility. The content of the social responsibility report can be studied, qualitatively analyzed and categorized as system construction, market performance, protection of workers' rights and interests, social issues, and environmental protection, involving five dimensions of a total of 17 projects. It was also indicated in 2017 that the main content of social responsibility reports disclosed by Chinese listed companies includes the details of charitable donations, environmental protection, as well as the protection of employees' rights and interests. The contents of social responsibility information disclosure of agricultural enterprises involve the disclosure of responsibility information for increasing agricultural income, ensuring food safety, upholding employee welfare, preserving the environment, and engaging in social public welfare undertakings.

However, there is still a lack of information about the social responsibility assumed by significant stakeholders such as consumers and creditors. Moreover, enterprises only disclose positive information and do not disclose negative information, which means that only favorable information is released. The vast majority of listed companies in China publish social responsibility reports with no negative information contained. Therefore, positive information alone is insufficient to evaluate the integrity of CSR reports objectively and impartially, let alone to assess the fulfillment of corporate social responsibility. To enhance the credibility of CSR reports, verifying the CSR report is crucial. However, there are still plenty of unverified CSR reports, which diminish the overall credibility of CSR reports published by Chinese listed companies (Wu and Hąbek, 2021). For example, various problems arise from the disclosure of social responsibility information by Chinese enterprises.

Praxis of CSR in China

The first-ever concept of social responsibility was raised by Oliver Shelton in a research study conducted in 1924 to demonstrate the necessity for corporations to be responsible for meeting the needs of both employees and society. However, currently, there are different views held by scholars and organizations both domestically and internationally on how social responsibility should be defined. Due to different concerns, there are various definitions of CSR according to different theories. The major theoretical basis of CSR includes corporate social responsibility theory, enterprise performance evaluation theory, and stakeholder theory. In his first study of CSR, which was conducted in the 1920s, It is argued that it is essentially a moral responsibility closely associated with the needs of human development. It is also elaborated on the social objectives and values of corporate development, thus constructing a basic content system for modern enterprises' social responsibility. In Howard Bowen's view, the CSR system involves three aspects. The first one is the subject of social responsibility, which is the enterprise itself. The second one is the party who fulfils CSR, which is the decision-making power within the enterprise managers. The third and final one is the voluntary principle of CSR, which is the level of corporate awareness of social responsibility. By explaining the concept of the "Iron Law of Responsibility," It is argued that corporate social responsibility shows two natures, economic and non-economic, and indicated the need to consider not only economic factors but also other social interests other than economic interests for the fulfilment of social responsibility.

The Carroll's pyramid of CSR is a well-known and widely accepted model in the field of CSR during 1970s. It consists of four layers: economic responsibility, legal responsibility, ethical responsibility, and philanthropic responsibility. The economic responsibility layer emphasizes that businesses have a responsibility to be profitable and create value for shareholders. The legal responsibility layer requires businesses to follow laws and regulations. The ethical responsibility layer goes beyond legal compliance and requires businesses to act in accordance with moral principles. The philanthropic responsibility layer encourages businesses to engage in voluntary activities that benefit society, such as charitable giving and community service.

McGuire's theory divides social responsibility into four elements: economic, legal, moral, and discretionary. The economic element is similar to Carroll's economic responsibility layer, while the legal element corresponds to Carroll's legal responsibility layer. The moral element emphasizes the importance of ethical behavior, similar to Carroll's ethical responsibility layer. The discretionary element includes voluntary actions, such as philanthropy, that go beyond legal and ethical requirements. Zheng Li and Rui Xiang argue that corporate social responsibility should not be limited to economic responsibility but should also encompass social welfare and moral considerations. According to stakeholder theory, businesses have a responsibility to consider the interests of all stakeholders, not just shareholders. Yimin Kang defines CSR as a range of responsibilities that businesses assume through their systems and practices, with the aim of serving the interests of all stakeholders while remaining profitable and following the law.

The concept of CSR has evolved over time, and there are different opinions among scholars and organizations on the definition and scope of social responsibility. However, it is generally agreed that CSR encompasses not only economic responsibility, but also social and environmental responsibility, as well as ethical and philanthropic responsibilities. This means that corporations are expected to take into account the interests of all stakeholders, including shareholders, employees, customers, suppliers, communities, and the environment, and not just focus on maximizing shareholder value.

Financial performance and evaluation theory

Studies on financial performance can be classified into two categories: one focusing on market indicators and the other on accounting indicators (Xing, 2014). Market indicators rely on transaction data in the capital market and focus on shareholder returns. In contrast, accounting indicators use financial statement data to reflect the operating performance of a company. Commonly used accounting indicators in prior literature include return on total assets (ROA) and return on net assets (ROE). ROA is the ratio of net profit to average net assets, indicating the capability of corporate shareholders to generate income for every dollar invested. A higher ratio indicates better profitability for shareholders. ROE, on the other hand, is defined as the ratio of net profit to total average assets. It reflects the profitability of the total assets owned by the enterprise and suggests not only the optimization and allocation of resources held by the enterprise but also its capability to deliver value.

The study on the relationship between corporate value and corporate social responsibility can yield three analytical results: positive correlation, negative correlation, and irrelevance. Regardless of whether the path of business decision-making is focused on "maximizing the value of the enterprise" or "maximizing shareholders' equity," companies should adhere to the principle of cost-effectiveness, benefit, and cost matching (Xiao, 2021). To explain the contradictions between different research results, it is important to consider the limitations of the study, which account for a large part of the variation. These limitations include the effect of different industries, differences in measurement that need to be examined, as well as economic and legal factors that may influence the outcomes.

Stakeholder theory

The theory of Corporate Social Responsibility (CSR) can be broadly divided into two genres: "Shareholder Supremacy" and "Stakeholder Doctrine." According to Huang (2021), shareholder supremacism has experienced both prosperity and decline. Since the 1980s, both shareholder supremacy and stakeholder doctrine have gained increasing recognition. Shareholder supremacists believe that the primary social responsibility of firms is to deliver maximum shareholder value (Friedman, 1970). According to Friedman, firms supporting CSR are effectively endorsing socialism and undermining the foundations of the free market. They argue that firms are obligated to maximize public interests only after generating maximum profits. In their view, corporate primary task is to maximize profits, followed by serving the public interest.

Bowen (1953) defines CSR as the progress made by enterprises toward public goals, social values decision-making, production, and operation. The undertaking of social responsibility is unaffected by external factors such as government and law. However, companies must consider their own circumstances before deciding whether to undertake social responsibility.

Scholars have proposed that the interests of shareholders are not limited to the goals pursued by enterprises. However, it was not until the exacerbation of tense labor relations by shareholder supremacy in the West during the 1980s that the management of enterprises was presented with numerous stock options to maximize shareholder value, which further widened the gap between the rich and the poor. Additionally, there was severe public criticism directed at the one-sided pursuit of corporate interests at the expense of the ecological environment. This led to a profound reflection on shareholder supremacy and the rise of stakeholder theory. As the social economy and culture developed, investors paid increasing attention to the social responsibilities assumed by firms. Carroll (1979) constructed a pyramid of CSR and proposed four types of responsibility performed by organizations: economic, legal, ethical, and philanthropic. This pyramid quickly gained recognition for CSR research. In 1984, Freeman systematically addressed stakeholder theory and proposed a major monograph on Strategic Management. The Stakeholder Act defines a stakeholder as any group or individual that can influence or be influenced by the achievement of goals and processes made by an organization.

The study of corporate social responsibility (CSR) emerged in China in the last two decades. To define social responsibility in the Chinese context, Shangkun Xu and Rudai Yang (2007) collected 2,811 descriptions of social responsibility events, based on six common dimensions between China and the West. Among them, three dimensions of social responsibility are consistent with the specific social and cultural background of China, including jobs, business ethics, social stability, and progress. This enriches the study of the connotation of social responsibility in China.

The corporate social responsibility refers to the legal and moral responsibilities assumed by an individual company for its stakeholders, such as employees, creditors, consumers, the social environment, and the disadvantaged in society. It also involves maximizing profits and assuming legal responsibilities to investors. Despite the late start of research on social responsibility in China, both domestic and foreign scholars pay attention to the judgment of corporate stakeholders for defining the concept of CSR. Corporate social responsibility is supposed to meet the needs of all stakeholders, integrate the industry and country's environment, and maximize company value on the basis of symbiosis.

The stakeholders management is key to fulfilling corporate social responsibility, which can demonstrate an enterprise's social responsibility to stakeholders. Based on this, it is concluded that the main task of CSR is to ensure economic returns for shareholders, establish credibility with creditors, reduce financing costs, enhance the sense of belonging and cohesion among employees, improve work efficiency, prioritize customers, improve the market share of enterprise products at lower promotion costs, maintain healthy cooperative relations with suppliers, accelerate capital turnover, lower operating costs, engage in social services and public welfare undertakings, and build a positive public image. These are significant not only for consolidating relations with various stakeholders but also for the sustainable and steady improvement of corporate performance. It is clear that there is a lack of clarity regarding the definition of CSR, which can influence the behavior of enterprises.

Drivers of disclosing CSR information

With the constant development of social, economic, and cultural factors, investors have increasingly attached significance to the social responsibilities performed by firms for decades. As argued by Friedman (1970), the most significant social responsibility placed on firms is to create maximum shareholder value. However, in the early stage of the development of CSR theory, the commitment to moral and social obligations was not yet a major component of CSR. Carroll (1979) constructed a pyramid of CSR and argued that organizations shoulder four significant types of responsibility, including economic responsibility, legal responsibility, ethical responsibility, and philanthropic responsibility. Currently, this pyramid is commonly adopted as the framework for research on CSR due to the introduction of ethical and philanthropic responsibility into the CSR framework. With in-depth study of the issue, there has been an increasing number of studies conducted on how Corporate Social Responsibility (CSR) relates to Firm Value (FV), including whether the disclosure of CSR reports has any impact on FV. Based on research by Xiao (2021), there are three common hypotheses raised about the relationship between the social and financial performance of firms, namely, negative association, neutral association, and positive association. The two main discourses on the correlation between CSR and company value are the social impact hypothesis and shift of focus hypothesis (Chen and Lee, 2016), which take opposite views on how CSR relates to FV. There is no consensus reached on the most appropriate theoretical classification of CSR research (Pan and Guan, 2021). With Mellahi's (2016) theory combined, it is concluded that there are both internal and external drivers of corporate social responsibility.

Internal drivers

There are various potential factors within the enterprise that could motivate the enterprise to improve its practice of disclosing information about social responsibility. On the one hand, it may be attributed to the pursuit of their own moral character by business owners or firm managers, which can be referred to as moral motivation. On the other hand, enterprises may treat the disclosure of social responsibility information as a means to create benefits for themselves, which is known as a tool-based motive. Among these two types of motivations, tool-based motives have attracted more attention for study. Enterprises seek to maximize their own interests and the disclosure of social responsibility information is a profitable tool that aligns with current practice (Ma, 2019). According to Feng (2016), higher levels of CSR information disclosure can release more high-quality signals to the outside world, which can improve the performance of enterprises. Yan and Guo (2020) found that companies with better carbon performance send positive signals to the public through carbon information disclosure, thus building a low-carbon image.

External drivers

From the perspective of external motivation, the information disclosure behavior of enterprises will be influenced by the external conditions and institutional environment they face. Therefore, in order to achieve political legitimacy or alignment with the orientation of social values, enterprises make information disclosure decisions accordingly. Based on the theory of legality, it is believed in research that the essence of environmental information disclosure by enterprises is the process of legitimacy management. Due to higher legitimacy pressure from the outside world, those enterprises with poor environmental performance tend to exert influence on the view of the outside world on the level of environmental management by disclosing more and higher quality environmental information. In this way, the environmental image of enterprises is improved, and negative market reactions are avoided. According to the legitimacy theory, the process of information disclosure is a tool used to reverse negative images, indicating a negative association between the disclosure of enterprise environmental information and its environmental performance (Gong and Duan, 2021).

Correlations between firm's value and disclosing CSR information

As suggested in the study by Chen and Lee (2016), there is a non-linear relationship between CSR and FV, meaning that the relationship is not absolute positive or negative. The conclusions drawn from existing research are based on the positive correlation, negative correlation, irrelevance, or U-shaped relationship between

CSR and corporate performance. However, there is still no consensus reached on this matter (Zhang et al., 2021). Furthermore, the disclosure of CSR information is considered a risky investment if a specific level has not been reached. Only when a specific level is reached, CSR can produce a positive effect on FV. In the developed world, well-developed laws and regulations have been put in place for disclosing CSR information. Since 2000, many Western countries have made it mandatory for enterprises to publish information on social responsibility (Wu and Hąbek, 2021). Therefore, the disclosure of CSR reports by many firms has been accepted as a voluntary behavior. In this context, there are numerous existing studies that focus on how the performance in voluntary environmental disclosure or the quality of CSR reports would impact the value of firms in developed countries.

However, in emerging economies, the disclosure of environmental performance is mandatory. For example, the Shanghai Stock Exchange and Shenzhen Stock Exchange announced in 2008 that specific firms were required to publish a CSR report with their annual report. In this context, mandatory CSR disclosure causes a change in firm behavior and leads to positive externalities at the cost of shareholders. In comparison, all listed companies in France have been mandated to disclose information on social and environmental conditions in their annual reports since 2001. A limitation of research in this area is that it did not consider the quality of disclosure of environmental performance by the firm, but only the existence of this behavior (Gerged et al., 2020). Additionally, it has been found that in the Gulf Cooperation Council, a region with heavy dependence on natural resources, there is a statistically significant relationship between corporate environmental disclosure (CED) and FV, as measured by Tobin's Q.

In the existing literature on developed countries, firm-level data was examined, but little attention was paid to developing countries. The time interval covered by the literature on developing countries is short, and the focus is placed on the earlier period. Due to the lack of data and limitations in different methods used to measure the quality of social responsibility fulfilled by firms, there are few studies on the quality of CSR in developing countries. This study follows the basic case study path of "Theoretical Overview – Case Report Vertical Analysis – Case Report and Excellent Company Horizontal Analysis – Case Characteristics, Problems and Reason Analysis – Perfect Countermeasures." Based on the results of existing research conducted both at home and abroad, it starts by introducing the concepts and theories associated with the disclosure of social responsibility information. It provides a summary of the disclosure of social responsibility information by China Resources SANJIU. Then, a comparison is drawn between the CSR reports issued by SANJIU and FOSUN PHARMA. Finally, several suggestions are made based on combining the current situation facing the Chinese pharmaceutical industry and the development of the company. The suggestions are aimed at improving the disclosure of corporate social responsibility information and providing references for other enterprises engaged in the pharmaceutical industry to improve the quality of disclosing social responsibility information.

The pharmaceutical industry is an exceptional industry due to its close association with the safety of people's lives, as well as the particularity of the products and business models of pharmaceutical enterprises, which, in turn, determines the unique social responsibility placed on them. In addition to economic benefits, pharmaceutical enterprises are also expected to protect public health and maintain social stability as part of their production and operation objectives. The 2018 "Problem Vaccine" incident exposed in China was a hard blow to the pharmaceutical industry, including pharmaceutical companies. This incident raised doubts about drug safety across the pharmaceutical industry.

Factors influencing the disclosure of CSR

The factors that influence the disclosure of CSR reports can be either external or internal. External factors are mainly reflected in legal and regulatory constraints, the preferences of stakeholders, and external supervision. Haixia Wu and Lisi Chen (2018) conducted research on 86 A-share food listed companies in Shanghai and Shenzhen stock markets from 2006 to 2016. They demonstrated that the formulation of legal policies had a positive effect on improving the quality of enterprise information disclosure to a significant extent after controlling for other variables.

However, the promotion effect of policies shows a certain time lag, which makes it necessary for the government to develop and enforce relevant policies and regulations for standardized disclosure by enterprises in annual reports, social responsibility reports, or internal control reports. In a study on stakeholder preferences, Chunhui Lian and Yuetang Wang (2018) focused on corporate social responsibility information and revealed that disclosing information on corporate social responsibility is conducive to improving consumers' purchase intentions and investors' intentions to make investments. Hengwang Ni, Changqing Li, and Zhihua Wei (2015) selected listed companies in China that voluntarily disclosed social responsibility reports from 2009 to 2013 as samples and adopted empirical research methods. They concluded that there is a positive correlation between media attention and the willingness of enterprises to disclose social responsibility information on a voluntary basis. Hanming Yang and Danhong Wu (2015) proposed to apply the framework of "institutional peer" to study the motivation of CSR disclosure given the exact economic basis, legal system, social culture, and other institutional environments.

Therefore, it can be seen that CSR disclosure is a concern for various institutional organizations or roles at different levels. The conditions or pressures associated with these institutional factors exert influence on the willingness and level of social responsibility information disclosure by different enterprises. According to the research results of Lan Guo (2016), an inverted U-shaped relationship exists between industry competition and corporate social responsibility. Due to the control imposed on the influencing factor for industry competition, there is a negative correlation between enterprise competitive position and social responsibility. In a study conducted from the perspective of the Big Four accounting firms, Chao Huang, Min Wang, and Wei Chang (2017) found that the international "Big Four" accounting firms were presented with higher litigation risks and attached more significance to the disclosure of non-financial information like corporate social responsibility, with the aim of improving the quality of corporate social responsibility information disclosure.

Regarding the internal influencing factors in CSR disclosure, research is mainly focused on the financial index of companies, industries, and the size of companies. There is a positive association between company size and information disclosure. The larger the company, the greater the willingness to disclose information. With regard to the research on corporate financial leverage, Lys, Naughton, and Wang (2015) proposed that the number and frequency of corporate participation in social responsibility activities showed a positive correlation with the scale of operating benefits. The listed companies that had publicly released social responsibility reports from 2009 to 2013 as the research object and found that most enterprises had disclosed their social responsibility information, particularly about environmental protection. The size of an enterprise shows a positive correlation with its willingness to disclose social responsibility information. Through an empirical study on the social responsibility information disclosed by listed companies in Malaysia, Haniffa and Cooke (2005) discovered that the higher the percentage of non-executive directors, the stronger the willingness of enterprises to disclose social responsibility information. Bialek (2015) argued that the level of information disclosure is subject to influence from the ownership structure formed by members of the board of supervisors, managers, government agencies, and investors. According to Liyan Feng, Xiang Xiao, and Tianjiao Zhao (2016), excellent economic performance is beneficial for enterprises to improve the quality of social responsibility information disclosure. Jian Du and Lingyan Cao (2016) found that the higher the ownership concentration, the more enterprises are willing to disclose social responsibility reports.

CSR disclosure and its economic consequences

Social responsibility information is classified as non-financial information and is regarded as a supplement to corporate information disclosure. As the social responsibility system develops, both domestic and foreign scholars have conducted numerous studies on social responsibility. These studies focus on how CSR disclosure makes a difference in the financial performance of companies. Whether the fulfilment of corporate social responsibility is beneficial to enterprises and conforms to the long-term development goals of enterprises has long been the focal point of many governments and entrepreneurs. There are three mainstream viewpoints on the correlation between corporate social responsibility and corporate performance: negative correlation, positive correlation, and irrelevance. In the academic circle, plenty of research has been conducted on its related theoretical analysis and empirical tests, but no consensus has been reached. These inconsistent research results may result from the difference in methods adopted to measure financial performance.

It is inevitable for the performance of social responsibility to impact corporate performance. Regarding corporate social responsibility performance, it has both positive and negative effects, and the difference in the final result is reflected in the implementation of social responsibility from the perspective of various stakeholders. Besides, the stakeholders of the enterprise can create benefits to make up for the enterprise's social responsibility in terms of cost (Guo, 2020).

Positive correlation

Based on the reputation theory, Edmans (2011) argues that fulfilling corporate social responsibility can help improve financial performance. First, excellent CSR performance can contribute to boosting product sales, as consumers' perception of corporate image and evaluation of corporate value are directly or indirectly influenced by their willingness and level of social responsibility fulfilment. A high performance in corporate social responsibility will not only enhance consumer loyalty to the company but also attract potential customers. Second, high social responsibility performance is effective in improving the reputation and popularity of an enterprise, attracting more talents, enhancing production efficiency, and increasing market share. Finally, a high performance in social responsibility can significantly reduce various non-systemic risks and the risk of enterprises getting stranded in a financial crisis.

That the higher the level of corporate social responsibility information disclosure, the greater the value of the enterprise. Empirical research methods and the exogenous hypothesis of corporate social responsibility was adopted to demonstrate that corporate social responsibility performance can play a significant role in improving corporate performance. To distinguish the nature of enterprise property rights, a study was conducted on Chinese state-owned enterprises and found that fulfilling social responsibility by state-owned enterprises was associated with enterprise performance. Furthermore, when the innovation performance of pharmaceutical enterprises is improved, corporate social responsibility plays a role in enhancing the innovation performance of pharmaceutical enterprises (Kang et al. 2020).

Negative correlation

Regarding the negative correlation between social responsibility disclosure and financial performance, domestic and foreign scholars have analyzed operating costs, disclosure modes, and the stakeholders of enterprises in fulfilling social responsibility. Hung and Wang (2014) revealed that listed companies required to disclose CSR information suffered damage within three years after the implementation of the mandatory disclosure policy, in terms of financial performance, investment expenditure, and market value. It was believed that the fulfilment of social responsibility consumes the resources of the enterprise, diminishing the resources needed for operation and management, thus causing the business performance of the enterprise to deteriorate. Feng Cong (2015) conducted empirical research using data from manufacturing enterprises for three consecutive years and discovered that the performance of enterprises in fulfilling responsibilities to employees was negatively correlated with the operating conditions of enterprises to the most significant extent. In cases of excellent performance, enterprises lacked the willingness to shoulder responsibilities to employees. Abhishek (2018) found that when enterprises failed to meet social expectations in fulfilling corporate social responsibility, the Indian government implemented mandatory CSR, both in terms of the amount of CSR spending generated and the activities it targeted. It fell short of expectations and had a negative impact on the profitability of the enterprise.

Lin et al. (2017) conducted observations on a panel dataset of the 100 most respected companies from the Fortune 500 companies. They made observations for a total of 1,000 company-years over the sample period from 2007 to 2016. Based on their observations, they established a two-way link model between corporate social responsibility (CSR) and corporate financial performance (CFP). The results suggest that CSR can have a negative effect on CFP. Additionally, a significant negative relationship was found between financial performance and the follow-up evaluation of corporate social responsibility. Guo (2020) found that the occurrence of a problem vaccine infringed on the interests of key stakeholders of Walvax Biotechnology, which diminished the stakeholders' satisfaction with the company. As a result, they showed resistance to the company, reduced their investment in corporate resources, and caused corporate performance to decline. Guo also found that the performance of social responsibility has an interactive effect on corporate performance.

Irrelevance

McWilliams and Siegel (2000) deduced the supply-demand model of CSR attributes among industries, enterprises, and products, and believed that CSR and financial performance had a neutral relationship without a significant correlation. Yanjun Jiang et al. (2011) conducted a study on the response of the market to the disclosure of social responsibility information using the event study method. Their findings suggest that the market response to the release of corporate social responsibility reports was insignificant. Zhaoguo Zhang et al. (2013) explored the intertemporal impact, using five-year data as the sample. They concluded that there was no significant correlation between the current CSR, the two lagging CSR, and the current corporate financial performance.

As mentioned above, the definition of corporate social responsibility information varies between different countries and regions. Particularly in developing countries like China, where regulations and laws remain immature, it is difficult to find uniform standard CSR reports with details. Additionally, the effect of disclosing social responsibility information and the quality of CSR reports differs between various countries and industries. In this chapter, China Resources SANJIU is taken as a case study to analyze the weaknesses of social responsibility disclosure in China and to provide suggestions for China Resources SANJIU and similar companies on how to improve their social responsibility performance.

CSR information disclosure case of China Resources SANJIU

China Resources SANJIU Co., Ltd. (China Resources SANJIU) is a large state-controlled pharmaceutical listed company that primarily engages in research, development, production, and sales of pharmaceutical products and relevant health services. The company officially joined the China Resources Group at the end of November 2007 and is affiliated with the healthcare department of China Resources, which also includes China Resources SHUANGHE and other pharmaceutical companies. Since its listing, the company has been rated among the "value of the top 100" and "Golden Bull 100" enterprises in China on the main board. China Resources SANJIU has been listed on the Shenzhen Composite Index, the China Securities 500, the MSCI Emerging Markets Index, and the FTSE Russell. Since 2009, China Resources SANJIU has published CSR reports, and in 2018 and 2019, it ranked BB level on the list of RKS ESG rated enterprises. In this chapter, China Resources SANJIU is used as an example to conduct an analysis and provide suggestions for China Resources SANJIU and other pharmaceutical firms on how to improve the quality of their CSR reports and help investors better understand the content of CSR reports published by pharmaceutical firms. For more information, please visit the official website of SANJIU.

Overview of China Resources SANJIU

The company was founded in 1985 as the Shenzhen Southern Pharmaceutical Factory. In 1999, five companies, including SANJIU Enterprise Group and Shenzhen SANJIU Pharmaceutical Co., Ltd., jointly established a joint-stock company. In September 2000, it was listed on the Shenzhen Stock Exchange (stock code 000999). The company officially joined the China Resources Group in 2008 and was renamed in 2010 from "SANJIU Pharmaceutical Co., Ltd" to "China Resources SANJIU Pharmaceutical Co., Ltd." The company's consumer health business covers nearly ten different categories, including colds, skin, gastrointestinal, cough, orthopaedics, and paediatrics, among others. The high incidence of medical accidents in recent times has led to severe tension in the doctor-patient relationship. In addition, the media has repeatedly exposed the fraudulent practices of some pharmaceutical manufacturing enterprises, such as "Kangtai Pharmaceuticals," the "vaccine incident," "Hansen Pharmaceuticals," the "four mill soup" cancer-causing rumors, and "Benevolence Pharmaceuticals" cold medicine that has been found to impact kidney development in children. These product quality and safety problems implicate pharmaceutical enterprises and put the public interest at risk, causing consumers to become increasingly concerned about the fulfilment of social responsibility across the pharmaceutical industry.

The China Resources SANJIU has a wide product line, covering a broad range of products. The company currently offers over 100 million varieties of 21 different products. As a well-known brand, "SANJIU" enjoys high recognition among consumers and across the pharmaceutical industry. WPP Group has consecutively released the "most valuable Chinese brand list" for many years, with China Resources

SANJIU consistently appearing on the list. For many years, the company has also ranked first in the cold cough category (traditional Chinese medicine) in the comprehensive ranking issued by the China Over-the-counter Medicine Association. In addition, the company has developed as many as ten products that have been ranked at the top of the list. In 2018 and 2019, the company's performance continued to improve, with operating income of 13.428 billion yuan and 14.702 billion yuan, respectively. Despite the impact of the pandemic in 2020, the company worked to maintain business stability and generated an operating income of 13.637 billion yuan, with a net profit of 1.597 billion yuan. For more information, visit the official website of SANJIU. Given the significant position and wide-ranging business of China Resources SANJIU in the Chinese pharmaceutical industry, it is crucial to examine its social responsibility and have a deep understanding of its CSR reports.

CSR information disclosure mode and development of China Resources SANJIU

The number of social responsibility reports disclosed by listed companies in China has been increasing year on year. In particular, the number of voluntarily disclosed CSR reports rose sharply, surpassing the number of mandatory CSR reports for the first time in 2017 and continuing to increase in the following two years (Wu and Hąbek, 2021). China encourages enterprises to publish independent social responsibility reports that include quantitative financial information. When preparing the report independently, the performance of social responsibility is detailed in the report through words, and supplemented with data, tables, photos, and case studies. China Resources SANJIU has mainly issued independent social responsibility reports over the past 12 years. From its official website, it can be seen that China Resources SANJIU has released social responsibility reports since 2009, and it is one of the earliest enterprises to issue independent social responsibility reports annually through external disclosure. The content of the report can be found in the investor sector on its official website.

Comparison of China Resources SANJIU CSR reports disclosure from 2009 to 2019

As argued by Xu (2019), the determination of the preparation standard is essential for enterprises to disclose standardized social responsibility information, which makes it more comparable. Table 3.1 shows the CSR reports published by SANJIU annually from 2009 to 2020, and the standard of CSR reports adopted by China Resources SANJIU.

From the above table, it is clear that the standard applied by China Resources SANJIU has been updated and enriched as national and international standards are improved. It can also be found out that there's no reference to its CSR report in 2009, which makes it difficult to compare the CSR report published in 2009 with the CSR reports of other firms. Under this circumstance, investors are unable to fully understand the problems within the CSR report and make well-informed decisions. The CSR reports released by China Resources SANJIU in 2010, 2011, and 2012 show a great progress in 2009. Although China Resources SANJIU adopted

"Guidance on the Performance of Social Responsibility by Central Enterprises" and "Guidelines on Social Responsibility of Listed Companies on the Shenzhen Stock Exchange," the two guidances are aimed mainly to guide behavior rather than the content of CSR report.

Table 3.1 Report preparation basis

Year	*2009*	*2010*	*2011*	*2012*	*2013*
Standard	N/A	"Guidance on the Performance of Social Responsibility by Central Enterprises," "Guidelines on Social Responsibility of Listed Companies on the Shenzhen Stock Exchange"	Same as 2010	Same as 2010	"Guide to the Preparation of CSR Reports in China 2.0"
Year	*2014*	*2015*	*2016*	*2017*	*2018*
Standard	"Guide to the Preparation of CSR Reports in China 3.0"	Same as 2014	Same as 2014	Same as 2014	"Guide to the Preparation of CSR Reports in China 4.0" "About The Central Enterprise Guidance on fulfilling social responsibility"
Year	*2019*	*2020*	*Year*	*2019*	*2020*
Standard	"Guide to the Preparation of CSR Reports in China 4.0" "About The Central Enterprise Guidance on fulfilling social responsibility" "Global Sustainable Development Reporting Standards for Advocacy"	Same as 2019	Standard	"Guide to the Preparation of CSR Reports in China 4.0" "About The Central Enterprise Guidance on fulfilling social responsibility" "Global Sustainable Development Reporting Standards for Advocacy"	Same as 2019

Source: Obtained by collating SANJIU's annual CSR reports.

During the period of 2013 to 2017, China Resources SANJIU adopted "Guide to the Preparation of CSR Reports in China" as the standard of its CSR reports, which has set out clear provisions for a series of details such as report content, compilation process, and general indicators. Since 2013, the quality of CSR reports of China Resources SANJIU has shown rapid improvement, which facilitates the comparison with CSR reports of other companies engaged in the same industry. This change has played a role in increasing the industry relevance of the report and improving the level of corporate social responsibility information disclosure to a significant extent. Back in 2016, as various preparation guidelines were developed (GRI standards have been developed to the fourth generation, China's preparation guidelines have been perfected to the third generation and the introduction of industry-specific system indicators), SANJIU made timely update on the premise for the preparation. Especially in the year of 2019, it also adopted "Global Sustainable Development Reporting Standards for Advocacy" as another basis, which enhanced the comparability of its CSR in the context of global competition.

Report review and continuity analysis

Table 3.2 displays the method used to analyze the continuity and reliability of CSR reports published by SANJIU, as per Xu (2019), indicating whether China Resources SANJIU published its annual CSR report for the years 2009 to 2020. "Yes" indicates that SANJIU published the report for the respective year, while "No" means that SANJIU did not release the report (same for report review). This table provides a clear overview of whether SANJIU has been publishing its annual CSR report consistently.

Based on the above Table 3.2, it is evident that China Resources SANJIU has been consistently publishing CSR reports since 2009, indicating the company's commitment to social responsibility. Moreover, China Resources SANJIU has conducted third-party reviews on its CSR reports since 2018, which enhances the objectivity of its disclosure of CSR information, ensures the comprehensiveness, accuracy, authenticity, and reliability of the information, and guarantees the correctness of details. Furthermore, the quality and standardization of CSR reports published by China Resources SANJIU have improved significantly over the last 12 years of development.

Report appearance and analysis

Table 3.3 illustrates the method employed by Xu (2019) to assess the completeness and readability of CSR reports released by SANJIU. It reveals the elements included or excluded in SANJIU's annual report from 2009 to 2020. "Yes" indicates that the element is present in SANJIU's annual CSR report for that respective year, while "No" indicates its absence. The table demonstrates the elements utilized by

Table 3.2 Report review and continuity analysis

Year	*2009*	*2010*	*2011*	*2012*	*2013*	*2014*
Whether issued CSR	Yes	Yes	Yes	Yes	Yes	Yes
Report review	No	No	No	No	No	No
Year	*2015*	*2016*	*2017*	*2018*	*2019*	*2020*
Whether issued CSR	Yes	Yes	Yes	Yes	Yes	Yes
Report review	No	No	No	No	No	No

Source: Obtained by collating SANJIU's annual CSR reports.

Table 3.3 Report appearance and length analysis

	2009	*2010*	*2011*	*2012*	*2013*	*2014*
Events	No	No	No	No	Yes	Yes
Contents	No	No	No	Yes	Yes	No
Graphs	No	No	Yes	Yes	Yes	Yes
Data	No	No	Yes	Yes	Yes	Yes
Colored	No	No	Yes	Yes	Yes	Yes
Executives signed	No	No	No	No	No	No
Length (pages)	14	8	23	34	30	50
	2015	*2016*	*2017*	*2018*	*2019*	*2020*
Events	Yes	Yes	Yes	Yes	Yes	Yes
Contents	No	No	No	Yes	Yes	Yes
Graphs	Yes	Yes	Yes	Yes	Yes	Yes
Data	Yes	Yes	Yes	Yes	Yes	Yes
Colored	Yes	Yes	Yes	Yes	Yes	Yes
Executives signed	No	No	No	Yes	Yes	Yes
Length	43	40	47	32	73	74

Source: Obtained by collating SANJIU's annual CSR reports.

SANJIU in its CSR reports, indicating the improvements made in annual CSR reports published by the company.

Based on the information presented in Table 3.3, it can be inferred that China Resources SANJIU began incorporating graphs and data, as well as colors, into its CSR reports starting from 2011. From 2014, the company made significant changes to its CSR reports, including an increase in length, addition of events and graphs, and the division of content into different sections, which continued through 2015, 2016, and 2017. When combined with Table 3.1 and Table 3.2, it is evident that China Resources SANJIU has made significant progress in its CSR reporting since 2018. With the incorporation of more guidelines into the standard, the information disclosed by China Resources SANJIU has become more practical and readable, resulting in high-quality CSR reports that are widely recognized in the industry.

Content analysis

Table 3.4 displays the content of annual CSR reports published by SANJIU from 2009 to 2020, with a comparison of the structure of reports released by SANJIU. The structure of the CSR report is divided into three sections, including a preface, main body, and conclusion, based on the standards adopted by SANJIU as shown in Table 3.1 and the method applied by Xu (2019). The main body, covering the primary work undertaken by SANJIU on social responsibility, is the most significant part. This table allows for a comparison of the structure of CSR reports released by SANJIU, facilitating the analysis of the improvement made for each section of its CSR reports in each year.

The table above shows that the CSR report published by China Resources SANJIU has significantly enriched its content since 2011, followed by a change in format from 2013 and a considerable increase in length from 2019. The year 2011 can be considered a revolutionary year for the disclosure of social responsibility information by China Resources SANJIU. The content covered by the main body was largely fixed in the years after 2011, including seven sections: Shareholders' Rights, Customers' Rights, Partners' Rights, Employee's Rights, Production Safety, Public Welfare Undertakings, and Environmental Protection and Sustainable Development. Furthermore, 2019 marked the year when China Resources SANJIU managed to keep up with international standards.

Comparison of CSR reports between China Resources SANJIU and FOSUN PHARMA

According to the ranking from the RKS ESG of pharmaceutical industry in 2020, FOSUN PHARMA ranks top (BBB level) across this industry while China Resources SANJIU ranks only sixth (BB level). In this section, the CSR reports published by these two companies are compared to analyze the advantages and disadvantages of China Resources SANJIU's CSR reports. The latest CSR report released by the FOSUN PHARMA, a leading enterprise in the pharmaceutical industry with a high level of scale and social responsibility development, is used as a reference for comparison with the China Resources in order to identify any problems with the disclosure of social responsibility information by the China Resources SANJIU.

Table 3.5 illustrates the differences between the CSR reports of China Resources SANJIU and FOSUN PHARMA. The FOSUN PHARMA has been publishing CSR reports since 2008, one year earlier than China Resources SANJIU. Both companies independently and annually disclose their CSR reports. However, FOSUN PHARMA refers to more standards than China Resources SANJIU, including the "Guide to the Preparation of CSR Reports in China," "Global Reporting Initiative Standards," and "Guidelines for Environmental, Social and Governance Reporting" from "Securities Listing Rules," issued by the Stock Exchange of Hong Kong. This results in FOSUN PHARMA's disclosure of social responsibility

Table 3.4 Content analysis

	2013	*2014*	*2015*	*2016*
Preface	1 Notes 2 Contents 3 Introduction 4 Company performance 5 Events in 2013	1 Notes 2 Introduction 3 Company performance 4 Company values 5 Events in 2014	1 Message from executive 2 Introduction 3 Company values	1 Notes 2 Introduction 3 Company performance
Main body	1 Corporate governance 2 Shareholders' rights 3 Employee's rights 4 Production safety 5 Environmental protection and sustainable development 6 Public welfare undertakings	1 Social responsibility organization 2 Shareholders' rights 3 Employee's rights 4 Customers' rights 5 Partners' rights 6 Public welfare undertakings 7 Production safety 8 Environmental protection and sustainable development	1 Events in 2015 2 Social responsibility 3 Company performance 4 Innovation 5 Partners' rights 6 Social performance 7 Employees' rights 8 Production safety 9 Public welfare undertakings 10 Environmental protection and sustainable development	1 Social responsibility 2 Quality culture 3 Innovation 4 Partners' rights 5 Shareholders' rights 6 Government's rights 7 Employee's rights 8 Production safety 9 Customers' rights 10 Employee's rights 11 Partner rights 12 Production safety 13 Public welfare undertakings 14 Environmental protection and sustainable development
Conclusion	N/A	Look into the future	1 Look into the future 2 Feedback form	1 Look into the future 2 Feedback form

	2009	*2010*	*2011*	*2012*
Preface	1 Notes 2 Introduction 3 Company performance	1 Notes 2 Introduction	1 Notes 2 Introduction 3 Organization table 4 Company performance 5 Company values 6 Communication and response	1 Contents 2 Notes 3 Introduction 4 Company performance 5 Company values 6 Organization 7 Development strategy
Main body	1 Shareholders and creditors' rights 2 Employee's rights 3 Suppliers and clients' rights 4 Customers' rights 5 Environmental protection and sustainable development 6 Public welfare undertakings	1 Social responsibility management 2 Main work in 2010	1 Shareholders' rights 2 Customers' rights 3 Partners' rights 4 Employee's rights 5 Production safety 6 Public welfare undertakings 7 Environmental protection and sustainable development	1 Shareholders' rights 2 Customers' rights 3 Employee's rights 4 Partner rights 5 Production safety 6 Environmental protection and sustainable development 7 Public welfare undertakings
Conclusion	Look into the future	Look into the future	Look into the future	N/A

	2017	*2018*	*2019*	*2020*
Preface	1 Notes	1 Notes	1 Notes	1 Notes
	2 Introduction	2 Contents	2 Contents	2 Contents
	3 Events in 2017	3 Executive's signature	3 Executive's signature	3 Executive's signature
		4 Introduction	4 Responsibility culture	
		5 Company organization		
Main body	1 Responsibility culture	1 Production management	1 Innovation	1 Events in 2020
	2 Company performance	2 Environmental protection and sustainable development	2 Customers' rights	2 Introduction
	3 Partners' rights	3 Company performance	3 Environmental protection and sustainable development	3 Responsibility culture
	4 Social performance	4 Employees' rights	4 Employees' rights	4 Partners' rights
	5 Employees' rights	5 Public welfare undertakings	5 Public welfare undertakings	5 Guarantee for quality
	6 Production safety			6 Innovation
	7 Public welfare undertaking			7 Environmental protection and sustainable development
	8 Environmental protection and sustainable development			8 Employees' rights
Conclusion	1 Look into the future	1 Look into the future	1 Look into the future	1 Look into the future
	2 Notes	2 Contents	2 Key performance in 2019	2 Key performance in 2020
	3 Feedback form	3 Feedback form	3 Contents	3 Contents
			4 Feedback form	4 Feedback form

Source: Obtained by collating SANJIU's annual CSR reports.

Table 3.5 Comparison of CSR reports between SANJIU and FOSUN

Items	*China Resources SANJIU*	*FOSUN PHARMA*
Name	Social responsibility report in 2020	2020 corporate social responsibility report
Starting year	2009	2008
Release frequency	Annual	Annual
Method	Independent report	Independent report
Basis	"Guide to the Preparation of CSR Reports in China 4.0" "About The Central Enterprise Guidance on fulfilling social responsibility" "Global Sustainable Development Reporting Standards for Advocacy"	"Guide to the Preparation of CSR Reports in China 4.0" "Global Reporting Initiative Standards" "Guidelines for Environmental, Social and Governance Reporting" from "Securities Listing Rules" "National Standards for the Social Responsibility Series"
5 Report structure	1.1 Notes 1.2 Contents 1.3 Executive's signature 2.1 Events in 2020 2.2 Introduction 2.3 Responsibility culture 2.4 Partners' rights 2.5 Guarantee for quality 2.6 Innovation 2.7 Environmental protection and sustainable development 2.8 Employees' rights and public welfare undertaking 3.1 Look into the future 3.2 Key performance in 2020 3.3 Contents 3.4 Feedback form	1.1 Executive's signature 1.2 Contents 1.3 Notes 1.4 Events in 2020 1.5 Introduction 2.1 Social responsibility strategy 2.2 Customers' rights and private security 2.3 Partners' rights 2.4 Employees' rights 2.5 Environmental protection and sustainable development 2.6 Public welfare undertaking 3.1 Feedback form 3.2 Contents 3.3 Report review
Length (pages)	74	142
Report review	No	Yes

Source: Obtained by collating SANJIU's annual CSR reports.

information being more reliable, standardized, and consistent with international standards compared to China Resources SANJIU. Although the main body sections of FOSUN PHARMA's CSR report are fewer than China Resources SANJIU's, they are more detailed. In terms of report length, FOSUN PHARMA's report is 142 pages, while China Resources SANJIU's is only 74 pages. However, both companies have a similar report structure. FOSUN PHARMA's CSR report is reviewed by SGS-CSTC Standards Technical Services CO., LTD, whereas China Resources SANJIU's report is not subjected to any third-party review, which affects the reliability of its social responsibility information relative to FOSUN PHARMA. Additionally, both companies disclose little negative information in their reports, mainly in the form of numbers of events, with no details provided. Based on the method adopted by Wu (2019), Table 3.6 presents a comparison of the space and content of each section of the CSR reports published by China Resources SANJIU and

Table 3.6 Comparison of corporate stakeholder concerns

Company	*China Resources SANJIU*		*FOSUN PHARMA*	
Content	*Length*	*Analysis*	*Length*	*Analysis*
Shareholder	0	The content was not specifically disclosed	10	Tables for analyzing shareholder's feedback
Supplier	6	There is less disclosure of specific case content	6	Supply chain optimization and green supply chain
Government	4	Less disclosure of relevant information	10	Strengthen supervision and anti-corruption
Employee	9	Focus on employee health	20	Multiple case and data descriptions
Consumer	17	Focus on product quality, innovation, and customer privacy protection	26	Focus on product quality, innovation, customer service and customer privacy protection
Environment	10	Mostly written narratives, lack of case support	28	Multiple case and data descriptions
Community	3	Mostly written narratives, lack of case support	22	Multiple case supporting

Source: Obtained by collating SANJIU's annual CSR reports.

FOSUN PHARMA. The table compares the contents of these reports to determine the level of attention paid by each company to various stakeholders, based on the various stakeholders mentioned in the 2020 CSR reports.

It can be argued that the CSR report published by the SANJIU has less space dedicated to its various stakeholders than the FOSUN Pharma. The report released by the SANJIU lacks information about shareholder's interest, and many sections such as supplier, environment, and community are mostly written as narratives with a lack of case support. In contrast, the CSR report published by FOSUN Pharma has a relatively equal emphasis on all aspects of the expression about various stakeholders, with its focus placed on employees, the environment, and the community, and more space dedicated to these areas, which makes the description objective and detailed.

Features of China Resources SANJIU CSR information disclosure

As seen in Table 3.4, the CSR report published by China Resources SANJIU has been structured more clearly since 2011, and the content of each section has been enriched over the years. This shows that the company is continuously improving its CSR reporting process and trying to make it more reliable and standardized. It is commendable that China Resources SANJIU has been publishing CSR reports annually since 2009, and the fact that they release it in March of the following year is indeed efficient. This timeliness is important because stakeholders rely on up-to-date information to make informed decisions. The emphasis on employee welfare in their CSR reports is also a positive aspect. It is noteworthy that the company has been developing its employee promotion system over the years, with the introduction of the "two-channel promotion system" in 2012 and the "performance culture" in 2016. However, it is concerning that the 2020 CSR report did not mention the "performance culture" solution that was introduced in 2016. It is important for companies to ensure that their CSR reports are comprehensive and up-to-date, and this omission raises questions about the reliability of the information disclosed.

The China Resources SANJIU always pays attention to employee welfare issues. Employee welfare is an important section in its CSR reports, and the level has been improving with the development of China Resources SANJIU. It announced a general system of promoting employees in 2011 but did not specify it. In 2012, China Resources SANJIU introduced a promotion mechanism called the "two-channel promotion system," which allows employees to choose between management or professional technical paths after reaching a certain technical level. In 2016, China Resources SANJIU introduced the "performance culture" to motivate employees by tying their personal performance to promotion. However, this was not mentioned in the CSR report in 2020. As a pharmaceutical company, the China Resources SANJIU has been dedicated to improving its social responsibility behavior to build a positive corporate image. In 2011, it did not have a department dedicated to fulfilling social responsibility. However, in 2014, it established a social responsibility work leading group, and in 2018, it established the SANJIU ESG working group to focus on improving its performance in fulfilling its social responsibilities.

Disadvantages of China Resources Group CSR information disclosure

From the analysis of Table 3.1, it can be argued that the CSR reports of the FOSUN PHARMAR are more standardized than the reports published by SANJIU. In comparison with the CSR reports issued by FUSUN PHARMAR, SANJIU's CSR reports have the following problems.

First, in the SANJIU's CSR reports, most of the details are included in a large paragraph of textual expression, which results in a lack of data consolidation and case studies. As a result, the report appears to be more rigid and less intuitive, which hinders stakeholders from understanding the corresponding statement. Furthermore, it provides no relevant communication channels with stakeholders, which is detrimental to communication and improvement with stakeholders in the enterprise. In comparison, the FOSUN's CSR reports are longer and provide more intuitive data and case studies. They also include a large number of external and internal links, allowing stakeholders to quickly and comprehensively grasp the content of the report.

Among Chinese pharmaceutical enterprises, SANJIU's social responsibility report is better than the vast majority of other enterprises in terms of its form and content. The SANJIU has been issuing its corporate social responsibility report for 12 consecutive years. While the form of the SANJIU's report was relatively novel in the first few years and its content was relatively abundant, it still has some shortcomings compared to the FOSUN PHARMAR's CSR report.

However, the SANJIU's report fails to disclose information sufficiently and completely regarding environmental protection, environmental management, energy conservation, and emission reduction. Specific data is not provided in these areas. In contrast, the FOSUN PHARMAR's CSR report has each section classified in terms of environmental protection, detailing climate and energy, water resources, waste, outdated products, biodiversity, and other aspects, each of which is supported by relevant data. Moreover, in the section regarding employee's interests, the SANJIU's CSR report focuses mainly on the health of employees, but with less case support. Even the promotion mechanism is illustrated only as a chart.

The FUSON PHARMAR is concerned about product quality throughout the report, including raw materials, product management, and other aspects of public concern, supported by a large number of statistics and charts over the years. However, drug safety issues facing the company are mostly positive or general expressions, with no details or negative information disclosed, which is inadequate in terms of neutrality and objectivity. On the other hand, the SANJIU's CSR report has less quantitative disclosure. While the report accurately describes poverty alleviation and cites specific data, other projects lack statistical descriptions. Therefore, it can be concluded that the content of CSR reports published by the SANJIU is insufficient.

Credibility in social responsibility reporting means that the information and data used by enterprises must be factual and reliable. To ensure the quality of the report, the collection, organization, recording, analysis, and disclosure of information should be verifiable. Additionally, the report should be validated by an independent third-party accredited organization and released in public for audit and certification. However, the current review mechanism of social responsibility reports is flawed, and public awareness of social responsibility report audit is low, resulting in inadequate credibility of the reports. As a consequence, the social responsibility report audit business has failed to develop smoothly, with many firms either not qualified or unwilling to undertake audits of social responsibility reporting. Social responsibility reports unchecked by independent third parties are more like promotional advertisements for enterprises, with only positive news reported. In terms of form, they are far from achieving their intended purpose.

From Table 3.2, it can be seen that none of the CSR reports published by the China Resources SANJIU were reviewed by third-party institutions, which undermines the credibility of its reports. In contrast, the CSR reports issued by the FOSUN PHARMA were reviewed by a third-party institution, allowing investors and shareholders to better understand the company and make more informed decisions. The CSR report released by the SANJIU lacked a third-party audit and fair evaluation, resulting in a lack of credibility and persuasiveness.

The principle of neutrality is an essential aspect of a credible and comprehensive CSR report. The report should present both positive and negative aspects of the company's social responsibility performance, including any challenges and setbacks, and highlight areas for improvement. The language used in the report should be objective and factual, without any selective disclosure or concealment of information. This approach ensures that stakeholders have a complete and unbiased view of the company's social responsibility performance, enabling them to make informed decisions and hold the company accountable for its actions.

The lack of disclosure of negative news and possible crises in the SANJIU's CSR reports could potentially lead to a lack of transparency and trustworthiness. It is important for companies to not only disclose their successes and positive news, but also any challenges or negative news they may face. This can help build trust with stakeholders and demonstrate the company's commitment to transparency and accountability. It is also important for companies to provide verifiable evidence to support their claims, so that stakeholders can have confidence in the information presented in the report.

If a company refuses to disclose negative information to the public, it will turn their CSR report into a tool for advertising and propaganda. Furthermore, inaccuracies in the report could push the company's behavior and statements to the extreme, which could ultimately affect the company's credibility and positive image. Therefore, when preparing social responsibility reports, companies should not only highlight what they have done, what results they have achieved, and what honors they have earned, but also provide details about the problems they may encounter in the process of business management, the risks they face, and the potential penalties they may be subjected to. By including both positive and negative information in the social responsibility report, companies can ensure the integrity of their corporate information disclosure. This integrity is beneficial for enterprises to understand their strengths and weaknesses and address any problems.

The China Resources SANJIU has introduced a "Performance Culture" to motivate its employees for job promotion but assessing its effectiveness has proven difficult. Under this culture, employees who receive more "thumbs up" online are considered to perform better than their peers. However, data fraud is prevalent, making it challenging to accurately evaluate an employee's performance. Additionally, the heterogeneity of customers makes it difficult to quantify what the employee is doing at work. This method of quantification is overly simplistic and may discourage employees from working dutifully. It fails to consider the complex nature of employee performance and customer interactions. Therefore, a more comprehensive evaluation method is necessary to ensure that employees are recognized for their hard work and that the company benefits from their improved performance.

Conclusion

Currently, there are two mainstream models, the shareholder model and the stakeholder model, which are widely recognized both domestically and abroad. Since the annual social responsibility report published by pharmaceutical companies is closer to the stakeholder model, it is suggested that the stakeholder model be adopted to classify the disclosure of social responsibility (Guo, 2013). In the main part of the report, the social responsibility assumed by the company can be disclosed from seven perspectives, including shareholder responsibility, customer responsibility, partner responsibility, government responsibility, employee responsibility, social welfare, and environmental protection. The SANJIU's CSR reports are complete with these sections, although there may be a need to optimize their length and space allocation.

A complete CSR report should have a clear structure that provides detailed information and ends with the practice of social responsibility disclosed in the main part. Additionally, the report should start by explaining the norms under which it was prepared. Since this is the company's first social responsibility report, it is necessary to explain the social responsibility concept, social responsibility strategy, and key performance model adopted by the company. A brief introduction of the company should also be included, along with an executive statement that explains the social responsibility assumed by the company and discloses relevant social responsibility information. The report should conclude with a future outlook, report reviews, reference indexes, and reader feedback. These elements will help the company to evaluate its performance and make necessary improvements. With a well-structured report, the company can effectively communicate its social responsibility efforts to stakeholders and build a positive reputation as a responsible corporate citizen. In addition to corporate governance and information disclosure, a company's responsibility toward its shareholders also includes disclosing negative information related to investor management system, growth, profitability, security, and shareholder responsibility. It is crucial for a company to provide accurate and transparent information to its shareholders, including information that may negatively impact the company's reputation or financial performance. By disclosing negative information, a company can demonstrate its commitment to transparency and accountability, which can help to build trust and loyalty among its shareholders.

Most of the information included in the CSR reports published by the SANJIU is provided through qualitative analysis rather than quantitative analysis. Furthermore, these reports lack case studies, which may reduce their credibility. In this chapter, it is suggested that the SANJIU could improve the credibility of its report by incorporating more quantitative data, such as ROE, ROA, R&D investment, employee training expenses, and case studies related to its CSR efforts. In addition, the SANJIU should consider introducing a third-party institution to review its reports, which would help to ensure that the reports are complete, accurate, and credible. By working with a reputable third-party institution, the SANJIU can demonstrate its commitment to transparency and accountability and provide stakeholders with a more comprehensive view of its social responsibility efforts.

To comprehensively improve the disclosure of social responsibility information and effectively communicate their social responsibility efforts, it is important for pharmaceutical enterprises to establish a system of social responsibility information disclosure tailored to their own development. This system should begin by improving the CSR strategy, integrating corporate awareness and values of social responsibility into the corporate strategy, and adopting a stakeholder-based social responsibility performance model that prioritizes product quality responsibility and consumer responsibility. Furthermore, it is essential to establish and improve communication channels between enterprises and stakeholders, understand the needs and expectations that stakeholders have for corporate disclosure of social responsibility information, and maintain open and effective communication channels. While the SANJIU has provided information about its channels for communication with stakeholders, it lacks a clear explanation. Therefore, it is suggested that the SANJIU can enhance the transparency of its communication channels and consider adopting additional communication methods to engage with stakeholders.

References

Chen, R. and Lee, C., 2016. The influence of CSR on firm value: An application of panel smooth transition regression on Taiwan. *Applied Economics*, 49(34), pp. 3422–3434.

Friedman, M., 1970. The social responsibility of business is to increase its profits. *The New York Times Magazine*, September.

Gerged, A., Beddewela, E. and Cowton, C., 2020. Is corporate environmental disclosure associated with firm value? A multicountry study of Gulf Cooperation Council firms. *Business Strategy and the Environment*, 30(1), pp. 185–203.

Gong, N. and Duan, M., 2021. The motivation and influencing factors corporate carbon information disclosure: an analysis of the constituent enterprises of SSE social responsibility index. *Journal of Environmental Economics*. **6**, pp. 31–52.

Guo, H., 2020. *The Research on the Impact of Pharmaceutical Corporate Social Responsibility on Corporate Performance: A Case Study of Waston Bio*. Master. Central South University of Forestry & Technology.

Guo, Y., 2013. *Quality Research on Pharmaceutical Corporate Social Reponsibility Information Disclosure——Take KM Pharmaceutical Company as an Example*. Master. Shandong University.

Jia, X., Liu, Y. and Liao, Y., 2016. Stakeholders pressure, corporate social responsibility, and firm value. *China Journal of Management*, 13(2).

Kang, Y., Zhu, X. and Li, X., 2020. Empirical study on the impact of corporate social responsibility to innovation performance of medical enterprises——A mediating role of dynamic capability. *Science & Technology Progress and Policy*, 37(11).

Lin, B., Cai, S. and Wang, W., 2017. The definition of variables in the study of CSR evaluation is analyzed. *Finance and Accounting Monthly*. Issue 8.

Ma, J., 2019. *An Analysis on the Motivation of Corporate Social Responsibility Information Disclosure for Publicly Listed Enterprises*. Master. Xiamen University.

Maignan, I. and Ferrell, O.C. 2004. Corporate social responsibility and marketing: an integrative framework. *Journal of the Academy of Marketing Science*. **32**(1), pp. 3–19.

Pan, J. and Guan, J., 2021. Summary of CSR theory. *Sweeping over the Management*.

Xiao, Z., 2021. Summary of CSR and financial performance and enterprise value research. *Academic Exchange*.

Xing, Y., 2014. *The Evaluation of Corporate Social Responsibility in Pharmaceutical Manufacturing and Its Impact on Corporate Performance*. Master. Chongqing Technology and Business University.

Yan, S. and Guo, X., 2020. Discussion of the status quo of social responsibility information disclosure of listed companies in China. *Chinese Market*.

Zhu, S., 2011. Corporate social responsibility, market evaluation and informativeness of accounting earnings. *China Journal of Accounting Studies*, (11), pp. 27–34+92.

4 Impact of environmental and social governance (ESG) on the performance of Chinese companies

Chenlei Wu and Bhabani Shankar Nayak

Introduction

Environmental, social, and governance (ESG) is an assessment of a company's social responsibility and its potential for sustainable financial development. The ESG investment concept originated in response to the Exxon Valdez oil spill in 1989, with the formation of the Valdez Principles (Environmentally Responsible Economic Alliance Principles). In 1990, KLD Research & Analysis created the first ESG index. This was followed in the 1990s by the publication of the first corporate governance code in the UK and the Dow Jones Sustainability Index, which illustrate the initial development of the ESG investment concept. In 2006, the United Nations created the Principles for Responsible Investment (UNPRI), promising to incorporate ESG issues into its investment analysis and ownership policies. UNPRI's impetus has played a significant role in the emergence of ESG investing. In 2010, Bloomberg Terminal integrated ESG data, further institutionalizing the dissemination of ESG information. Currently, more than a quarter of global assets under management are invested in accordance with ESG principles, with the highest proportion of sustainable investment in the European region. There is also an increasing focus on ESG investment in China.

According to a report by McKinsey published in October 2017, over a quarter of global assets under management were invested in accordance with ESG principles. Among them, the European region had the highest proportion of sustainable investment, reaching 52.6% at the beginning of 2016 alone. In contrast, just 0.8% of Asian countries outside of Japan invested in ESG principles, although the gap was narrowing as ESG principles became more prevalent in emerging markets. The number of sustainably managed assets outside of Europe has grown significantly faster than in Europe over the last decade (Bernow et al., 2017). As a result, ESG investment concepts are relatively mature in Europe and America and can serve as a reference standard. Other regions are also paying increasing attention to the concept of ESG investment.

ESG investments deserve to be valued because studies have shown that ESG information is related to many economically meaningful impacts (Amel-Zadeh and Serafeim, 2018). One of the most researched questions is whether ESG disclosure practices translate into positive firm performance (FP). Corporate performance is

DOI: 10.4324/9781003437307-5

often narrowly defined and should be combined with a wide range of financial ratios to provide a good and recognized benchmark for firm performance. FP can be divided into corporate financial performance and market performance. In the European and American areas, there have been extensive empirical and critical studies on the relationship between ESG standards and corporate financial performance (CFP). Although some scholars argue that ESG cannot improve CFP and corporate profitability, the majority of scholars believe that the business case of ESG investment is well-founded in experience. While there is less literature on the relationship between FP and market performance, most findings suggest a non-negative relationship between FP and market performance. This demonstrates the importance of ESG as a sustainability concept for research into the value of corporate investment in sustainable finance.

While ESG may not yet be widely known in China, the government's emphasis on sustainable and eco-friendly development through various policies and regulations suggest that the importance of ESG investment is recognized in the Chinese market (Zhao et al, 2018). However, there is a lack of both empirical and critical studies on the impact of ESG on the Chinese market. Moreover, few studies have examined how ESG indicators affect the performance of listed companies in China by dividing firm performance into corporate financial performance and market performance.

The impact of ESG on firm performance can be divided into two parts: the impact of ESG on corporate financial performance and the impact of ESG on market performance. The relationship between ESG and corporate financial performance has been extensively discussed in the literature. Not only are the reasons why ESG affects corporate financial performance debated, but also empirical analyses are conducted using samples. Three common findings have emerged: first, ESG positively affects corporate financial performance (Xie et al., 2019; Paolone et al., 2021); second, ESG has a negative impact on firm financial performance (Poelloe, 2010; Peiris and Evans, 2010); and third, some scholars have argued that there is no correlation between ESG and corporate financial performance (Han et al., 2016; Qiu et al., 2016). The relationship between ESG and market performance has also been studied by the authors. Some believe that there is a negative relationship between ESG and market performance (Brammer et al., 2006; Landi and Sciarelli, 2019; Demers et al., 2021), while most of them believe that market performance is positively affected by ESG (Sahut and Pasquini-Descomps, 2015; Peiris and Evans, 2010; Buallay, 2019). An alternative view is that there is no correlation between ESG and market performance (Landi and Sciarelli, 2019). However, most of the literature describes the situation in the US and European markets, and studies with Chinese markets as a sample are very scarce.

The development process of ESG in China reflects the importance of government promotion. It is worth considering whether the increase in the number of ESG scores disclosed by companies is related to the impact of ESG on corporate performance, in addition to policy promotion. Comparing the research results in Europe, America, and China, we find that most of the literature on the Chinese market only discusses the single relationship between ESG and corporate financial performance or ESG and market performance, and lacks empirical research that combines the two. Moreover, the Chinese market lacks research on the three sub-components of ESG.

Environmental and social governance (ESG) and corporate performance

Traditional company management models have focused solely on the interests of shareholders and maximizing their profits by improving financial performance. However, many companies are now advocating for a sustainable management model that is oriented toward all stakeholders, including shareholders, consumers, and customers. Environmental, Social, and Governance (ESG) is an extension and enrichment of the concepts of responsible investment and the green economy, and it is an important measure of a company's sustainable management model (Deng and Cheng, 2019).

The ESG approach is not focused on short-term profits, but rather on sustainable returns in the long term. It mainly examines three non-financial indicators: Environmental factors, Social factors, and Corporate Governance. According to Camilleri (2015) and Alareeni and Hamdan (2020), Environmental factors include areas such as climate change, air and carbon emissions, biodiversity, energy efficiency, and waste management. Social factors represent customer satisfaction, data protection, human rights, and community relations. Governance relates to the top level of corporate authority, including the composition of the board of directors, the relationship between shareholders and management, and the existence of financial fraud in the company.

From an investor perspective, Amel-Zadeh and Serafeim (2018) conducted a survey with European and American investors and found that the use of ESG information has been primarily motivated by economic rather than ethical motives. ESG information is relevant for assessing the reputation of the company, legal and regulatory risks, and can reduce the asymmetry of internal and external information, making stakeholders more accountable to the company. Respondents also believed that ESG information has investment value, as it can be used to make appropriate investment choices by predicting the future financial performance of a company and the performance of its shares in the market. Furthermore, many investors suggested that governments and enterprises should guide the supervision and disclosure of ESG information according to the needs of investors. Green bonds or thematic indexes can serve as a laboratory for the market to understand how to price social preferences.

From a corporate perspective, companies are increasingly required to comply with strict environmental, social, and other regulations and disclose information on ESG in response to pressure from the government, non-governmental organizations, and stakeholders (Alareeni and Hamdan, 2020).

From the perspective of the government, ESG is a key driver for sustainable financial development. It can help investors understand the impact of ESG on investment value and encourage companies to incorporate ESG into their corporate strategic deployment, increasing their awareness of environmental protection. This will ultimately help build a modern economic system, address environmental pollution problems, and achieve sustainability for the whole society (Deng and Cheng, 2019).

Growth of ESG in China

China has made significant efforts to promote green finance and ESG investment. In 2016, the People's Bank of China issued guidelines for green credit, and in 2017, it established a green finance committee to promote the development of green finance in China. In addition, the China Securities Regulatory Commission (CSRC) issued guidelines on corporate social responsibility reporting in 2008, which included ESG disclosure requirements. Furthermore, in 2018, the CSRC issued guidelines for the issuance of green bonds, which required the disclosure of environmental information and the use of proceeds from green bonds. These initiatives have helped to promote the development of ESG in China and have encouraged companies to disclose ESG information.

In 2016, the government issued "Several Opinions on Promoting the Sustainable and Healthy Development of Venture Capital" (Guo Fa [2016] No. 53), which introduced the concept of responsible investment. The ESG-related system was further improved in the "Guidance on Building a Green Financial System" jointly issued by the People's Bank of China and seven other ministries. Additionally, in the same year, the China Banking and Insurance Regulatory Commission (CBIRC) proposed that the banking industry and financial institutions establish and improve their environmental and social risk management systems, integrate ESG requirements into their credit-granting processes, enhance environmental governance information disclosure, and increase communication and interactions with stakeholders. This year marked the first national-level promotion of ESG development in China.

In 2018, the China Securities Regulatory Commission (CSRC) amended the "Code of Corporate Governance for Listed Companies," which mandated listed companies to disclose ESG information. The Shanghai Stock Exchange (SSE) and the Shenzhen Stock Exchange (SZSE) issued guidelines on ESG information disclosure, which were expected to take full effect in 2020. The China Securities Investment Fund Association released its first guidelines on green investment and later published a report on the ESG evaluation system for listed companies in China. This year could be considered as another significant push by regulators and industry associations for the development of ESG in China.

In 2020, the CSRC implemented mandatory ESG disclosure principles for listed companies, in line with an agreement made with the Ministry of Environmental Protection. This move is expected to enhance the quality and quantity of ESG data on Chinese listed stocks. In 2021, the government work report required the inclusion of a clear carbon-neutral target (dual carbon target), which provided an excellent opportunity for the development of China's ESG investment system. This brought new challenges and opportunities for the development of Chinese enterprises.

The above process of ESG development demonstrates that ESG has been actively promoted with the attention and support of the Chinese government and industry associations, despite its relatively late start and only receiving its first boost in 2015. Driven by the appeal for reform, listed companies have also begun to prioritize ESG issues. In 2018, over 60% of Shanghai Stock Exchange companies disclosed some ESG information, which was a 235% increase from the previous year. In 2020, a total of 1,021 A-share companies released ESG annual reports, significantly surpassing the 371 in 2009. This indicates that the number of companies issuing ESG reports is increasing. Since 2018, China A-shares have been included in the MSCI Emerging Market Index, and their weight has been increasing in recent years. However, official statistics from MSCI indicate that the ESG scores of Chinese A-share listed companies remain low. The majority of A-share companies still rank at the bottom of the seven ESG rating categories, with more companies in the B, BB, and CCC categories. The proportion of high-ranking companies in China falls significantly below the overall level of emerging markets. This illustrates that ESG is gaining importance in the Chinese market, but ESG ratings of listed companies still require further development.

The actual development of ESG in the Chinese market began when the government started paying attention to it and introduced various policies to promote its growth. Companies have since followed the national policy, resulting in an increasing number of companies disclosing their ESG scores. However, the disclosed ratings have not been high. This raises questions about whether the rise in ESG disclosures by companies is driven solely by policy or if it reflects the impact of ESG on firm performance. If ESG has a positive impact on firm performance in the Chinese market, it would be more conducive to the future development of ESG in China. However, if there is a negative impact, even with government support, companies may be less inclined to promote ESG development in the future.

Impact of ESG on corporate financial performance

The first perspective is that ESG does not have a positive impact on corporate financial performance, a view supported by much literature (Peiris and Evans, 2010; Poelloe, 2010; Landi and Sciarelli, 2019). This impact can be explained in terms of each of the three sub-components of ESG. For example, if a company complies with environmental laws and regulations, it may incur additional costs, thereby reducing the firm's efficiency and profitability and having a negative impact on its financial performance. Smith, Yahya, and Marzuki (2007) found that disclosing environmental information has been negatively related to corporate financial performance, with a higher level of environmental disclosure associated with a lower return on assets.

Corporate social responsibility activities can also negatively impact corporate financial performance, as they generate additional costs resulting from agency problems and inefficient resource allocation, which can reduce a company's competitiveness in the market. Margolis and Walsh (2003) noted that two issues of misappropriation and misallocation are likely to arise when enterprises engage in social responsibility activities. Executives may divert funds and resources that originally belonged to all stakeholders, and then misallocate these resources.

The relationship between corporate governance activities and CFP is typically linked to the characteristics of the board of directors. This is because the board of directors plays a crucial role in supervising the performance and activities of senior management, as well as in designing and implementing strategies (Jensen and Meckling, 1976). Generally, if the board of directors is independent or large, corporate governance activities are positively associated with corporate financial performance. However, O'Connell and Cramer (2010) argued that board size was significantly and negatively correlated with corporate financial performance. Another perspective is that ESG has a positive impact on corporate financial performance (Sahut and Pasquini-Descomps, 2015). ESG information disclosure can increase transparency and mitigate the problem of information asymmetry among stakeholders. Through ESG disclosure, the lemon problem can be effectively addressed by reducing information asymmetry between managers and external investors. When investors receive reliable signals sent to the market by the company, their confidence in the company increases, and the cost of raising funds decreases. Brammer and Pavelin (2008) argued that ESG disclosure reduced the level of information asymmetry between the firm and its stakeholders. ESG disclosure can also influence investors' perceptions of a company's future financial prospects by communicating information to the outside world that can benefit the company's value.

This impact can be explained in terms of each of the three subcomponents of ESG. The additional costs for firms to conduct activities in accordance with environmental regulations can increase, but strict environmental regulations also lead to more competition and foster innovation. Innovation can increase efficiency, offset additional costs, and even generate new revenue. Aerts et al. (2008) demonstrated that analysts could make more accurate earnings forecasts when presented with more environmental disclosures. Karagozoglu and Lindell (2000) argued that corporate environmental strategies had a positive impact on finance and competition.

Corporate social responsibility activities can help companies build and enhance their corporate reputation capital, which increases their ability to attract resources and ultimately improves their financial performance (Fombrun et al., 2000). Ferrell, Liang, and Renneboog (2016) demonstrated that corporate social responsibility activities did not cause agency problems and actually improved shareholder benefits. In fact, corporate social responsibility activities can lead to higher returns for investors by improving the corporate financial performance and shareholder wealth. Saleh et al. (2011) found a significant positive correlation between corporate social responsibility and corporate financial performance. Kim et al. (2013) argued that companies could increase stakeholder value and overall company value by engaging in corporate social responsibility activities. Empirical research also supports a positive correlation between corporate social responsibility and financial performance.

When companies engage in ESG activities, especially governance activities, they can stimulate the management or technology of the company to innovate. These innovations increase efficiency and lead to improved corporate financial performance. Additionally, companies with good corporate governance mechanisms can provide more useful information available in their financial statements, which can help strengthen their operations. The more information is disclosed about corporate governance activities, the more competent managers are hired, and the better the financial performance of the company (Hermalin and Weisbach, 2012). Xie et al. (2019) believed that a moderate level of disclosure was positively related to company efficiency and concluded that governance activities have a more positive impact on company efficiency. Paolone et al. (2021) conducted a study on the pharmaceutical industry and found that ESG indicators contributed to improved financial performance, with governance-related scores having a greater impact. Luan and Tang (2007) found that the appointment of independent outside directors has a positive impact on corporate financial performance. Esteban-Sanchez et al. (2017) stated that banks with better corporate governance perform better in terms of CFP.

The last perspective is that there is no correlation between ESG and corporate financial performance. Although this viewpoint is not mainstream, it can still provide a new idea for research. Qiu et al. (2016) concluded that there was no correlation between environmental disclosure and corporate financial performance since environmental disclosure scores include both positive and negative factors, making it a noisy measure. Trumpp and Guenther (2017) argued that there could be a nonlinear relationship between environmental performance and corporate financial performance, particularly a U-shaped relationship. Therefore, it is not possible to singularly describe the positive or negative correlation. Han et al. (2016) believed that there was no statistically significant relationship between corporate social responsibility activities and corporate financial performance. In summary, ESG and its three sub-components may have a negative impact on CFP by increasing additional costs and reducing the efficiency of the firm. However, ESG may also act as a stimulus to corporate innovation, enhance corporate reputation, and reduce the cost of raising funds, thus having a positive impact on CFP. It is also possible that the two are in a neutral relationship, with no correlation between ESG and its three sub-components and corporate financial performance.

ESG and corporate financial performance in China

In most literature on the Chinese market, ESG indicators usually have an impact on corporate financial performance. However, most of this influence is caused by the theoretical system. As the government pushes to institutionalize ESG in the Chinese legal and political system, companies need to disclose ESG information, which can build good corporate reputations and improve corporate financial performance. However, economically efficient companies incur more costs for ESG disclosure, and there are costs for further improvements as ESG performance improves. Nevertheless, Liu and Anbumozhi (2009) believe that the current ESG information disclosure in China is still in its infancy. Compared with other countries, the government's supervision pressure and market competition mechanism in China are relatively low, suggesting that ESG may not have a significant impact on corporate financial performance.

However, Guoyou et al. (2013) argue that ESG can influence corporate financial performance. With the globalization of the economy, whether Chinese companies disclose ESG indicators or not and the extent of ESG indicator disclosure is affected by international trade. If Chinese companies supply their products to different countries, they must meet the standards required by different countries/regions. For example, the Environmental Management System (ISO 14001) has requirements for suppliers, production methods, and product use in manufacturing plants. This has implications for the willingness of Chinese companies to report on their ESG indicators, further affecting corporate financial performance. For different industries in the Chinese market, ESG indicators have a greater impact on financial performance for state-owned enterprises and green enterprises (Weber, 2014). The energy sector, such as power companies, also shares these findings (Zhao et al, 2018). This is because government regulations and guidelines have a greater impact in China compared to the size of the company. State-owned enterprises are more susceptible to government supervision than ordinary enterprises, and green enterprises and energy enterprises are more responsive to national policies, such as the carbon neutrality policy and the recent introduction of electricity restrictions in response to the epidemic.

Impact of ESG on market performance

In Europe and the US, the impact that ESG can have on market performance has been described in the literature (Peiris and Evans, 2010; Buallay, 2019; Alareeni and Hamdan, 2020). As the financial accounting of the firm is no longer sufficient to support the needs of shareholders, the sustainable competitive advantage of companies has become important. The impact of ESG on market performance, in other words on the future value of a company, is therefore worth being studied (Buallay, 2019). ESG can partially explain the firm performance in the market since those investors can see a company's ability to mitigate risk and predict trends from its ESG score (Sahut and Pasquini-Descomps, 2015). Some studies have also found that companies with high ESG perform better in the market (Deng and Cheng, 2019; Alareeni and Hamdan, 2020). In the three sub-components of ESG, environmental regulations stimulate corporate innovation and improve company efficiency, which in turn has a positive impact on the performance of the company in the market; corporate social responsibility activities can improve corporate reputation and bring companies a competitive advantage in a rational market, as Kim et al. (2013) stated that CSR activities reduced the risk of companies; corporate governance also improves corporate efficiency through innovation, thereby affecting company performance in the market.

However, some studies have found a negative correlation between ESG and market performance. Brammer, Brooks, and Pavelin (2006) studied the relationship between corporate social performance and market performance by using stock returns as a measure and British listed companies as a sample. They found that companies with high scores on comprehensive social performance indicators received low stock returns. Landi and Sciarelli (2019) stated that investors who follow the ESG investment philosophy could not obtain excess returns in the Italian market. Demers et al. (2021) tested whether ESG performance would become a factor of stock price elasticity during a crisis and found that ESG scores could not have a positive impact on market performance. Furthermore, they argued that only when more traditional corporate accounting indicators such as financial performance, liquidity, and profitability are combined with market-based measures of equity risk can they jointly explain a company's stock returns.

Finally, some argue that there is no correlation between ESG and market performance. Landi and Sciarelli (2019) explored whether investors who follow the ESG investment philosophy could obtain excess returns in the Italian market. However, they found that the impact of ESG investment on the market premium was not positive or statistically significant. Trumpp and Guenther (2017) show that there is a non-linear relationship between environmental performance and market performance. In conclusion, the mainstream view in Europe and the US is that ESG may have a positive, negative, or no impact on the market performance of a firm.

ESG and market performance in China

Most of the literature also suggests that ESG indicators can impact firm performance in the Chinese market. Deng and Cheng (2019) used data from Chinese A-share listed companies to establish an empirical model, using corporate financial indicators as a control variable to study the relationship between ESG indexes and stock market performance. The research shows that ESG has a positive impact on stock market performance. Li et al. (2020) found that the bond default rate of Chinese companies was not only related to financial performance but also to ESG performance, both of which affect the credit and operational risks of the firm. Feng, Goodell, and Shen (2021) examined the importance of the quality of ESG disclosure in assessing the risk of share price collapse in the Chinese market, starting with the risk of share price collapse. Additionally, the relationship between ESG indicators and the market performance of companies during a special period has also been studied. Broadstock et al. (2021) used the China CSI 300 Index as a dataset to study the role of ESG performance in the market during the financial crisis triggered by the COVID-19 global pandemic.

The impact of ESG on CFP and market performance is not uniformly agreed upon, mainly due to the inability to mediate the process between the firm's ESG indicators and its financial performance. There is no uniformity in the range of commonly used market or accounting indicators (Peloza, 2009). Moreover, the concept of ESG and its three sub-components complicate the conclusions about the relationship between ESG and firm performance. Companies choose their desired ESG strategy based on their different motivations, leading to different implications for firm performance. Studies focusing on different types of ESG activities may draw distinct conclusions about the relationship between ESG and firm performance (Xie et al., 2019).

ESG is an essential standard for measuring sustainability with different implications for investors, enterprises, and governments. The research question raised by the development of ESG in China is whether it has an impact on firm performance. A critical discussion of research findings in Europe, the US, and China follows the research question, ultimately revealing that ESG and its sub-components have both positive and negative effects on corporate financial performance and market performance. Additionally, some argue that there is no correlation between ESG and its sub-components and CFP and market performance of companies. Furthermore, while compiling the literature on the impact of ESG indicators on firm performance in the Chinese market, it was found that ESG is only in its infancy in China, resulting in a scarcity of published literature on the impact of ESG on firm performance in conjunction with corporate financial performance and market performance.

Conclusions

In the Chinese market, there is a positive correlation between ESG and firm performance in terms of both corporate financial performance and firm market performance. Higher levels of ESG disclosure have a positive impact on firm performance, as higher ESG is associated with better financial, operational, and market performance. These findings are consistent with several previous studies that show ESG's positive impact on corporate financial performance (Brammer and Pavelin, 2008; Friede et al., 2015; Xie et al., 2019; Paolone et al., 2021) and that ESG positively affects firm market performance (Buallay, 2019; Deng and Cheng, 2019; Li et al., 2020; Broadstock et al., 2021). Increasing corporate social responsibility activities can improve a company's market performance. Such activities can enhance a company's reputation, reduce its market risk, and provide a competitive advantage in a rational market. This perspective is in line with studies by Kim et al. (2013) and Broadstock et al. (2021). Hence, it can be concluded that corporate social responsibility activities are highly significant and practical in improving the market capitalization of China's FTSE A50 listed companies.

Corporate governance activities have a positive impact on the financial performance of firms. Higher levels of corporate governance activities can improve a firm's financial performance, as indicated by return on equity (ROE). This is because increased information disclosure on corporate governance activities helps companies attract more competent managers, resulting in improved financial performance (Hermalin and Weisbach, 2012). Furthermore, the development of corporate governance activities can lead to innovation in a company's management or technology, which increases efficiency and, consequently, improves corporate financial performance (Xie et al., 2019). This perspective is consistent with studies by Luan and Tang (2007), Esteban-Sanchez et al. (2017), and Paolone et al. (2021).

It is clear that Environmental Information Disclosure (EID) has a positive or negative impact on company performance. However, this study found no correlation between EID and firm performance in the Chinese market, which is consistent with previous studies (Han et al, 2016; Landi and Sciarelli, 2019). The Bloomberg score used to measure EID covers both positive and negative environmental disclosures, making it a noisy measure of a company's environmental performance. Moreover, there may be a U-shaped relationship between environmental performance and Corporate Financial Performance (CFP), making the model used in this study unsuitable for exploring the relationship between environmental activities and firm performance (Trumpp and Guenther, 2017). Furthermore, companies may only symbolically comply with environmental policies without making significant efforts toward them, which may contribute to the lack of correlation between EID and firm performance in the Chinese market (Haque and Ntim, 2018).

ESG has huge implications for the Chinese government, Chinese companies, and investors. For the government, the positive impact of ESG on firm performance means that promoting the development of ESG in China can be a win-win situation for all. Not only does it promote the establishment of a green financial system, which will help achieve future carbon neutrality targets, but it will also have a positive impact on firm performance. Companies will be more proactive in cooperating and complying with government regulations. Additionally, the Chinese government, the China Securities Regulatory Commission, and other regulatory authorities can introduce more policies on ESG information disclosure in the future to increase the number of companies disclosing ESG information and improve the quality of their ESG scores, thereby improving communication and interactions with stakeholders. For companies, the positive impact of ESG on firm performance means that Chinese companies should pay more attention to ESG information disclosure and improve their ESG scores rating. It is recommended that they consider ESG to provide reliable financial information. For investors, understanding ESG and its importance in business is crucial. ESG should be used as an alternative measure of investment choice to get better returns on investment, in addition to basic company financial statements.

One of the challenges facing China and Chinese companies is the lack of a systematic disclosure framework and standards for ESG. The current disclosure efforts of listed companies in China are still not satisfactory enough to fully meet the requirements of ESG evaluation. Another challenge is the lack of localized applications of ESG scoring standards. Factors such as carbon emissions and climate risk need to be adjusted according to China's national conditions. A third challenge is the quality and validity of the databases used for ESG evaluation. As an emerging market for ESG development, China lacks domestic service agencies that provide effective and reliable data.

References

Aerts, W., Cormier, D. & Magnan, M. 2008, "Corporate environmental disclosure, financial markets and the media: an international perspective", *Ecological Economics*. [E-journal]. Vol. 64, no. 3, pp. 643–659. Available at: https://doi.org/10.1016/j.ecolecon.2007.04.012. Accessed 25th November 2021.

Alareeni, B.A. & Hamdan, A. 2020, "ESG impact on performance of US S&P 500-listed firms", *Corporate Governance (Bradford)*. [E-journal]. Vol. 20, no. 7, pp. 1409–1428. Available at: https://doi.org/10.1108/CG-06-2020-0258. Accessed 22nd September 2021.

Amel-Zadeh, A. & Serafeim, G. 2018, "Why and how investors use ESG information: evidence from a global survey", *Financial Analysts Journal*. [E-journal]. Vol. 74, no. 3, pp. 87–103. Available at: https://doi.org/10.2469/faj.v74.n3.2. Accessed 28th September 2021.

Bernow, S., Klempner, B. & Magnin, C. 2017, "From 'why'to 'why not': sustainable investing as the new normal", *McKinsey & Company*. [Online]. Available at: https://www.mckinsey.com/industries/private-equity-and-principal-investors/our-insights/from-why-to-why-not-sustainable-investing-as-the-new-normal. Accessed 22nd September 2021.

Brammer, S. & Pavelin, S. 2008, "Factors influencing the quality of corporate environmental disclosure", *Business Strategy and the Environment.* [E-journal]. Vol. 17, no. 2, pp. 120–136. Available at: https://doi.org/10.1002/bse.506. Accessed 25th November 2021.

Brammer, S., Brooks, C. & Pavelin, S. 2006, "Corporate social performance and stock returns: UK evidence from disaggregate measures", *Financial Management.* [E-journal]. Vol. 35, no. 3, pp. 97–116. Available at: https://doi.org/10.1111/j.1755-053X.2006.tb00149.x. Accessed 15th November 2021.

Broadstock, D.C., Chan, K., Cheng, L.T.W. & Wang, X. 2021, "The role of ESG performance during times of financial crisis: evidence from COVID-19 in China", *Finance Research Letters.* [E-journal]. Vol. 38, pp. 101716. Available at: https://doi.org/10.1016/j.frl.2020.101716. Accessed 25th November 2021.

Buallay, A. 2019, "Is sustainability reporting (ESG) associated with performance? Evidence from the European banking sector", *Management of Environmental Quality.* [E-journal]. Vol. 30, no. 1, pp. 98–115. Available at: https://doi.org/10.1108/MEQ-12-2017-0149. Accessed 28th September 2021.

Camilleri, M.A. 2015, "Environmental, social and governance disclosures in Europe", *Sustainability Accounting, Management and Policy Journal (Print).* [E-journal]. Vol. 6, no. 2, pp. 224–242. Available at: https://doi.org/10.1108/SAMPJ-10-2014-0065. Accessed 19th November 2021.

Demers, E., Hendrikse, J., Joos, P. & Lev, B. 2021, "ESG Didn't immunize stocks during the COVID-19 crisis, but investments in intangible assets did", *Journal of Business Finance & Accounting.* **48**, pp. 433–462.

Deng, X. & Cheng, X. 2019, "Can ESG indices improve the enterprises' stock market performance?—an empirical study from China", *Sustainability (Basel, Switzerland).* [E-journal]. Vol. 11, no. 17, pp. 4765. Available at: https://doi.org/10.3390/su11174765. Accessed 22nd September 2021.

Esteban-Sanchez, P., de la Cuesta-Gonzalez, M. & Paredes-Gazquez, J.D. 2017, "Corporate social performance and its relation with corporate financial performance: international evidence in the banking industry", *Journal of Cleaner Production.* [E-journal]. Vol. 162, pp. 1102–1110. Available at: https://doi.org/10.3390/su11174765.Accessed 28th September 2021.

Feng, J., Goodell, J.W. & Shen, D. 2021, "ESG rating and stock price crash risk: evidence from China", *Finance Research Letters*. [E-journal]. pp. 102476. Available at: https://doi.org/10.1016/j.frl.2021.102476. Accessed 26th September 2021.

Ferrell, A., Liang, H. & Renneboog, L. 2016, "Socially responsible firms", *Journal of Financial Economics.* Vol. 122, no. 3, pp. 585–606.

Fombrun, C.J., Gardberg, N.A. & Barnett, M.L. 2000, "Opportunity platforms and safety nets: corporate citizenship and reputational risk", *Business and Society Review (1974).* [E-journal]. Vol. 105, no. 1, pp. 85–106. Available at: https://doi.org/10.1111/0045-3609.00066. Accessed 7th October 2021.

"Guidance on Building a Green Financial System". 2016. Available at: http://www.pbc.gov.cn/goutongjiaoliu/113456/113469/3131684/index.html. Accessed 28th October 2021.

Guoyou, Q., Saixing, Z., Chiming, T., Haitao, Y. & Hailiang, Z. 2013, "Stakeholders' influences on corporate green innovation strategy: a case study of manufacturing firms in China", *Corporate Social-Responsibility and Environmental Management.* [E-journal].

Vol. 20, no. 1, pp. 1–14. Available at: https://doi.org/10.1002/csr.283. Accessed 15th October 2021.

Han, J., Kim, H.J. & Yu, J. 2016, "Empirical study on relationship between corporate social responsibility and financial performance in Korea", *Asian Journal of Sustainability and Social Responsibility.* [E-journal]. Vol. 1, no. 1, pp. 61–76. Available at: https://doi.org/10.1186/s41180-016-0002-3. Accessed 26th November 2021.

Haque, F. & Ntim, C.G. 2018, "Environmental policy, sustainable development, governance mechanisms and environmental performance", *Business Strategy and the Environment.* [E-journal]. Vol. 27, no. 3, pp. 415–435. Available at: https://doi.org/10.1002/bse.2007. Accessed 12nd November 2021.

Hermalin, B.E. & Weisbach, M.S. 2012, "Information disclosure and corporate governance", *The Journal of Finance (New York).* [E-journal]. Vol. 67, no. 1, pp. 195–233. Available at: https://doi.org/10.1111/j.1540-6261.2011.01710.x. Accessed 15th November 2021.

Jensen, M.C. & Meckling, W.H. 1976, "Theory of the firm: managerial behavior, agency costs and ownership structure", *Journal of Financial Economics.* [E-journal]. Vol. 3, no. 4, pp. 305–360. Available at: https://doi.org/10.1016/0304-405X(76)90026-X. Accessed 12nd October 2021.

Karagozoglu, N. & Lindell, M. 2000, "Environmental management: testing the win-win model", *Journal of Environmental Planning and Management.* [E-journal]. Vol. 43, no. 6, pp. 817–829. Available at: https://doi.org/10.1080/09640560020001700. Accessed 22nd October 2021.

Kim, J., Chung, S. & Park, C. 2013, "Corporate social responsibility and financial performance: the impact of the MSCI ESG ratings on Korean firms", *Journal of the Korea Academia-Industrial Cooperation Society.* [E-journal]. Vol. 14, no. 11, pp. 5586–5593. Available at: https://doi.org/10.5762/KAIS.2013.14.11.5586. Accessed 28th October 2021.

Landi, G. & Sciarelli, M. 2019, "Towards a more ethical market: the impact of ESG rating on corporate financial performance", *Social Responsibility Journal.* [E-journal]. Vol. 15, no. 1, pp. 11–27. Available at: https://doi.org/10.1108/SRJ-11-2017-0254. Accessed 28th November 2021.

Li, P., Zhou, R. & Xiong, Y. 2020, "Can ESG performance affect bond default rate? Evidence from China", *Sustainability (Basel, Switzerland).* [E-journal]. Vol. 12, no. 7, pp. 2954. Available at: https://doi.org/10.3390/su12072954. Accessed 17th November 2021.

Liu, X. & Anbumozhi, V. 2009, "Determinant factors of corporate environmental information disclosure: an empirical study of Chinese listed companies", *Journal of Cleaner Production.* [E-journal]. Vol. 17, no. 6, pp. 593–600. Available at: https://doi.org/10.1016/j.jclepro.2008.10.001. Accessed 28th November 2021.

Luan, C. & Tang, M. 2007, "Where is independent director efficacy?" *Corporate Governance: An International Review.* [E-journal]. Vol. 15, no. 4, pp. 636–643. Available at: https://doi.org/10.1111/j.1467-8683.2007.00593.x. Accessed 28th November 2021.

Margolis, J.D. & Walsh, J.P. 2003, "Misery loves companies: rethinking social initiatives by business", *Administrative Science Quarterly.* [E-journal]. Vol. 48, no. 2, pp. 268–305. Available at: https://doi.org/10.2307/3556659. Accessed 17th October 2021.

O'Connell, V. & Cramer, N. 2010, "The relationship between firm performance and board characteristics in Ireland", *European Management Journal.* [E-journal]. Vol. 28, no. 5, pp. 387–399. Available at: https://doi.org/10.1016/j.emj.2009.11.002. Accessed 17th October 2021.

Paolone, F., Cucari, N., Wu, J. & Tiscini, R. 2021, "How do ESG pillars impact firms' marketing performance? A configurational analysis in the pharmaceutical sector", *The Journal of Business & Industrial Marketing.* **37**(8), pp. 1594–1606.

Peiris, D. & Evans, J. 2010, "The relationship between environmental social governance factors and U.S. stock performance", *The Journal of Investing.* [E-journal]. Vol. 19, no. 3, pp. 104–112. Available at: https://doi.org/10.3905/joi.2010.19.3.104. Accessed 17th October 2021.

Peloza, J. 2009, "The challenge of measuring financial impacts from investments in corporate social performance", *Journal of Management.* [E-journal]. Vol. 35, no. 6, pp. 1518–1541. Available at: https://doi.org/10.1177/0149206309335188. Accessed 17th October 2021.

Poelloe, A. 2010, Is there a trade-off between social responsibility and financial performance. *Erasmus University.* Retrieved from http://oaithesis. eur. nl/ir/repub/asset/8254/ Poelloe,% 20A, 20287713.

Qiu, Y., Shaukat, A. & Tharyan, R. 2016, "Environmental and social disclosures: link with corporate financial performance", *The British Accounting Review.* [E-journal]. Vol. 48, no. 1, pp. 102–116. Available at: https://doi.org/10.1016/j.bar.2014.10.007. Accessed 17th October 2021.

Sahut, J. & Pasquini-Descomps, H. 2015, "ESG impact on market performance of firms: international evidence", *Management International (Montréal).* [E-journal]. Vol. 19, no. 2, pp. 40–63. Available at: https://doi.org/10.7202/1030386ar. Accessed 24th October 2021.

Saleh, M., Zulkifli, N. & Muhamad, R. 2011, "Looking for evidence of the relationship between corporate social responsibility and corporate financial performance in an emerging market", *Asia-Pacific Journal of Business Administration.* [E-journal]. Vol. 3, no. 2, pp. 165–190. Available at: https://doi.org/10.1108/17574321111169849. Accessed 24th October 2021.

Smith, M., Yahya, K. & Marzuki Amiruddin, A. 2007, "Environmental disclosure and performance reporting in Malaysia", *Asian Review of Accounting.* [E-journal]. Vol. 15, no. 2, pp. 185–199. Available at: https://doi.org/10.1108/13217340710823387. Accessed 24th October 2021.

Trumpp, C. & Guenther, T. 2017, "Too little or too much? Exploring U-shaped relationships between corporate environmental performance and corporate financial performance", *Business Strategy and the Environment.* [E-journal]. Vol. 26, no. 1, pp. 49–68. Available at: https://doi.org/10.1002/bse.1900. Accessed 24th October 2021.

Weber, O. 2014, "Environmental, social and governance reporting in China", *Business Strategy and the Environment.* [E-journal]. Vol. 23, no. 5, pp. 303–317. Available at: https://doi.org/10.1002/bse.1785. Accessed 24th October 2021.

Xie, J., Nozawa, W., Yagi, M., Fujii, H. & Managi, S. 2019, "Do environmental, social, and governance activities improve corporate financial performance?" *Business Strategy and the Environment.* [E-journal]. Vol. 28, no. 2, pp. 286–300. Available at: https://doi.org/10.1002/bse.2224. Accessed 29th October 2021.

Zhao, C., Guo, Y., Yuan, J., Wu, M., Li, D., Zhou, Y. & Kang, J. 2018, "ESG and corporate financial performance: empirical evidence from China's listed power generation companies", *Sustainability (Basel, Switzerland).* [E-journal]. Vol. 10, no. 8, pp. 2607. Available at: https://doi.org/10.3390/su10082607. Accessed 29th October 2021.

5 Scientific research in universities and their impacts on regional economic development in China

A study of Zhejiang from 2009 to 2017

Jie Cheng and Bhabani Shankar Nayak

Introduction

China's economy has progressed from high-speed growth to high-quality development, and it now faces the daunting task of optimizing its economic structure and changing its development mode. Yang (2018) shows that transforming the potential driving force of economic growth is also the internal demand of building a modernized economic system. China's economy has progressed from high-speed growth to high-quality development, and it now faces the daunting task of optimizing its economic structure and changing its development mode. Yao and Chen (2013) show that the report to the 19th CPC National Congress identified the strategy of rejuvenating the country through science and education as one of the seven strategies to be firmly implemented for a decisive victory in building a moderately prosperous society in all respects. To build an innovative country, China needs to constantly strengthen the force of science and technology, improve its transformation capacity and promote the development of productive forces. What's more, to fully realize the contribution of science and technology to economic growth, while constantly relying on science and technology to promote economic development, we must also consistently improve colleges and universities' scientific research capabilities and cultivate high-quality people to suit the needs of the times.

This research engages with the current situation of scientific research in colleges and universities in Zhejiang Province, finds the relationship between scientific research in colleges and universities and regional economy through relevant models, explores the causes and difficulties, and gives suggestions for the process of promoting regional economy by scientific research in colleges and universities. The aim of this chapter is to take Zhejiang as a case to analyze the current development process of university scientific research, explore the logical relationship between university scientific research and regional economy, optimize the efficiency of university scientific research to promote regional economy on this basis, and give relevant suggestions for the cooperation model of different stakeholders.

Wang (2016) notes that scientific research in colleges and universities, which is the core of the national innovation system, has traditionally been strongly linked to the development of regional economies. The national economic development varies with different regions. If the scientific research of colleges and universities

DOI: 10.4324/9781003437307-6

can be integrated into the characteristics of regional economy, it will create greater value and have diversified influences on the local government, enterprises, and residents. Yao and Chen (2013) show that with the great support of the state, scientific research in colleges and universities has shown a good situation, but its role in promoting regional economic development has not been very clear, such as the way and effect of promoting and facing problems.

The research ability of universities and regional economy has always been the focus of scholars' attention. As the country attaches importance to high and new technology, more and more research has begun to put into how to take science and technology as the fundamental driving force of productivity. The focus of scholars' research and the problems they want to solve are mainly in three aspects. The first is to study the relationship between university scientific research and regional economy and the role that university scientific research can have on regional economy. The second is what kind of model should be built to measure. The third is what problems exist in promoting regional economic development and the corresponding countermeasures. In terms of the overall impact of university scientific research on regional economies, scholars mainly analyze the driving role of university scientific research ability on regional economic growth and its quality from the perspective of the relationship between universities, enterprises, and governments. Li (2006) points out that the improvement of regional economic quality was aided by the transformation of scientific and technological achievements at universities. Basic research in colleges and universities may deliver tremendous benefits to local firms and the regional economy by transforming scientific and technological achievements, and it is also the major approach to realize the value of scientific research in colleges and universities.

Wang (2016) points out that scientific research activities of universities are conducive to opening up emerging industries in regional economy and helping transform the structure of traditional industries. The development of regional economy also needs science as the primary productive force. Yang and Yi (2018) point out that scientific research in universities can cultivate scientific and technological talents and provide technical support for regional economy. The scientific research activities of colleges and universities can improve the innovation ability of students. As a result, organizations and society will have a big number of high-quality compound talents to meet their needs and adapt to the changing times.

In terms of research methods, to more accurately assess the impact of university research ability on regional economic quality, a bridge needs to be built between them. Xu (2007) shows that university scientific research ability is a comprehensive index, and it can cover the evaluation of scientific research investment, scientific research production, the transformation of scientific and technological achievements, resources, and environment. He used principal component analysis to analyze colleges and universities in nine provinces and cities along the east coast of China and drew objective conclusions.

Lv (2002) shows that data envelopment analysis (DEA) is also a common research method for this kind of research. She selected and evaluated the scientific and technological innovation ability of colleges and universities in 25 provinces and cities to judge the relative effectiveness of their scientific and technological innovation ability. Xu (2007) believes that Correlation analysis is a statistical tool for examining the relationship between two or more random variables that have the same status, and it is also a commonly used method in academic circles to study the relationship between variables. Xu and Jin (2010) show that the quantitative interdependent relationship between two or more variables is determined using regression analysis, which is a statistical analytic tool and focuses more on using independent variables to predict dependent variables, so it is very suitable for studying the relationship between universities and regional economy. Therefore, they constructed a regression model to analyze the impact of government-industry-university cooperation on regional economic growth.

Scholars have expressed different views on the current problems of scientific research in colleges and universities. Li (2006) shows that the conversion rate of scientific research accomplishments in universities is quite low, and it is required to improve the conversion form and strengthen assistance. The ultimate goal is to transform scientific research achievements into actual productivity. However, neither universities themselves nor enterprises and government pay enough attention to it. As a result, a substantial number of scientific research accomplishments are unable to play a meaningful role, or the study process is suspended and terminated. Xu (2018) shows that the layout structure of scientific research in universities lacks rationality and characteristics. Because colleges and universities are such an essential element of the area economy, scientific research in these institutions should be tightly linked to the local industrial pattern. But now many universities do not have long-term scientific research goals, more follow the overall trend of scientific research, lack of practical based on the local. Sun (2005) believes that the scientific research ability of colleges and universities needs to be improved, and high-level scientific research talents are in short supply and the loss is serious. The foundation of scientific research at universities and colleges is scientific research talent. However, as universities do not attach importance to or even increase pressure on scientific research, and the government does not provide reasonable subsidies and policy support, more and more scientific research talents give up scientific research and turn to teaching or other fields. As a result, a large number of scientific research activities lack talents, which will also affect the sustainable development of scientific research.

The theory of economic growth has undergone many changes and improvements. Xu (2007) points out that in classical economic theory, Adam Smith, Ricardo, and Malthus believed that economic growth was related to capital and labor. Economic growth is largely driven by external forces, and the role of technology and human capital has not yet been realized. There are limits to how much capital and labor can contribute to economic growth. Due to political factors and changing times, economists began to explore other drivers of economic growth. Xu (2018) points out that endogenous economic growth model can support the promotion effect of university and college scientific research on regional economy. The mid-1980s saw the emergence of endogenous economic growth theories. Its basic notion is that the economy can expand sustainably without relying on external forces, and that endogenous technological advancement is the most important factor in achieving this. It emphasizes imperfect competition and growing rewards.

The theory of regional economics has also experienced two stages of development, namely the stage of regional equilibrium theory and the stage of regional disequilibrium theory. Xu (2007) shows that the theory of regional balanced development points out that after the flow of production factors among regions, the economic development of each region will eventually be balanced. Therefore, the theory advocates balanced distribution of productivity and investment within the region, and balanced development of various industries, so as to ensure the healthy development of regional economy.

The theory of regional uneven development is opposite to that of the theory of regional development with equity. Xu (2007) shows that the regional disequilibrium theory holds that the differences between regions are constantly expanding and will not tend to balance. And the theory is more in line with the current economic situation. Therefore, it is more reliable to choose the theory of regional unbalanced development when studying how to promote regional economic growth.

The triple helix theory was born in the 1990s, based on the concept of the triple helix in biology, proposed by Henry Etzkowitz. The government, enterprises, and colleges and universities together constitute the three major elements of economic society, which are closely related and interact with each other. Liu (2018) believes that the triple helix theory can effectively explain the linkage between all stakeholder groups in the process of university research promoting regional economic growth. However, such theoretical outlooks follow the Solow (1956, 1970) growth model which is Eurocentric in letter and spirit. The causal analysis does not engage with conditions of economic growth. It lacks perspectives of political economy. Similarly, Cobb and Douglas' (1928) production function model of economic growth follows a similar path which provides cause and effect relationship within economic growth without engaging with conditions of economic growth and development. Scholars, like Zhang (2018), have used such narrow ideologically driven Eurocentric models to understand trade war between China and USA. Xu (2018) believes that technological innovation is a major driver of current productivity growth and has a significant role in fostering regional economic progress. Joseph Schumpeter, the author of modern innovation theory, stressed the importance of technological innovation for economic development and proposed that "innovation" is the establishment of a new production function, including new products, new technology, new markets, new suppliers, and new organizational forms.

Theories of economic growth

The emergence of "surplus" leads to the accumulation of capital, which in turn increases the demand for labor, and at this time the scale of employment and production continues to expand, which in turn leads to the emergence of "surplus", and so on, and economic growth is realized. Adam Smith creatively distinguished productive labor from unproductive labor and guided subsequent scholars to focus on the substantive production field. At the same time, Adam Smith also linked economic growth with capital and division of labor, emphasizing the huge effect of capital accumulation and division of labor on economic growth. Before Adam Smith identified the essence of economic growth, the mercantilist emphasized economic growth, but could not distinguish between economic growth and the growth of money and wealth.

Ricardo's economic theory emphasizes the relationship between income distribution and economic growth, and his theoretical system of economic growth is based on the law of diminishing marginal productivity. He also emphasized the importance of capital accumulation to economic growth, but he innovatively proposed the law of diminishing marginal productivity for additional labor on a given land. Malthus's theory was about the link between population growth and economic growth. When studying per capita income growth, population change cannot be regarded as a purely exogenous variable. In conclusion, early economic theories did not recognize the importance of science and technology, but gradually recognized the role of human capital in promoting economic growth.

In the mid-1980s, Romer proposed the endogenous economic growth hypothesis, which was based on the growth model of exogenous technical advancement. The model's distinguishing feature is that it begins with technology internalization and always emphasizes understanding of economic growth and development mechanisms based on creativity or knowledge goods. It is critical for developing countries to have a process for generating and implementing new concepts or ideas in order to achieve long-term economic progress. This necessitates that government policymakers prioritize education development and science and technology investment, as well as foster and preserve innovation. In this stage, human capital and technological advancement are critical, and new equipment and materials might represent technological advancements.

The theory of endogenous economic growth has opened up a new perspective for the study of economic growth. Since then, more and more attention has been paid to technological progress and innovation. The assumptions of technological endogeneity and increasing returns to scale better match the reality of economic growth. If a country can have more human capital, knowledge accumulation and rapid technological renewal, then the country will achieve higher economic growth rate and national income level. The endogenous economic growth theory also points out the intervention way for the government. The government should strengthen knowledge education, encourage technological innovation, increase support in education subsidies, intellectual property protection, and research and development funding, and formulate appropriate policies for the long-term development of national and regional economies.

The main idea of the theory of regional balanced development is that the elements flow and maintain balance between regions. But this theory also has certain flaws. First of all, for some less developed regions, capital and other resources are not available to promote the development of all industries in the region. Second, the theory also ignores the effects of scale and technological progress. In a perfectly competitive market, the existence of markets does not reduce regional differences, but increases them. As more developed regions have more resources and markets, capital and labor will be attracted to them, leading to economies of scale, which will only widen the gap between developed and less developed regions. The theory of regional balanced development is too idealized, and it cannot accurately explain the regional economic growth in reality. The notion of regional imbalanced development has more practical application in the early stages of economic growth.

The theory of regional disequilibrium considers that the flow between factors is disequilibrium. The flow of factors exists between the economically developed area and the less developed area. Capital and labor will continue to flow from the less developed to the more developed regions, a cycle that will only make the less developed regions poorer and the more developed regions richer. At this time, if there is no government to carry out macro-control, the differences between regions will become bigger and bigger.

The growth pole theory is also an important representative of the regional unbalanced development theory, which holds that the economic growth rate is different between different industries, different sectors, and even different regions. Growth pole refers to the element of the sector that has dominant effect in the economy and can promote the development of other sectors. It occupies a central position in the regional economic growth, and the innovation ability is a necessary element of the growth pole. If a growth pole can be implanted in the regional economy, it will drive the development of the entire regional economy.

The triple helix theory emphasizes the important relationship among universities, enterprises, and government, which restrict and influence each other. If the relationship among them can be well coordinated, it will bring benefits to the society. In the era of knowledge economy, colleges and universities are playing more and more diverse roles in the economic society, and their status is becoming more and more important. If we can deal with the relationship between government, enterprises, and efficiency, and give full play to the role of scientific research ability of colleges and universities, it will have a great impact on regional economy. At the same time, government and enterprises should also give corresponding support and cooperation to jointly promote the improvement of regional economic quality.

Joseph Schumpeter first proposed the theory of technological innovation. After Schumpeter, Western scholars conducted in-depth studies on the relationship between technological progress and economic growth. At the time, economic growth could not be described just by capital and labor force, prompting a new development of technological innovation theory, resulting in the formation of four schools: neo-classical, neo-Schumpeterian, institutional innovation, and state innovation. The theory of technical innovation considers invention to be a precondition for technological growth and claims that it can be separated into two types:

Progressive and breakthrough innovation. No matter what kind of innovation, it will have a great impact on economic development in the era of knowledge economy. The theory of technological innovation provides a guarantee for technology to promote economic development. Scientific research in colleges and universities is valued by businesses and governments because of its strong talent pool and infrastructure advantages, and it should play an important role in encouraging regional economic development.

Role of colleges and universities in economic development

Colleges and universities have been providing a steady stream of scientific research talents and technological achievements for the country's scientific research undertakings and are important places to promote the development of national economy. In universities and colleges, a growing number of academics are focusing on the link between scientific research and economic development. Due to the regional characteristics of economic development, in order to make the research more realistic, scholars have also made a series of studies according to different regions.

Li (2006) shows that the scientific and technological achievements of university scientific research could promote the improvement of regional economy through transformation. University-based scientific research is frequently the result of a unique discovery in basic research, which is the source of applied research. Compared with colleges and universities, enterprises lack perfect facilities, teachers, resources, and government support for scientific research environment, while colleges and universities have unique advantages. At the same time, colleges and universities play a role in the production of talents and knowledge, so they can maximize their worth by converting fundamental research into applied research. Colleges and institutions in the area should make most of their scientific research services and deeply integrate into each link of the local industrial chain, and exert the driving force of scientific research through university-industry cooperation.

Wang (2016) shows that scientific research activities of colleges and universities can promote the transformation and upgrading of industrial structure in the region, help traditional industries update and improve their technological level, and increase the speed of economic growth. In the knowledge economy age, the process of industrialization is accelerating, and industries relying on science and technology emerge in endlessly. As an important national innovation institution, scientific research in colleges and universities is always on the road of cutting-edge science and technology, which can guide emerging industries, speed up the upgrading of traditional industries, quickly transform regional resources into industrial advantages, and improve the industrial structure and product quality. Faced with the development and modernization of the industrial sector, the labor force of labor-intensive enterprises is decreasing, while those enterprises relying more on science and technology are thriving. In such a fierce competitive environment, enterprises must rely on powerful scientific research forces if they want to remain invincible. Although businesses and the government both play important roles in fostering economic growth, university research has a distinct advantage. First of all, university scientific research has a long-term research foundation, so it can help enterprises transform technology into benefits in the shortest time, and the cooperation between universities and enterprises can also form a virtuous cycle. Second, university scientific research can help some small and medium-sized enterprises with weak scientific research strength and lack of funds. Finally, scientific research in universities is often based on regional characteristics, so it can better fit the local industrial chain structure. At the same time, the industrialization of college students' research results can also drive the new development of emerging industries and professional fields.

Yang and Yi (2018) show that scientific research of colleges and universities can not only provide scientific and technological achievements directly, but also provide more scientific and technological talents for enterprises. In the process of scientific research activities in colleges and universities, college students can exercise their scientific research ability and accumulate more professional knowledge. Therefore, when they enter enterprises and society after graduation, they can easily be competent for work and create value.

Although the overall scientific research ability of Chinese universities has been improved, there are still many problems to be solved, so scholars also put forward some views. Li (2006) points out that the largest issue right now is the conversion rate of scientific research breakthroughs in universities. Most universities do not set up special intellectual property management institutions; internal management is chaotic and lacks certain rules and regulations. This will easily lead to the loss of intellectual property rights, and the operation channels of achievement transformation will be affected, thus leading to the failure of university scientific research to effectively improve the quality of regional economy. Enterprises and governments also lack attention to scientific research in universities. Universities struggle to put their research findings into practice due to a lack of government backing and business collaboration. Universities themselves are not closely connected with the region, and lack some docking mechanisms and platforms, resulting in a low conversion rate of scientific research achievements.

Xu (2018) believes that the layout structure of scientific research in universities lacks rationality and characteristics. First of all, many universities' scientific research activities are not based on the local, and blindly pursue large and comprehensive. In addition, the focus of scientific research is also focused on the comparison between universities, losing the original purpose of scientific research. This directly affects the regional industrial pattern and innovation ability and affects the effective improvement of regional economic quality. Second, universities have little knowledge of regional industry and do not organize scientific research activities according to local features, resulting in universities' scientific research activities failing to truly benefit the regional economy and local industry. Sun (2005) points out the lack of support and training for scientific research talents in universities. Universities and governments do not deeply realize the importance of university research ability to improve regional economic quality, resulting in the waste of high-level research talents.

Yang and Yi (2018) point out that the government should play a huge role in the process of scientific research in colleges and universities and equip colleges and universities with more infrastructure construction such as laboratories and research institutes. Scientific research in colleges and universities often requires huge capital investment. As the research results are uncertain, neither enterprises nor universities themselves are willing to bear this part of the cost, which makes it difficult to carry out many scientific research projects. As the person in charge of macro-control, the government needs to support these factors outside the market that are conducive to promoting economic development.

Yang and Yi (2018) point out that in addition to infrastructure construction, the government should also put forward corresponding incentive policies, such as tax reduction benefits for scientific research projects and certain rewards for talents. Introducing a certain market competition mechanism can also help universities improve their enthusiasm for scientific research and follow the direction of the market. Li (2006) points out that the government should set up a sound management mechanism to help the scientific research achievements of colleges and universities to be successfully transformed into products or industries. In the initial stage, it is necessary to provide a lot of market information for colleges and universities, guide the combination of the direction of scientific research and the direction of the market, and also provide technical or financial support for colleges and universities. In the medium term, it is necessary to help colleges and universities establish a perfect team of brokers and provide a large number of brokers who understand business, law, and market trends, so as to provide support and protection for the transformation of scientific research achievements in colleges and universities. In the later stage, perfect patent protection system should be established to protect the scientific research achievements of universities and increase the confidence and motivation of scientific research talents.

Li (2006) points out that colleges and universities need to adjust their educational structure, distinguish between research-oriented talents and practice-oriented talents, and attach importance to the cultivation of research-oriented talents. To improve the employment rate and increase the number of students, many colleges and universities will ignore the perfection of the education system for research-oriented talents, resulting in the inability to improve the level of scientific research in colleges and universities. Colleges and universities should shoulder the responsibility and mission for regional economic growth and should not blindly pursue short-term benefits. Therefore, more research-oriented courses should be set up to increase students' interest in scientific research, and more research-oriented talents should be recruited instead of just focusing on routine courses.

Yang and Yi (2018) point out that colleges and universities should put forward local characteristics in curriculum setting. In setting up the curriculum system, we should pay attention to the combination of local characteristic industries and increase innovation, so as to promote the sustainable development of regional economy. Nowadays, many colleges and universities are stagnant in curriculum provision and fail to make progress according to the transformation of local industrial structure and the development of The Times, leading to talent training that cannot meet the market demand. Yang and Yi (2018) point out that in addition to the curriculum system, colleges, and universities should also establish a resource integration mechanism, increase academic exchanges between colleges and universities, and encourage sharing and reference. Colleges and universities should integrate regional information and share and exchange it, which is conducive to improving efficiency and promoting regional economic development.

Peng (2015) points out that the educational level of colleges and universities should be optimized. Graduate education needs to be valued, and undergraduate education needs to increase diversity. Diversified courses should be introduced in undergraduate education to make talent training more comprehensive. Postgraduate education should increase the proportion of scientific research, improve the evaluation and assessment mechanism, and increase a series of incentive systems, so that postgraduate training can be more profound. The colleges and universities should attach importance to discipline construction and resource sharing. Talent training system should be combined with local industrial characteristics and the trend of The Times. Only in this way can we provide high-quality scientific research projects and high-quality talents for the regional economy.

Liu (2018) points out that enterprises should establish information and resource-sharing platforms with colleges and universities. On the one hand, enterprises provide universities with original technology and a large amount of funds, which can promote the progress of scientific research achievements in universities. On the other hand, universities provide talents and scientific research projects to enterprises, which can reduce the cost of enterprises and increase their technical strength. Finally, enterprises and universities can achieve a win-win result. Li (2006) points out that cooperation modes between enterprises and universities should be diversified, including joint establishment of companies, enterprises providing scientific research funds, joint establishment of laboratories, etc. Different enterprises may have different advantages. As a start-up enterprise, some enterprises may not have sufficient capital, but have strong technical force. Therefore, they can choose to provide scientific research personnel for university cooperation. In addition, some enterprises are rich in capital but lack technical force, so they urgently need transformation. At this time, scientific research projects and scientific research talents in universities are their important resources. Therefore, it is important to cooperate with universities by providing funding for their scientific research.

Li (2006) believes that enterprises should improve their sense of social responsibility in the process of cooperating with universities. On the one hand, we should pay attention to the development direction of regional economy and follow the trend of The Times and adjust the industrial structure for transformation. On the other hand, enterprises should vigorously help university scientific research by providing financial support and information sharing. At present, many enterprises are unwilling to spend on cost transformation in order to improve their profits, which leads to the inability to meet the needs of regional industrial structure adjustment. At the same time, some enterprises are not willing to trust the scientific research level of universities and worry about the interruption of the scientific research process. Therefore, in the process of cooperation with universities, capital chain fracture and scientific research personnel withdrawal often occur. This is a bad result for both universities and enterprises. Universities and enterprises should enhance trust at the early stage of cooperation by signing agreements, assigning researchers to each other for study, and holding seminars and academic conferences to enhance mutual understanding. The enterprises and universities should enhance the transparency and diversity of cooperation, so as to create more high-quality scientific research projects more efficiently and jointly promote the development of regional economy.

The scientific research carried out by colleges and universities belongs to basic research. How to promote the improvement of regional economic quality is the key to transform the basic scientific research results into actual productive forces and form high-tech products or high-tech industries. With the advent of knowledge-based economy, the total output value of high-tech industry accounts for more and more of the entire regional economy, and science and technology become the potential power to promote economic growth. Due to lack of capital and limited technology, most enterprises cannot carry out scientific and technological research and development, especially the basic scientific research in the early stage, often facing the risk of high investment cost and small return. Therefore, companies often choose the form of patent purchase and technology transfer. The form of university-enterprise cooperation is very common, for example, enterprises invest funds for scientific research in universities, enterprises establish specialized research institutes in universities, and university researchers cooperate with enterprise researchers to develop research.

In addition to the actual productivity boost, university research activities can also provide human capital. First of all, there are a large number of academic talents in universities. They are the leaders of original research, and some breakthrough innovations are created by these researchers, which is an important factor in improving the quality of regional economy.

Second, in the process of scientific research activities, these research talents can also get the opportunity to exercise. In such a virtuous circle, the scientific research ability of colleges and universities will continue to improve. Finally, colleges and universities can gather high-quality talents from all over the world through enrollment. After the training of higher education and scientific research activities, they will be cultivated into high-level inter-disciplinary talents and then exported. Colleges and universities send a large number of high-tech talents to enterprises every year, which can meet the needs of various positions in enterprises. Human capital also plays an important role in improving regional economic quality.

Scientific research abilities of colleges and universities in Zhejiang

Scientific research input ability, scientific research output ability, scientific research achievement transformation ability, and environment and resource abilities are central to properly evaluate the scientific research capacity of colleges and universities in Zhejiang. Liang and Zhang (2014) show that the scientific research investment capacity of colleges and universities refers to the quantity and quality of scientific resources invested in scientific research activities. In general, scientific research at colleges and universities necessitates a significant capital commitment. Because Zhejiang province has traditionally placed a high value on scientific and technology research, viewing scientific and technological forces as the primary driving factor for the growth of productive forces, government, enterprise, and private capital inputs are all more than enough.

It is clear from Table 5.1 and Figure 5.1, the growth rate of investment in scientific research funds of colleges and universities in Zhejiang province is progressively increasing, showing that scientific research activities of colleges and universities in Zhejiang Province are being supported and developing in a good environment. It is expected that with the emphasis on science and technology and

Table 5.1 Investment in university research funds in Zhejiang universities

	2009	*2010*	*2011*	*2012*	*2013*	*2014*	*2015*	*2016*	*2017*
Investment in scientific and technological activities (10,000 yuan)	447,772	596,839	660,167	718,381	722,863	750,889	847,205	972,426	1,091,217
Expenditure on scientific and technological Activities (10,000 yuan)	391,720	539,237	635,506	686,972	675,602	725,606	751,587	873,965	994,536

Data source: China Ministry of Science and Technology, China National Bureau ofStatistics.

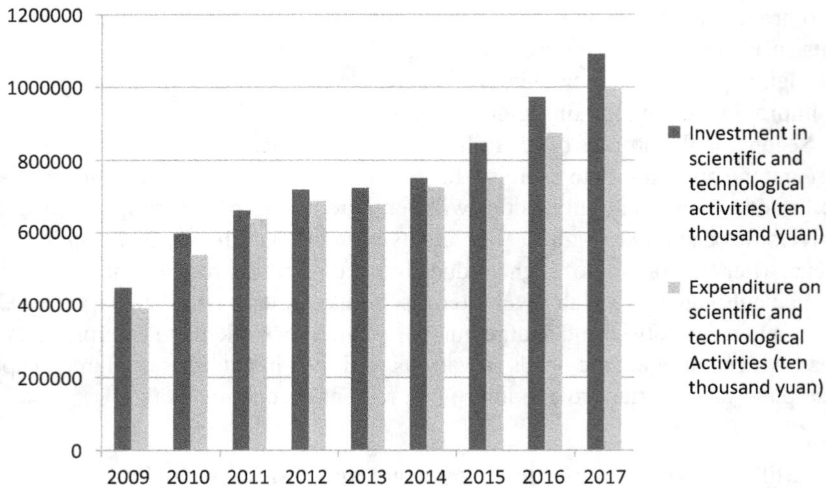

Figure 5.1 Investment in university research funds in Zhejiang universities.

scientific research ability of colleges and universities, the capital investment of colleges and universities in Zhejiang province will be increased by a larger proportion.

Input of science and technology investment, R&D personnel in colleges and universities, and research and development project number are also the important indicators of university scientific research ability. The foundation of academic science and technology research is high-quality scientific research professionals. Human capital is a critical component of innovative research. The amount of research and development subjects in colleges and universities may reflect the capability of scientific research and technology on the one hand.

It is clear from Table 5.2 and Figure 5.2, scientific research personnel and project investment in colleges and universities in Zhejiang province have shown an increasing trend. In recent years, the growth rate has also been increasing, showing a good trend of development.

Table 5.2 Research personnel and project investment in Zhejiang universities

	2009	*2010*	*2011*	*2012*	*2013*	*2014*	*2015*	*2016*	*2017*
Science and technology activists (people)	53,160	56,822	60,216	62,209	64,507	65,855	74,942	87,309	89,458
RD personnel input (person)	12,000	13,000	12,900	13,400	14,200	14,100	16,100	17,700	20,000
Research and development projects (items)	22,235	22,391	22,193	23,938	25,264	25,510	28,514	32,389	36,800

Data source: China Ministry of Science and Technology, China National Bureau of Statistics.

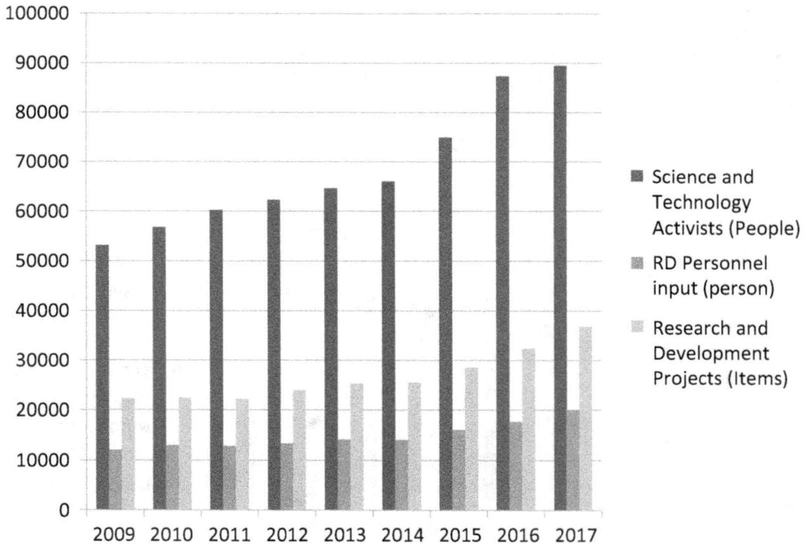

Figure 5.2 Research personnel and project investment in Zhejiang universities.

The output of scientific research achievements is the most direct symbol to measure the total importance of scientific research and technical ability of universities. Luo, Wang, and Fan (2012) show that scientific research activities in colleges and universities go through many links, such as basic research, applied research, and achievement transformation, and each link has different emphases, different forms of expression and evaluation. In terms of basic research, publishing scientific papers and scientific works is the focus of this stage. The amount of patent applications and legitimate invention patents are crucial indicators of how well university scientific research is being applied. Patent is a kind of industrial intellectual property, and the number of patents in a country is an important index to measure its technological innovation ability.

Table 5.3 and Figure 5.3 depict the output of scientific research achievements of colleges and universities in Zhejiang province generally shows a trend of fluctuating growth, and the output capacity of scientific research is affected by many

Table 5.3 Scientific research achievements in Zhejiang universities

	2009	*2010*	*2011*	*2012*	*2013*	*2014*	*2015*	*2016*	*2017*
Publish scientific papers	44,553	46,236	45,876	45,385	43,374	39,632	43,304	49,592	53,471
Publishing scientific and technological works (species)	1,730	1,549	1,533	1,546	1,553	1,374	1,822	2,013	1,949
Number of patent applications (pieces)	5,860	7,950	9,053	10,750	12,085	12,488	15,949	18,063	18,319
Valid invention patent (piece)	7,437	13,086	17,075	9,902	11,831	13,222	16,624	21,081	24,579

Data source: China Ministry of Science and Technology, China National Bureau of Statistics.

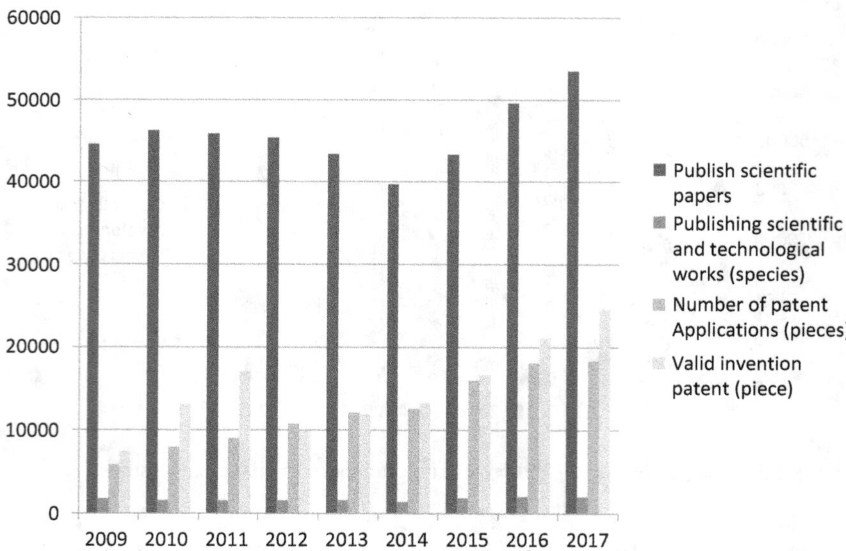

Figure 5.3 Scientific research achievements in Zhejiang universities.

factors, such as human capital, scientific research environment, and capital investment. So there's a lot of uncertainty. Zhejiang province has always attached great importance to the output of scientific research achievements of colleges and universities. The government gives great support and there is also a large number of school-enterprise cooperation, so the output of scientific research achievements has been in the forefront of the country.

Xu and Jin (2010) point out that only by transforming the achievements of scientific research into products or industries can the potential productive forces be turned into actual productive forces and drive the development of regional economy. As a result, the potential of university scientific research results to transform

Table 5.4 Transformation of scientific research achievements in Zhejiang universities

	2009	*2010*	*2011*	*2012*	*2013*	*2014*	*2015*	*2016*	*2017*
Patent ownership transfer and licensing number (pieces)	140	164	245	67	76	112	203	344	613
Number of national or industry standards (items)	15	9	12	17	12	6	16	20	56

Data source: China Ministry of Science and Technology, China National Bureau of Statistics.

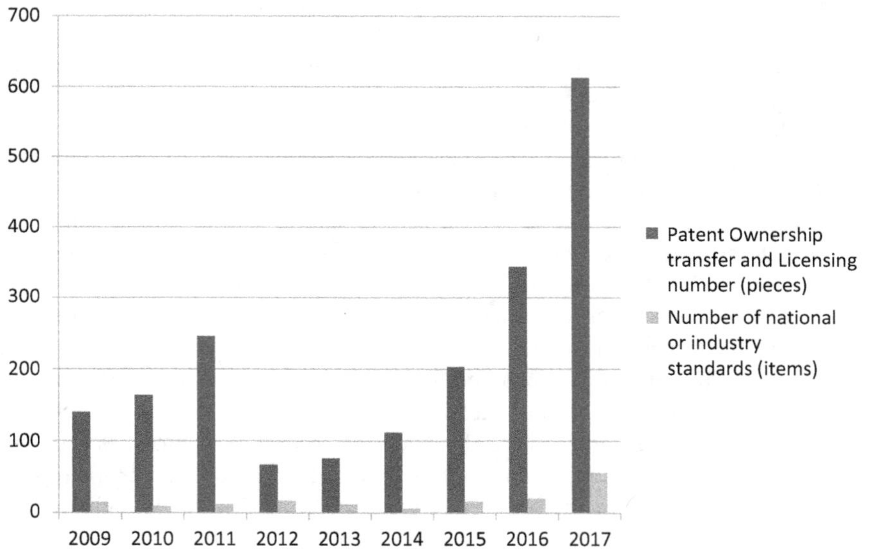

Figure 5.4 Transformation of scientific research achievements in Zhejiang universities.

is an essential metric for assessing a university's contribution to economic development. On the one hand, technology transfer and patent sale are the common forms of transformation of scientific research achievements in colleges and universities. On the other hand, national and industrial standards developed in response to college and university scientific research activities can also reflect the practical role of scientific research in colleges and universities. The scientific research ability of colleges and universities must face the market and society, and transform the basic research into actual productive forces, so as to play a maximum role.

It can be seen from Table 5.4 and Figure 5.4 that in Zhejiang province, the transformation of scientific research achievements of colleges and universities exhibits a fluctuating growth tendency. The number of patent accomplishment transfers has increased dramatically in recent years, as has the number of national or industrial standards. Peng (2015) shows that the resources and environment of scientific research in universities are the basis of scientific research activities. Full-time teachers are the leaders of all kinds of scientific research projects. They decide the research direction and overall planning of scientific research activities and have a great influence on the final success of scientific research achievements. Students in colleges and universities are the main force of scientific research activities, with strong innovation and action power. Most scientific research activities are carried out by them. Therefore, the number and level of graduate students also affect the final formation of scientific research results. Scientific research institutions are important places for scientific research activities. Only with sufficient scientific research institutions and perfect equipment and facilities can scientific research activities be carried out smoothly. To some extent, the number of institutions indicates the strength of universities' scientific research capabilities.

Table 5.5 and Figure 5.5 show all indicators of scientific research resources and environment in colleges and universities in Zhejiang province show a trend of continuous growth with a fast growth rate, which lays a good foundation for scientific research activities in colleges and universities.

It can be seen from each index that Zhejiang province has always had a relatively high investment and attention in scientific research in colleges and universities, and the four abilities are also showing a rising trend. The main reasons are as follows. First of all, Zhejiang province is located in the eastern developed region, and the industrial structure transformation has been approaching the completion stage, with a large proportion of tertiary industry and technology-driven industry. Therefore, the scientific research ability of colleges and universities also improves with the transformation of regional industrial structure. Second, the economic level of Zhejiang province has been in a leading position in the country, the government has abundant funds, enterprises are also booming. Therefore, it provides economic foundation and opportunities for university scientific research. For example, a large amount of government funds can be used to purchase more scientific research equipment, and enterprise project support and talent demand will also make university scientific research full of power. Finally, the number and quality of colleges and universities in Zhejiang have always been leading the country. A large number of high-quality talents gather from all over the country, including not only college students but also a large number of teachers, which is an important basis for the development of scientific research in colleges and universities.

Universities are natural greenhouses for original basic research since they bring together a big number of high-tech skills and scientific research equipment. Although the amount of scientific research input and output of colleges and universities in Zhejiang province is very considerable, the quality of scientific research needs to be improved, and the ability of scientific research achievement transformation is also lacking. In the process of improving regional economic quality, the scientific research ability of colleges and universities plays a guiding role in some regional characteristic industries and high-tech enterprises. Therefore, it is necessary to concentrate on original basic research to lay a good foundation for the subsequent practical achievements. The research content should not be limited to general technology development. Although it reduces risks for enterprises, it

Table 5.5 Research resources and environment in Zhejiang universities

	2009	*2010*	*2011*	*2012*	*2013*	*2014*	*2015*	*2016*	*2017*
Number of full-time teachers (persons)	49,516	50,969	52,296	54,154	56,000	58,076	59,472	60,477	62,357
Number of postgraduate students in school (person)	43,381	47,991	51,846	54,369	57,801	60,511	63,528	67,232	74,404
Number of science and technology activity institutions (units)	575	471	494	524	595	601	634	717	823

Data source: China Ministry of Science and Technology, China National Bureau of Statistics.

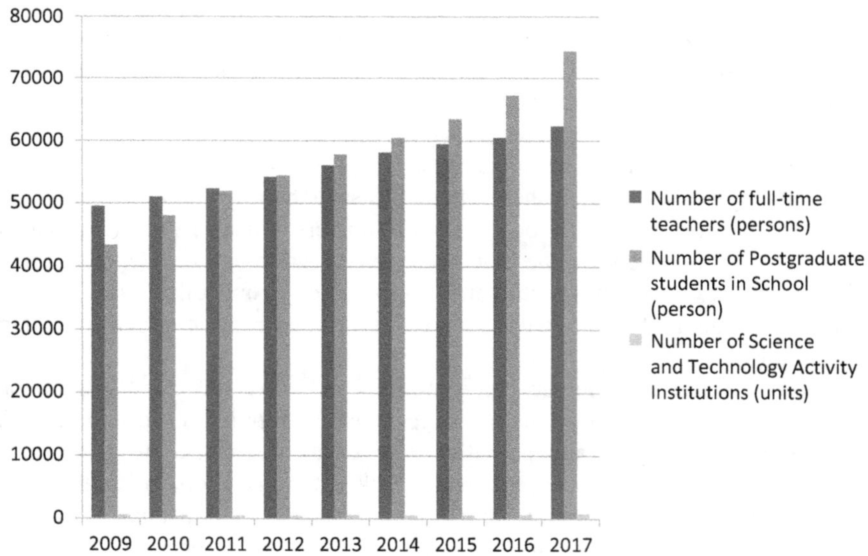

Figure 5.5 Research resources and environment in Zhejiang universities.

wastes precious resources of universities. Therefore, universities should also select some innovative projects with potential when choosing the direction of scientific research activities.

The scientific research activities of colleges and universities should not be limited to the inside of colleges and universities. Only by exporting the original basic research discoveries can the value of colleges and universities' scientific research capabilities be fully realized. Although many colleges and universities have departments and agencies to manage scientific and technological achievements, few of them have set up special intellectual property management agencies. In addition, due to insufficient or unprofessional internal personnel and unclear rules and regulations, a large number of patents and intellectual property rights have not gone through a good way of transformation, which makes many excellent scientific and technological achievements buried. The conversion rate of scientific research results plays a crucial role in improving the regional economic quality of universities and colleges. It is also transforming original basic research into productivity. As a result, colleges should place a greater emphasis on the administration and transformation of scientific research findings, while also emphasizing the importance of original basic research operations.

Pattern of cooperation between university research, enterprises, and government

In the era of knowledge economy, high-tech industry has become the mainstay of economic development. Scientific research activities of universities can not only provide enterprises with the most advanced scientific and technological force, but also transport a large number of high-quality talents. Therefore, the close connection between universities and enterprises can greatly improve productivity. However, the pattern of collaboration between university scientific research and businesses has a number of flaws. To save money and risk, many enterprises cooperate with universities in scientific research projects, which are basic and repetitive. Although this can indeed help enterprises save their own development costs, it not only wastes precious resources such as university teachers and researchers, but also is not conducive to the pioneering and breakthrough development of regional economy. When universities and enterprises carry out collaborative innovation, they should unify their goals and interests as much as possible and strengthen communication.

The cooperative attitude between enterprises and universities is also an important factor affecting the cooperation between them. Universities need a lot of funds to carry out scientific research activities, a large part of which comes from enterprise support. However, many enterprises lack enthusiasm for participation and keep a cautious attitude toward the transformation and industrialization of pioneering scientific research achievements with unclear market prospects, low commercialization degree, and large initial investment, so they lack initiative investment. In addition, teachers and researchers in universities and colleges do not have a strong awareness of market participation and focus on teaching activities. Scientific research activities are not connected with local industries and enterprises and do not pay attention to the development direction of regional economy, resulting in unsatisfactory application effects of scientific research results. As a result, it is vital to develop the sense of collaboration between businesses and universities, as well as to expand the substance and methods of collaboration, such as indirectly transforming them into productive forces through technical consultation and services, patent transfer and other forms. In addition, the company can also provide funds to support the scientific research activities of colleges and universities by setting up high-tech enterprises and establish research centers or high-level research alliances between universities and enterprises, and other forms of direct productivity transformation through university-industry cooperation.

Conclusion

The government should emphasize the value of colleges and universities' scientific research capabilities in boosting regional economic quality, do a good job of matchmaking, and build a suitable platform for communication between colleges and universities, enterprises, and the market. The government plays a dominant role in the early stages of the cooperation between colleges, and the government. It should be based on the planning for regional economic development needs. It helps to bridge development gaps and strengthen technological innovations. The long term goal of such partnership is to develop science education for the social and economic development of the country and its people. It provides relevant industrial information and market prospect forecast for colleges and universities, and the government takes the lead in implementing a batch of original research to help colleges and universities formulate reasonable scientific research direction and improve original research ability. At the same time, information on the market and regulations should also be provided to enterprises to help them make reasonable decisions and accelerate the transformation of scientific and technological achievements.

Perfecting the management system of industrialization of scientific research achievements and perfecting the intermediary service system is an important goal of government work. The government needs maintain policy transparency to transform scientific education and research for all irrespective of their regional, gender and class backgrounds. At the same time, we should strengthen the support for talents, formulate preferential policies and measures, and focus on supporting a number of scientific research teams, incubating scientific research projects, actively encouraging teachers to apply for undertaking various scientific research projects, and mobilize the enthusiasm of scientific research personnel.

References

Cobb C. W., Douglas P. H. (1928). A theory of production. *The American Economic Review*, 18(1), pp. 139–165.

Liu Lijuan. (2018). Research on promoting regional economic development by universities in Hebei Province. *Tianjin University of Finance and Economics*.

Luo Yafei, Wang Haifeng, Fan Xiaoyang. (2012). International comparison on the degree of coordination between economic development and HERD investment. *Science Research Management*, **4**, pp. 116–123.

Lv Haiping (2002). Research on Zhejiang University science and technology innovation courage and its promotion of regional economic development. *Zhejiang University of Technology*.

Peng Xiang. (2015). Research on the supporting role of higher education to regional economic development in Chongqing. *Chongqing Technology and Business University*.

Solow R. (1956). A contribution to the empirics of economic growth. *Quarterly Journal of Economics*, 70, pp. 65–94.

Solow R. (1970). *Growth Theory*. Oxford University Press, Oxford.

Sun Wenxiang. (2005). An empirical study on the regional differences between university R & D strength and economic growth. *Science and Technology Management Research*, 2.

Wang Weiping. (2016). Evaluation of regional innovation system based on provincial data from 2007 to 2013. *Journal of Education, Renmin University of China*, 3, pp. 123–135.

Xu N. (2007). Research on the role of university science and technology ability on regional economic development. *Dalian University of Technology*.

Xu Y. (2018). Research on the impact of scientific research funds investment on economic growth in Shaanxi Province. *Xi'an University of Technology*.

Xu Yingzhi, Jin Naili. (2010). Research on the Impact of government-industry-university cooperative innovation on regional economic growth in universities. *Science Research Management*, 1.

Yang Hui, Yi Lanli. (2018). Research on the promotion of regional economic development by science and technology in local universities: a case study of Qinhuangdao area. *Science and Technology of China Universities*, 7, pp. 74–75.

Yao Xiaoqiu, Chen Yujuan. (2013). Comparison of R&D performance of institutions of higher education and research institutions in Zhejiang Province (浙江省高校与研究机构R&D投入差异及绩效比较). *Research in Science and Technology Management*, 33(11), pp. 103–107.

Zhang, Y. (2018). The US–China trade war: a political and economic analysis. *Indian Journal of Asian Affairs*, 31(1/2), 53–74.

6 Impact of money laundering regulations on banks in China

Mingchi Yang and Bhabani Shankar Nayak

Introduction

Money laundering is primarily the process of transforming "dirty" proceeds obtained from certain criminal activities such as drug trafficking, illegal gambling, and tax evasion into clean form money. The problem of money laundering has become a significant concern in the world today because it is a method used by criminals to make profits. Therefore, if money laundering can be effectively restrained, the scale of criminal activities will be reduced, as this will reduce the incentives to undertake criminal activities. This chapter focuses on China, an influential and fast-developing country that has taken an active part in the battle against money laundering by introducing policies and legislation to enhance their ability to prevent, detect, and control money laundering.

China, as a country regarded as one of the crucial economic centers in the Asia Pacific region, established an open-door policy to the world in the 1980s and implemented a market economic system in the 1990s. This move attracted a significant amount of foreign investment into China's market (FESR, 1999). However, criminals from foreign countries also considered China as a suitable place to commit money laundering, resulting in a vast stream of 'hot' money entering the Chinese market. The Chinese government has recognized the importance of combating criminal activities such as money laundering by enhancing anti-money laundering legislation and introducing money laundering regulations. As 'dirty' proceeds are often laundered through financial institutions, especially banks (Geiger and Wuensch, 2007), banks play a crucial role in combating money laundering (Takats, 2011). Despite the measures implemented to eliminate money-laundering activities in China, the volume of 'dirty' money in the country remains significant.

Money laundering has become a significant global criminal activity that can be carried out across different countries. Money launderers aim to transfer the 'dirty' proceeds obtained from criminal activities, such as drug trafficking, smuggling, and gambling, into clean money using various means to conceal the source of those proceeds (Levi, 2002). To complete the process of money laundering, three steps must be followed: placement, layering, and integration. The first step, placement, involves money launderers placing their illegal proceeds into the legal financial system, such as banks. This is often the riskiest step for the launderer as large

DOI: 10.4324/9781003437307-7

amounts of money need to be placed, which may attract attention from officials (for instance, bank staff). This step can be carried out in various ways, such as dividing the money into several portions to reduce suspicions, using illegal proceeds to purchase foreign currency from foreign exchange companies, repaying existing loans, and more. The second step, layering, is the most complicated step in money laundering. Its aim is to cover up the source of illegal funds by carrying out financial movements of the 'dirty' funds. For example, the criminal may move the money across countries, separate them into different investments in foreign markets, and frequently move them around to take advantage of differences in legislation in different countries and evade detection by law enforcement agencies. In the integration step, the 'dirty' proceeds have been integrated entirely, and the money launderers will receive them in a clean form that appears to be from legal sources. These funds can then be used for any consumption (Reuter and Truman, 2004).

Money laundering was not considered a criminal activity until 1986, although it had existed for a long period (Unger, 2013a). The prime reason why it was listed as a criminal behavior was due to the bad influence it brought to society. At that time, the existence of money laundering was almost equivalent to that of drug trafficking (FATF, 2012). Criminal activities such as money laundering endanger economies and harm the stability of government systems (Yang, 2002). Money laundering has an impact on breaking the stability of financial institutions and systems, impairing investment from foreign countries and leading to a misjudgment of international capital flows (Tanzi, 1996). Based on Unger and van der Linde's (2013) classification, the impact of money laundering on the world can be categorized into three aspects. The first aspect is economic impacts; massive money laundering activity leads to unfair competition, distorts market prices, and harms investments. The second aspect is the effect it has on society; it exacerbates corruption and bribery among public employees who serve in legal institutions because they can make a profit by using their power to help money launderers hide the original source of funds obtained through criminal actions. Concerning political impact, it is worrisome that launderers exchange their 'dirty' money for political power, thereby further encouraging corruption within legal systems.

Furthermore, according to Cassella (2004), terrorists could use money laundering in the future to reverse the process and launder legal funds for the purpose of carrying out terrorism. However, it is difficult to accurately estimate the extent of money laundering in practice, despite the availability of statistical data (Harvey, 2008). According to a survey conducted by the International Monetary Fund (IMF), the amount of "dirty" money involved in money laundering is estimated to account for 2%–5% of the global gross domestic product (GDP), making money laundering the largest industry in the world (IMF Survey, 2001; Schroeder, 2001). Additionally, a study showed that the amount of "dirty" money being laundered globally was estimated at 2.85 trillion US dollars (Walker and Unger, 2009). However, these two estimations are considered unreliable because the methods used to measure the extent of money laundering cannot be replicated, even though they are commonly used in various literature (Barone and Masciandaro, 2011; Schneider and Windischbauer, 2008). The reason for the doubts regarding the statistics estimated by the IMF is that the approaches used to arrive at the estimation have not been clearly explained, and the disclosure of Walker's model is deficient (Masciandaro and Barone, 2008). Nevertheless, the negative impact of money laundering on the economy is undeniable, even though the level of impact cannot be quantified (Barone and Masciandaro, 2011). As a result, finding a proper method that can generate a credible calculation of the degree of money laundering remains a great challenge (Harvey, 2009).

Buchanan (2004) argues that globalization benefits not only the legal economy but also the illegal economy, as it provides money launderers with new financial instruments and trading opportunities, and improves the liquidity of financial markets. This allows them to move illicit money around the world and avoid national controls, with dirty funds flowing to countries with weaker regulations. The ease of setting up and shutting down a laundering system is also enhanced by globalization. Furthermore, globalization strengthens communication between launderers and makes investigations more difficult, as launderers are able to transact across multiple jurisdictions, increasing the volume of legal obstacles. Empirical evidence by Mundlak (1978) supports the notion that international cooperation improves anti-money laundering regulations and reduces the scale of criminal activities in a country. This underscores the importance of promoting and developing international cooperation in the fight against money laundering and crime worldwide (Ferwerda, 2009).

Due to the negative impact of money laundering, a consensus has been reached worldwide to inhibit this practice. Governments in different countries have implemented similar measures for anti-money laundering purposes, either by increasing punishments for criminals who engage in money laundering, thereby reducing the incentives for people to commit crimes, or by implementing regulations that prevent the proceeds obtained from criminal activities from being laundered through regulated institutions (van den Broek, 2011). Since 1988, a Convention prohibiting drug trafficking held by the United Nations in Vienna marked an important beginning for countries to cooperate with each other to solve this problem (Ryder, 2008). Subsequent anti-money laundering regulations have regarded this Convention as a basis when enacting related provisions, even if money laundering was not explicitly mentioned in it (Stessens, 2000). The first time that anti-money laundering was proposed was in a Global Programme established in 1997, with the objective of supporting the UN Convention mentioned earlier by improving the anti-money laundering capabilities of Member States and assisting them in detecting, seizing, and confiscating illegal proceeds (UNODC, 2013a). In 2000, another UN Convention was held which took into consideration all serious crimes, rather than being limited to the drug trafficking problem. Conventions against corruption and the suppression of financial terrorism were subsequently held in 2002 and 2003 (UNODC, 2013b). In the same year as the UN Convention held in Vienna, an organization called the Financial Action Task Force (FATF) was formed in Paris with the aim of aligning countries to fight against money laundering (FATF, 2013b). In 1989, the 40 Recommendations were established to provide specific requirements for combating money laundering, with the role of regulatory authorities being defined and a framework for implementing these regulations being provided (FATF, 1990). These recommendations have been widely accepted and utilized by 188 countries (FATF, 2013a).

China has been considered one of the vital economic centers in the Asia Pacific region. With the establishment of an open-door policy to the rest of the world in the 1980s and a market economic system in the 1990s, more and more foreign investments have been flowing into China, resulting in an increasing volume of sino-foreign joint venture enterprises (FESR, 1999). However, China is also considered to be an attractive country for criminals in foreign countries to undertake money laundering, and a massive stream of 'hot' money has been accessing the Chinese market. Despite the Chinese government's efforts to enhance legislation in all fields of finance, the absorptive capacity of 'dirty' money in China remains quite strong. According to research by Walker in 1998, with the amount of origins for laundered money in different countries measured, China has become the third-largest country with an estimated amount of 131 billion dollars per year (the United States being the largest country with 1.32 trillion dollars per year, and Russia being the second largest country with 147 billion per year). China has also been the fifth largest destination country for money laundering activities, with the United States being the top country with 538 billion dollars of laundered money, followed by the Cayman Islands with 138 billion dollars, Russia with 120 billion dollars, Italy with 105 billion dollars, and China with 94 billion dollars. The amount of laundered money presents an increasing trend year by year. According to Ye, J., et al. (2011), based on data from 2004, the amount of illegal profits through money laundering in China has risen to as much as 200 billion Chinese Yuan (RMB), which takes up nearly 2% of China's GDP. This amount is considered to be underestimated.

Based on Song Yang's research in 2002, money launderers in China use three main approaches. Firstly, mainland Chinese launderers take advantage of branches of financial institutions in the Hong Kong Special Administrative Region (HKSAR) where the relevant legislation is distinct from that in mainland China, making it easier for them to escape judicial adjudication. According to Crane (2001), the volume of suspicious transactions in HKSAR is over 20,000 with a value of about 640 million dollars, which led to approximately 2,600 investigations. However, only 61 of these investigations resulted in prosecutions and a mere 36 transactions were convicted. Secondly, money launderers in China also use underground banks that are established illicitly. According to Liu (2000), the volume of 'dirty' money laundered each year through these banks in China exceeds 200 billion RMB. The third approach involves the relationships between profiteers and launderers and may involve the corruption of public employees. The 'dirty' money obtained through corruption can be laundered by either investing it into legal corporations established by themselves or their family members, creating a false impression that the money was obtained through legal means, or by investing it into various projects or transferring the funds to foreign markets (Huang, 2002).

Banks play a crucial role in combating money laundering, more so than other regulated entities (Shehu, 2005). Since "dirty" money is often laundered through international financial institutions, particularly banks, the banking sector is the primary focus in anti-money laundering efforts (Takats, 2011). However, detecting money laundering can be difficult for banks, as launderers use various methods to avoid suspicion. They may use fake names to open bank accounts and divide illegal proceeds into smaller amounts deposited in different banks. In China, launderers can also transfer funds in and out of Chinese banks by investing in sino-foreign joint ventures or foreign enterprises, despite strict foreign exchange regulations (Yang, 1997). Complying with anti-money laundering regulations is a challenging responsibility for banks worldwide, and there is often a conflict between compliance and the objective of making profits. As a result, banks may prioritize regulatory risk management over combating money laundering (Favarel-Garrigues et al., 2011).

In the past few decades, China has introduced numerous countermeasures to control the severity of criminal activities, particularly money laundering. As banks play a vital role in enabling criminals to launder "dirty" money, anti-money laundering (AML) laws and regulations have been put in place for Chinese banks. Along with other types of financial institutions, banks have a significant responsibility to combat money-laundering activities in accordance with AML legislation and related regulations. Since the terrorist attacks on September 11, 2001, regulations concerning the supervision of cash management in Chinese banks have been modified. China has also established a reporting system for suspicious financial transactions (Liang, 2002). The modified regulations forbid illegal actions such as corruption of public employees who use individual accounts to store non-individual money in order to transfer those funds into their own pockets (Yang, 2002).

China has made significant efforts to combat money-laundering activities. In March 1997, the Chinese Criminal Law was revised to harmonize it with the Vienna Convention, and Article 191 was added to suppress money laundering (Guo, 2004). After the 9/11 terrorist attacks, Article 191 was revised again to include terrorist activities in the predicate crime category. Since April 1, 2001, depositors wishing to open bank accounts have been required to provide identification, similar to the Know Your Customer (KYC) rule in the United States, which allows banks to obtain basic information about their customers such as their names, addresses, and backgrounds. In June 2001, the Bank of China established the first anti-money laundering (AML) committee in China (China News Agency, 2002). Three months later, a special AML task force with unified leadership and arrangements for AML execution was established throughout the banking system in China (Financial News, 2001). In April 2002, the Bank of China convened a conference to discuss ways to collaborate with other countries and implement effective countermeasures to control money laundering (China News Agency, 2002). In January 2003, the People's Bank of China (PBoC) adopted three administrative regulations to combat money laundering: the Rules for Anti-Money Laundering by Financial Institutions, the Administrative Measure for the Reporting of Large-Value and Suspicious RMB Payment Transactions, and the Administrative Measure for the Reporting by Financial Institutions of Large-Value and Suspicious Foreign Exchange Transactions (Schulte-Kulkmann, 2006).

There are various criticisms and concerns about the effectiveness of anti-money laundering regulations. Some economists argue that these regulations may not effectively prevent money laundering and could even be counterproductive. Coase (1960) and Stigler (1964) suggest that laws targeting money laundering specifically may miss the underlying causes of illegal activity. Masciandro's (1998) model suggests that anti-money laundering regulations may have a negative impact on banks' efficiency, which could result in a lower efficiency of legislation. Rahn (2001) goes even further, arguing that anti-money laundering legislation may not be effective at all and could stimulate criminal activity by making it more difficult for honest individuals to protect their assets. He suggests that these regulations could create new criminal industries to evade the new laws, which in turn creates more demand for police services. An alternative argument suggests that the basic legal framework is insufficient in controlling money-laundering activities. This is due to the high incentives for individuals to engage in such activities, as long-term benefits exist and because of the unpredictability of prosecution and the high expenses of deterrence (Djankov et al., 2002). It is unlikely that appropriate legal tools are being used to make legislation on money laundering react and achieve its objective, as assumed in the simplest framework that evaluates the impact of regulations. This is due to imperfections in enforcing the judicial system itself (Djankov et al., 2002; La Porta et al., 2004), as well as the lack of proper legal tools provided by all relevant laws to inhibit crimes.

In China, there is still a gap in the contribution of the private sector to the battle against money laundering, despite the public sector being regulated and the public being motivated through the media to fight against such activities. While banks play an important role in anti-money laundering, it is necessary for China to involve industries in the private sector other than banks in the campaign to combat money laundering. It would be better to integrate both the public and private sectors (Li, 2009) to stop money laundering.

Macroeconomic perspectives on money laundering

The work follows Masciandaro's (1999) macroeconomic analysis of money laundering and anti-money laundering regulations within a theoretical and normative framework. The theory assumes a closed economy. It starts with the initial liquidity, Y, obtained through fraudulent practices in a given economic system, with a fraction of θ being laundered, where $0 < \theta < 1$. This means that, at the first stage, an amount of θY needs to be placed. However, this "dirty" money is valueless unless its illegal source is disguised through money laundering actions. This is why the layering stage is urgently needed to implement.

However, undertaking layering actions will give rise to aggregate transaction costs, including technical costs that arise when adopting specific money laundering technology and costs resulting from resistance to anti-money laundering regulations. The latter costs are positively correlated to the effectiveness of anti-money laundering regulations. That is, the expenses for money launderers undertaking money laundering will increase when the regulations are more effective. The aggregate transaction costs, derived as T, can be written as $T = c\theta Y$, where c refers to transaction costs as a proportion of the total money to be laundered. After the layering stage, the original liquidity has now become "clean," and the new liquidity will be the amount difference between the money laundered and the aggregate transaction costs, $\theta Y - c\theta Y$, which can be rewritten as $(1 - c)\theta Y$. This amount of money may be used by criminal agents in legal ways, for instance, to consume or invest in the market or kept in banks for saving. Nevertheless, there is also a possibility that they use this money in an illegal manner, for example, reinvesting it into criminal activities. Assuming that money is used both in legal and illegal ways, it has to be financed by "clean" liquidity. The proportion of money being reinvested in illegal actions takes up α of the new liquidity. This amount needs to go through the money laundering cycle again and is expected to generate returns of R_i. Therefore, the new illegal liquidity is $\alpha(1 - c)(1 + R_i)\theta Y$. If money laundering operations being repeated again and again in the same manner (values of the parameters being constant), let L be the amount of money to be laundered, the aggregate volume of illegal flows of fund will be:

$$L = \frac{\theta Y}{\left[1 - \alpha(1-c)(1+R_i)\right]} \tag{6.1}$$

Let M denote the multiplier of money laundering, which indicates how much money laundering could expand. To determine how these parameters affect the multiplier, we need to take partial derivatives of each parameter:

a Proportion (c) that aggregate transaction costs take up:

$$\frac{\partial Y}{\partial c} = \frac{-\alpha\theta(1+R_i)Y}{\left[1-\alpha(1-c)(1+R_i)\right]^2} < 0 \tag{6.2}$$

This implies that the lower the proportion (c) that aggregate transaction costs account for in processing money laundering, the lower the effectiveness that anti-money laundering regulations have, and the stronger the multiplier effect will be. Conversely, reducing money laundering requires support from effective regulations.

b. The expected return (R_i) on laundered money:

$$\frac{\partial L}{\partial R_i} = \frac{\alpha\theta(1-c)Y}{\left[1-\alpha(1-c)(1+R_i)\right]^2} > 0 \tag{6.3}$$

This indicates a positive relationship between the returns on money laundering and the multiplier effect, i.e. higher expected return (R_i) on criminal activities enlarges the multiplier effect.

Following the same logic, we can also conclude that the larger the amount of initial liquidity (Y), the larger the fraction (θ) of illegitimate money that criminal agents decide to launder, as well as the larger the portion (α) reinvested in criminal activities, can stimulate money laundering. To push the multiplier up to its maximum value (mmax), aggregate transaction costs need to be eliminated (i.e., $c = 0$), and all of the illegal proceeds need to be laundered (θ). The maximum liquidity that can be reinvested, denoted as Mmax, will then be equal to: Mmax = mmax$Y$.

Although this model is helpful for understanding how money-laundering processes are completed and reveals factors that can affect the global volume of money laundering; it is a mechanical model and the assumptions behind it are difficult to fully realize in practice (Matthews and Thompson, 2014).

Microeconomic perspectives on anti-money laundering

Gary S. Becker's Rational Offender theory is central to understanding anti-money laundering as an economic crime. According to Matthews and Thompson (2014), by following the economics of Becker's theory, offenders go through two stages. The first is the decision-making stage, where offenders have to decide whether to engage in criminal activities or not. This decision is made based on an individual's expected utility of benefits obtained by undertaking criminal activities. Generally, individuals may choose to commit a crime if, after assessing the potential payoffs and the price of being detected and convicted, as well as subsequent punishments once arrested, they find that the profits of a crime have a higher expected utility than doing other legal work (Entorf and Hannes, 2002). The second stage is to trade-off between the expected return of the criminal activities and the confidentiality of illegal activities, which incurs expenses. Let β be the probability of ensuring legality and is correlated with confidentiality (C), that is, $\beta = \beta(C)$.

Money launderers have to buy some confidentiality provided by banks if they are risk averse; confidentiality is valuable to them because disclosure raises the risk of being detected and suffer penalty. Higher confidentiality means lower risk (Walter, 1993). The purchase of confidentiality can be a form that accepting a lower expected return or higher risk than that in a situation without consideration of confidentiality (since C represents the percentage of purchasing, i.e. $0 < C < 1$). Let p_C stand for the price of confidentiality, the expected return on investing in illegitimate actions being denoted as $E(R)$, the remaining wealth after purchasing confidentiality being denoted as W. The expected utility function, U, can be formed by considering the expected investment profits (denoted as $E(\pi)$) and confidentiality:

$$U = U[E(\pi), C] \tag{6.4}$$

The first-order condition will be:

$$U_1' > 0,\ U_2' > 0$$

The remaining wealth of the offender can be written as:

$$W = W_0 - p_C C \tag{6.5}$$

where W_0 is the initial wealth before the purchase of confidentiality.

The expected profit of the crime is therefore:

$$E(\pi) = \beta(C)\left[1 + E(R)\right]W + [1 - \beta(C)]k \tag{6.6}$$

where k is negative (i.e. $k < 0$) since it represents penalty and punishment, the first-order partial derivative of $\beta(C)$ is:

$\frac{d\beta}{dC} > 0$, this indicates that the higher the percentage of confidentiality, the higher the probability that legality can be secured.

The second order partial derivative is:

$\frac{d^2\beta}{dC^2} \leq 0$, this indicates that the positive relationship is in a diminishing manner.

Combining equations (6.5) and (6.6), the expected profits can be rewritten as:

$$\text{У}(\pi) = \beta(C)x1 + \text{У}(K)\text{ъ}(\text{Ц}_0 - p_C C) + x1 - \beta(C)\text{ъл} \tag{6.7}$$

To evaluate the relationship between the percentage (C) of confidentiality and the expected profits ($E(\pi)$), first-order condition is shown as below:

$$\frac{\partial E(\pi)}{\partial C} = \frac{\partial \beta}{\partial C}\left[1 + E(R)\right]\left(W_0 - p_C C\right) - \beta p_C\left[1 + E(R)\right] - \frac{\partial \beta}{\partial C}k = 0 \tag{6.8}$$

It can be rewritten as:

$$\left[\frac{\partial \beta}{\partial C}\left(W_0 - p_C C\right) - \beta p_C\right]\left[1 + E(R)\right] - \frac{\partial \beta}{\partial C}k = 0 \tag{6.9}$$

Assume two extreme cases: when the percentage purchasing of confidentiality is zero ($C = 0$) and when the percentage purchasing of confidentiality is one ($C = 1$).

Primarily, let us consider the first case, which means that offenders are detected by officials because they fail to conceal their criminal activities. In the meantime, it implies that they fail to secure legality which causes their "dirty" activities being brought to light. In this case:

Both $C = 0$, $\beta = 0$. First, substituting them into equation (6.7), we can get $E(\pi) = k$, which indicates that once they are arrested, they cannot obtain their expected profits, instead, only penalties are waiting for them. Then substituting them into equation (6.9), it is easy to find that:

$$\frac{\partial E(\pi)}{\partial C} = \left[\frac{\partial \beta}{\partial C}\left(W_0\right)\right]\left[1 + E(R)\right] > 0 \tag{6.10}$$

This implies that the offenders' expected return on their illegal activities will rise as they increase their confidentiality. The slope of the expected return is positive, so that the expected return curve is upward sloping starting at $C = 0$.

Now, let us consider the other extreme case, if criminals disguise their actions completely, which means they successfully escape from being arrested and can fully enjoy the fruits of their victory. In this extreme case:

$C = 1$ and $\beta = 1$, substituting them into equations (6.7) and (6.9) separately, we can see their expected profits are now: $E(\pi) = [1 + E(R)]W$. The first-order condition at $C = 1$ will be:

$$\frac{\partial E(R)}{\partial C} = \left(-p_C\right)\left[1 + E(R)\right] < 0 \tag{6.11}$$

Indicating that the slope of the expected return at this point is negative, that is to say, the expected return curve is downward sloping in this specific point. Therefore, the shape of the expected return may be an upward convex arc, to check if there exists a maximum or minimum, the second-order condition is obtained:

$$\frac{\partial^2 E(\pi)}{\partial C^2} = \frac{\partial^2 \beta}{\partial C^2}\left(W_0 - p_C C\right) - \frac{\partial \beta}{\partial C} p_C < 0 \tag{6.12}$$

This shows that a maximum exists.

Furthermore, in order to evaluate the properties of the model, we totally differentiate equation (6.8), we can get:

$$\frac{\partial^2 \beta}{\partial C^2}\left[1+E(R)\right]\left(W_0 - p_C C\right)dC - \frac{\partial \beta}{\partial C}\left[1+E(R)\right]p_C dC - \frac{\partial \beta}{\partial C}\left[1+E(R)\right]C dp_C$$

$$-\frac{\partial \beta}{\partial C}\beta dC - \beta dp_C\left[1+E(R)\right] - \frac{\partial^2 \beta}{\partial C^2}kdC = 0 \tag{6.13}$$

$$\frac{dC}{dp_C} = \frac{\frac{\partial^2 \beta}{\partial C^2}\left[1+E(R)\right]\left(W_0 - p_C C\right) - \frac{\partial \beta}{\partial C}\left[1+E(R)\right]p_C - \frac{\partial \beta}{\partial C}\beta - \frac{\partial^2 \beta}{\partial C^2}kdC}{\frac{\partial \beta}{\partial C}\left[1+E(R)\right]C + \beta\left[1+E(R)\right]} < 0 \tag{6.14}$$

This shows that the consumption of confidentiality will reduce if the price of purchase rises.

The numerator of equation (6.14) is negative while the denominator is positive, set the numerator to be: $\Delta < 0$, and follow the same framework, we can obtain:

$$\frac{dC}{dk} = \frac{\Delta}{\frac{\partial \beta}{\partial C}} < 0 \tag{6.15}$$

$$\frac{dC}{dE(R)} = \frac{\Delta}{\frac{\partial \beta}{\partial C}\left(W_0 - p_C C\right) - \beta p_C} > 0 \tag{6.16}$$

The implication of this model is that increasing the penalty (k) for the criminals on their money-laundering activities will increase the risk of banks for engaging in it, which drives up the price (p_C) of purchasing confidentiality. Moreover, an increase in the purchase of confidentiality (C) will further drive up the cost of confidentiality, therefore reduces the consumption of confidentiality and will harm the effectiveness of money laundering which lead to a reduction of the scale of money laundering.

The model discussed above exhibit how the decision of whether to engage in money laundering for individuals being made. We can explore the incentive for the bank to participate in the illegal activities basing on the analysis of the rational tax evader (Allingham and Sandmo, 1972; Cowell, 1990). The bank's decision is making between achieving profit π_A from participating in money laundering activity without being detected and profit π_B if being detected. Obviously π_B is less than π_A and it is possible for π_B to be negative since penalty occurs once the bank is detected. Banks can certainly choose not to engage in illegal actions and earns a profit of π_C where $\pi_A > \pi_C > \pi_B$. Penalty rate (θ) for money laundering should be greater than one ($\theta > 1$) in order to ensure this condition. In other words:

$$\pi_B = \pi_C - \theta\left(\pi_A - \pi_C\right) \tag{6.17}$$

Let π_L and π_{NL} represent the profit from engaging laundering and non-laundering activities respectively, the expected profit (π_R) from conducting both activities will be:

$$E\left(\pi_R\right) = \gamma\pi_L + (1-\gamma)\pi_{NL} \tag{6.18}$$

where γ is the proportion of profit from money laundering. The expected profit from laundering is:

$$E\left(\pi_L\right) = E\left[(1-\rho)\pi_A + \rho\pi_B\right] \tag{6.19}$$

where ρ is the possibility of being detected. The utility function describing the behavior of the bank is described by:

$$E\left[U\left(\pi_R\right)\right] = E\left\{U(\gamma\left[(1-\rho)\pi_A + \rho\pi_B\right] + (1-\ \gamma)\pi_{NL}\right\} \tag{6.20}$$

It is clear that effective enforcement of money laundering regulations and policies increases the probability of detection by regulatory authorities, leading to a reduction in laundering activity. Similarly, if the penalty for money laundering is increased, banks will shift from money laundering to honest activities. Anti-money laundering regulations can help reduce laundering activities if they include severe penalties that have negative consequences for the bank. Such penalties increase the risk of detection, driving up the cost of confidentiality and, therefore, reducing the consumption of confidentiality.

The problem of money laundering has received significant attention worldwide due to its harmful impact on the global economy. While China has actively participated in the international market and made efforts to address the issue, it still requires more time to meet international standards for anti-money laundering. To this end, a series of laws and regulations have been gradually enacted in China to prevent and enforce against money laundering. A Financial Intelligence Unit (FIU) has been established to receive and analyze large and suspicious transactions, and a framework has been put in place to regulate and supervise its operations. Additionally, the scope of money laundering in Chinese Criminal Law, which was previously narrowly defined, has been expanded to include contemporary crime circumstances in China. The investigation of money laundering has been enhanced, and the anti-money laundering law regarding confiscation and forfeiture has been revised, while prosecution and punishment have been strengthened. Ultimately, China has developed an anti-money laundering regime.

History of money laundering in China

Money laundering has existed in China for a long time, even in ancient times. However, during those times, people in China did not have a clear understanding of the concept of money laundering. In this chapter, a chronological account will be provided to offer insight into the cultural, social, and political perspectives of money laundering, highlighting the development and significance of studying this issue. The first part of this section will introduce money laundering in its early form in ancient times, with several examples provided. In the second part, the development of triad societies and their methods of conducting money laundering will be briefly described. The third part will demonstrate money-laundering activities before the economic reforms of the 1980s. Finally, the last part of the chapter will focus on the resurgence of money laundering activities after the economic reforms of the 1980s.

Money laundering activities in ancient times

Although the concept of money laundering did not exist in ancient times, it appeared in various forms, such as through the misappropriation of public properties. Prior to 2000 BC, there were no private properties, and all property in the country belonged to the governor (usually the emperor) by law. In this situation, many unscrupulous merchants who sought to embezzle public properties achieved their goals by moving the assets to remote areas or even outside of the jurisdiction for investment purposes. By doing so, the risk of being reported to the authorities could be reduced. If these merchants were lucky enough to evade detection by the authorities, they would keep the assets for themselves. However, if they were caught, severe punishments such as the death sentence or banishment would be imposed on them (Chinaculture, 2006). There were criminals groups known as 'tomb robbers' conducted money laundering by stealing jewelry or antiques from the tombs of wealthy individuals in order to make a profit by selling them. This was a serious crime during the late Han Dynasty (206 BC to AD 220). The tomb robbers had legal identities in their daily lives and needed to conceal their criminal activities because if caught by the authorities, they would face severe punishment according to the law. To launder their illegally obtained proceeds, they usually worked as antique dealers to sell the antiques they acquired or exchanged the jewelry at pawnshops for cash (PHPWind, 2008).

In the Qing dynasty, Shen He held the position of Prime Minister during the reign of Emperor Qianlong (1711–1799). He became notorious in Chinese history for his corruption, as he used his high political status and the trust he gained from the emperor to accept huge bribes. Corruption by government officials at the time was severely punished, but Shen He continued to accept bribes despite the risks. In order to launder his illegally obtained proceeds, he established pawnshops and sold some cheap items he owned. Those who wanted to bribe Shen He could either pay a much higher price to redeem a low-value item or swap low-value items with their valuable bribes. As Shen He received these bribes, he satisfied the requests of those involved, thereby laundering the bribes. This made it difficult for authorities to investigate him since his superfluous assets could be explained as profits from his legal business (Li, 2009; World Financial Report, 2006).

Links between triads and money laundering

In the 17th century, rather than individuals conducting criminal activities, what dominated the underworld of Chinese communities were the triads. The triads were originally established by the remnants of the Ming dynasty (1368–1644), with the aim of overthrowing the rule of the Qing government and rebuilding the Ming dynasty. The triads had a clear structure, nicknames for different levels of their posts, training programs, different responsibilities and duties in different teams, ceremonies for entering the organizations, strict discipline, codes, and figure signal communication techniques, and identification recognition systems (Li, 2009). Over time, the criminal activities undertaken by the triads expanded, including the smuggling of salt and drugs such as marijuana, the operation of illegal casinos, the trafficking of women and forcing them into prostitution, and kidnapping. The negative influence of the triads was particularly strong in China in the early 1920s when numerous triad societies existed. In Shanghai, the most well-known triad among these was called the "Qing Bang," which was mainly led by Jinrong Huang, Yuesheng Du, and Xiaoling Zhang.

There were several ways in which "Qing Bang" laundered their illicit funds obtained from their criminal activities. According to He (2002), the first way was to collude with political power. They invited Kewen Yuan, the second son of President Shikai Yuan, into "Qing Bang" and offered him a high position in the gang. Secondly, allying with local warlords provided "Qing Bang" with military protection for their criminal actions. This was a win-win situation, as the local warlords provided protection for "Qing Bang" in committing crimes and helped maintain its monopoly position, while in return, they accepted large amounts of funds from "Qing Bang" to fill their military expenses. The third way was to collaborate with foreign forces. One of the ringleaders of "Qing Bang," Jinrong Huang, acquired support from the French Ambassador and obtained the position of Police Commissioner in the French administrative area in Shanghai. As a result, the criminal activities undertaken by "Qing Bang" were protected by both domestic and foreign military forces and therefore developed smoothly. Fourthly, "Qing Bang" had taken an active part in financial businesses in order to further launder their criminal proceeds. One of the ringleaders, Yuesheng Du, started by dabbling in the Shanghai Commodity and Stock Exchange, where he became a board member. Later, Yuesheng Du established the Zhong Hui Bank, whose primary business was helping to launder dirty proceeds. However, the bank was ranked poorly at 47th in Shanghai's banking system due to its sluggish business. The criminal proceeds were primarily obtained through gambling and drug trafficking, and other drug traffickers would be charged a huge amount of commission fees if they wanted to launder their money through Zhong Hui Bank.

In 1935, Xiaoling Zhang and Yuesheng Du implemented a hostile takeover of an important trading bank, Tong Shang Bank, by spreading rumors that resulted in a large volume of money being withdrawn from the bank and causing a credit crisis. As a consequence, Zhang and Du became the governor and vice governor of Tong Shang Bank, and the bank became a tool for money laundering. What was worse, Yuesheng Du took charge of China Bank of Communication as its managing director, as well as holding posts in Pu Dong Bank, Guo Xin Bank, Ya Dong Bank, and becoming one of the commissioners of Shang Hai Bank Consortium. As a result, these criminals had almost full control of the banking system in Shanghai.

The last method used by "Qing Bang" to launder their criminal proceeds was to involve themselves in more fields, such as entertainment, food production, fishing, and transportation. The purpose of these businesses was to conceal their criminal funds and make them appear legitimate. The reason why they had to operate more businesses was to survive in an unstable society where political power was constantly changing. It was highly risky for the triads to rely on a single political power. Once the political power changed, they would suffer asset confiscation by the new party since their illegitimate actions were protected by the previous one. Moreover, politicians who offered help to the triads with the return of financial support from them were not willing to be included in scandals that might ruin their careers. Therefore, it was necessary to cover their funds with legitimate businesses, reducing the risk of being exposed to the public.

Money laundering activities before the economic reform

Following Japanese invasion of China (1937–1945), when Shanghai was invaded, the Japanese invaders made use of triads to acquire intelligence against China. To leave open the possibility for the future, it was important for triad groups to launder their proceeds. They feared public outrage and conviction for treason. However, if they laundered their funds, they might escape punishment if Japan was defeated by China. The triads were used by both the Japanese invaders and the Nationalist Party to collect intelligence against the Communist Party and to suppress the public during the Second World War. In 1949, when the Communist Party took power in China, these triad groups were severely suppressed. As a result, the ringleaders of the triads escaped to Hong Kong or Taiwan, while the rest of them were gradually wiped out on the mainland China.

In 1949, when the People's Republic of China was established, the government attempted to implement a pure socialist economic system, which aimed to achieve a higher level of equality and provide greater control of production to the workers. The system involved the banning of all types of private property. The government drew up three rounds of 'Five-Year' Plans to explore a new pattern of socialist economy. The objective was to achieve socialist industrialization, transform handicraft industries and agriculture industries, and integrate capitalist technology while accelerating the development of trade. During the first five years, Enlai Zhou, the prime minister of New China, stated that "capitalism will be used for constructing the 'New China' and ultimately coalesce into communism".

The 'Three-anti campaigns' took place between 1951 and 1952, targeting anti-corruption, anti-waste, and anti-bureaucracy. During this time, capitalists were punished with severe penalties by the government (Spence, 1991). During the second Five-Year-Plan, the Great Leap Forward occurred, which resulted in a sharp drop in agricultural output. The irregular and chaotic production conditions led to the production of large amounts of low-quality goods at high expenses. For example, steel produced from low-quality iron could not even be used for construction (Chan, 2001).Even worse, the Great Cultural Revolution began in 1966 with the aim of 'removing the bourgeoisie' from the Communist Party. Workers suffered from frozen wages without bonuses, which resulted in a lack of incentives to work and poor production. Confusion and clashes erupted as people went on strike, and unfortunately, influential politicians and factory owners became victims of the uprisings (William et al., 1991).

During the decades between the 1950s and 1980s, Marxism dominated the public sphere in China, with imperialism, feudalism, and capitalism being criticized. It was compulsory for the public to attend anti-capitalism courses, and intellectuals were subjected to socialist education, which rigidly controlled people's ideology. To diminish income inequality, individual ownership of agriculture and handicrafts was transformed into collective ownership (He, 2009). This discouraged the motivation for criminals to conduct crimes such as predicate offenses or money laundering. Consequently, these crimes were not a major issue in society. During this period, China had no interest in either engaging with capitalist countries or building up international cooperation. As a consequence, China was isolated from the influence of the outside world, and industries were self-sufficient businesses without foreign assistance. Therefore, China was not obligated to comply with international anti-crime laws and regulations. Even so, it was difficult for international criminals to penetrate China or take advantage of it to facilitate criminal activities due to the close confinement on financial institutions, rigid social and educational environment, which lowered the incentives for international criminals to undertake money laundering in China. During this period, China was poor and based on agriculture, and people had no incentives to steal or convert money because there was nothing valuable. People who acquired any visible wealth would be viewed with suspicion under a heavily controlled regime.

Resurgence of money laundering after the economic reforms

With the implementation of economic reform and opening-up policies in the 1980s, political education was reduced, and consuemrism began to dominate people's ideology, which stimulated their material desires and resulted in an increase in social problems, including the rise of criminal activities in China. Anti-crime strategies were mainly focused on organized crime, economic crime, and public order, and the confiscation of illegal proceeds was seen as a reward for successfully investigating crimes. However, the terminology of money laundering was newly introduced in

China, and there was a lack of legislation and regulation in this area. Money laundering activities were rarely recognized and reported during this time. The major money launderers were drug traffickers, primarily located in southern and western China. At the time, drug trafficking was not considered a severe harm to China since China acted more as a drug transport link rather than a producer and consumer of drugs.

In the 1980s, regulations for anti-money laundering were implemented in order to combat international drug trafficking. These regulations targeted the finances of drug traffickers, and the concept of predicate offenses of money laundering was narrowly defined. However, at the time, the attention that law and policymakers paid to money laundering was insufficient, as the harm caused by money laundering was not seen as significant. The establishment of the Financial Action Task Force (FATF), which was created to combat drug trafficking, failed to meet China's requirements since drug trafficking was not a major social problem in China at the time. In the early 1990s, China was less enthusiastic about anti-money laundering compared to other countries, such as the United States. It took time for China to better understand how international cooperation worked across nations, as well as the routines and disciplines involved, and to learn how to meet international requirements, despite having opened up to the outside world. Little effort had been made with regard to anti-money laundering, and the terminology of money laundering was not clearly demonstrated in law and regulations (Li, 2009).

In the late 1990s, there was a surge in money-oriented crimes involving corruption, and the problem of money laundering became significant in China. Criminal proceeds obtained through drug trafficking, smuggling, organized crime, and corruption were reported to be a vast amount, which threatened the stability of economic reform in China. According to Yang (2006), the amount of money laundered each year was estimated to be approximately 30–40 billion Chinese Yuan, making China a "magnet" for money laundering. Although the accuracy of these estimates was doubted by Levi and Reuter (2006), they still indicate that money laundering was a noted social problem in China that urgently needed to be addressed.

It is evident that the phenomenon of money laundering has occurred since ancient times in China and has developed over thousands of years, with fluctuations in its evolution. This illustrates the importance of money laundering and the informal value transfer system in Chinese history, in economic, social, and political aspects. Money laundering has been both taken seriously and neglected by the public. It is necessary to comprehend this chapter in order to understand the development of China and to gain more awareness of the difficulties associated with China's development. In a historical view, money launderers sought to conceal their illegal proceeds obtained from serious crimes such as drug trafficking, smuggling, gambling, sex trade, burglary, embezzlement, and corruption. In the past, criminal proceeds could be laundered by either self-laundering or by mixing them with the legal income of operating businesses. There were also other approaches such as using financial and non-financial institutions or the underground banking system to launder criminal proceeds or laundering them outside the jurisdiction. At present, these traditional money-laundering methods are still applicable for criminals to escape from being detected and punished.

Impacts of anti-money laundering regulations on banks in China

The problem of money laundering has become a threat to the Chinese economy and has been taken seriously by the Chinese government. The sources of authority regarding money laundering in China are mainly from primary legislation and anti-money laundering regulations. To disclose, combat, and prevent money laundering in both the legal system and financial institutions, laws and regulations have recently been developed and revised in China (Li, 2009). Evaluating the effectiveness of anti-money laundering regulations is a challenging task worldwide. It is difficult to measure the magnitude of money laundering and how well the anti-money laundering regime works, and the accuracy of previous studies and their measurements is questioned. Currently, there is little empirical work being undertaken to examine the relationship between anti-money laundering regulations and the reduction of its scale in China. This chapter, based on the general anti-money laundering structure of Levi and Reuter (2006), will discuss the effectiveness of anti-money laundering regulations on the banking system in China. Specifically, it will focus on the prevention step of money laundering, which includes administrative and regulatory sanctions, regulation and supervision, reporting, and customer due diligence.

Financial institutions play a unique role in financial transactions, which suggests that the Chinese Financial Institution Anti-Money Laundering Regulation (CFIAMLR) will have a significant impact on financial institutions (Takats, 2011). This impact results from both the anti-money laundering duty of financial institutions to monitor suspicious transactions and the objectives to make profits while managing operational and reputational risks. Clement (2001) suggests that there are direct incentives to treat anti-money laundering regulations seriously, particularly when dealing with reputation and legal matters. Banks are legally required to systematically and comprehensively monitor each client from account opening to account closure. The impact of anti-money laundering regulations on regulated banks can be seen in the active implementation of these regulations and the punishment of non-compliant liable individuals and financial institutions.

Administrative and regulatory sanctions

In recent years, China has made efforts to enhance its AML regulations and enforcement, including the adoption of a risk-based approach to AML supervision and the implementation of new technologies to improve the efficiency and effectiveness of AML monitoring and investigation (Wang, 2013). Additionally, the PBC requires financial institutions to establish and improve their internal control systems to effectively prevent and control money laundering risks. The regulations also require financial institutions to conduct customer identification and due diligence, monitor transactions, and report suspicious transactions to relevant authorities (Wang, 2013). Failure to comply with these regulations can result in fines, suspension of business, revocation of business licenses, and criminal prosecution. Furthermore, the Chinese government has established specialized agencies to combat money laundering, such as the Anti-Money Laundering Monitoring and Analysis Center, which is responsible for collecting and analyzing suspicious transaction reports and providing support for law enforcement agencies in investigating and prosecuting money laundering cases (Li, 2009).

According to Article 46 of the PBC regulation, any actions that violate AML regulations will be penalized in accordance with punishments defined in related laws and administrative regulations. Depending on specific circumstances, the PBC has the right to confiscate criminal profits, impose fines, or give out warnings if there is no corresponding provision on penalization (People's Bank of China, 2011). If the amount of criminal profits exceeds 500,000 Chinese yuan, the offender could be fined up to five times the criminal gains. If the illegal gains are below 500,000 yuan, the fine could be imposed in a range of 500,000 yuan to 2 million yuan. If these regulations are violated, the responsible directors, senior managers, and liable staff will be warned or bear a fine ranging from 50,000 to 500,000 Chinese yuan. These parties will be prosecuted for their criminal liability by laws once a crime is perpetrated. The damage to reputation will persistently affect not only the extension of business but also the maintenance of existing clients. These constraints enable financial institutions to comply with the money laundering countermeasures and execute them compulsorily or willingly (Li, 2009).

The actions taken by the government to resolve conflicts between the responsibility and confidentiality of Chinese banks reflect the effectiveness of AML regulations. For Chinese financial institutions, secrecy and confidentiality are often prioritized over compliance with AML regulations. Banks have little motivation to comply with AML regulations if they are not protected by legal provisions in criminal and civil liability when violating any restraint on information disclosure imposed by regulatory, legislative, and administrative provisions (Guo, 2004).

In 1995, Articles 29 and 30 of the Commercial Bank Law in China failed to clarify that financial institutions were exempt from regulations requiring reporting of large and suspicious transactions. Recently, in line with FATF Recommendation 14, a clear distinction has been made between the responsibility of complying with AML regulations and the rules of bank confidentiality and privacy. The provisions regarding bank secrecy have been revised, and protections for financial institutions and their staff reporting large and suspected transactions have been added to prevent criminal and civil penalties. However, there are still areas that need improvement. For instance, details about compensation for financial institutions when privacy and confidentiality rules are breached for the sake of combating money laundering are not clearly outlined (Li, 2009).

The effectiveness of Chinese anti-money laundering regulations has significantly improved through administrative and regulatory sanctions. According to the AML report of 2006 by the Chinese Anti-Money Laundering Bureau (2007), the PBC completed site investigations of all financial institutions between 2004 and 2006. In 2006, 725 PBC branches inspected 3,378 banks, which represented an increase of approximately 14% in the number of PBC branches and nearly 1% in the quantity of banks inspected compared to 2005. About one-fifth of banking institutions (662 in total) received warnings, fines, or administrative penalties from

257 PBC branches, resulting in a fine of 40.5 million Chinese yuan. This amount was 28% less than that in 2005. The number of PBC branches with administrative authority increased by 11%, and it was reported that the number of banking institutions that actively sought to prevent violations also increased by 10%.

According to the FATF assessment, the PBC's site inspections shifted their focus from merely investigating the establishment of anti-money laundering regulations to examining the implementation of regulations on reporting large and suspicious transactions, customer due diligence, and record-keeping. In 2006, 76% of the banks being inspected and punished failed to report on large and suspicious transactions, 32% fell short of checking customer due diligence, and 18% did not keep records of customers' identification and transactions. The number of banking institutions identified as failing to implement an anti-money laundering internal control system decreased from 74% to only 10% (Liang, 2002). The data demonstrates China's initial determination to combat money laundering. Over a period of three years, China made significant efforts in implementing anti-money laundering inspections by the PBC, which had a significant impact on local PBC branches. The PBC branches have actively participated in the battle against money laundering, with the scale of banks being inspected constantly expanding and a reported reduction in the number of banks lacking a complete anti-money laundering internal control system (China News Agency, 2002).

Generally speaking, the Chinese financial institutions' anti-money laundering regulation appears to be effective in strengthening the AML internal control system by imposing threats and punishment. However, during the first round of national site inspection of anti-money laundering, it was observed that the punishment was limited to warnings, fines, or other administrative punishments, indicating that the primary objective of the inspection is to improve the AML control system as a whole, rather than to penalize poorly regulated banks. Moreover, criminal penalties have not been reported for violations of the CFIAMLR. It is challenging to measure whether the administrative punishments imposed on banking institutions are as effective as those derived from criminal sanctions.

Reporting of money laundering

Financial institutions in China have been obligated to report large and suspected transactions since 2003. However, there is still a gap between the anti-money laundering regulations in China and the standards set by the FATF, such as its recommendations 5–16 that deal with Record-Keeping and Suspicious Transactions Reports. Although the first version of the anti-money laundering regulation was a contributing factor, the duty for financial institutions to report large value and suspicious transactions was not specific enough. This lack of specificity failed to provide clear and precise guidance for financial institutions, such as banks, to comply with these rules in various financial institutions when compared with international standards.

Since 2006, China has formulated administrative measures for reporting large value and suspicious transactions. These measures are specifically categorized and clarified with detailed guidance. The Chinese Financial Institutions Anti-Money Laundering Regulation provides a threshold for large value transactions and numerous methods of identifying suspicious transactions. For instance, financial institutions monitor daily transactions over 500,000 dollars for companies or 100,000 dollars for individuals, as well as any single transfer of cash over 200,000 Chinese yuan. The Chinese Financial Institutions Anti-Money Laundering Regulation has generated numerous methods of identifying suspicious transactions, involving 18 methods that are applied to banking financial institutions (Li, 2009).

The China Anti-Money Laundering Monitoring and Analysis Centre has expanded the scale of anti-money laundering monitoring, particularly with regard to fund monitoring and case investigations. Through the intranet, 296 banks have submitted reports of monitoring. The People's Bank of China has carried out administrative investigations and established a cooperation system with law enforcement agencies, resulting in 1,599 administrative investigations and 1,239 crime clues provided by the PBC. Law enforcement agencies have been facilitated to participate in 2,750 crime investigations, contributing to the suppression of nearly 100 money laundering cases (Chinese Anti-Money Laundering Bureau, 2007).

According to the 2006 Anti-Money Laundering report, the number of reports of large value and suspicious transactions being sent to the China Anti Money Laundering Monitoring and Analysis Centre has increased. Out of a total of 314 banks, 296 provided reports of large value and suspicious transactions (Zhong, 2006). The amount of large value transactions reported to the China Anti Money Laundering Monitoring and Analysis Centre was 134 million, with 124 million being in Chinese currency. This represents an increase from 9.3525 million in 2005, or an increase of 21.78%. As for suspicious transaction reports, 1.535 million reports of suspicious transactions in Chinese currency were submitted to the China Anti Money Laundering Monitoring Analysis Centre, compared to only 283,400 in 2005 and 36,100 in 2004. Regarding the assessment of these reports, over 1,070 suspicious transaction reports had been identified for administrative investigation, including 137 billion Chinese yuan and 1 trillion US dollars, approximately 80,000 transactions, and 4,926 bank accounts (FATF, 2007a & b).

The significant increase in the number of large and suspicious transaction reports suggests that financial institutions in China have considerably improved their awareness of anti-money laundering and have taken an active role in fulfilling their obligations by detecting more instances of money laundering. However, the large volume of anti-money laundering reports may also indicate that the quality of these reports is in doubt. The high volume of reports for large value and suspicious transactions has created heavy pressure for the China Anti Money Laundering Monitoring and Analysis Centre. It has been reported that the Centre lacks sufficient staff to manage the vast number of suspicious transaction reports it receives (FATF, 2009).

The First Mutual Evaluation Report on AML, as recorded by FATF (2007), revealed that suspicious transactions were predominantly reported by banks and postal deposit institutions throughout China. This may be because money launderers prefer the conventional banking system over other sectors, such as securities, despite the banking system's enhanced anti-money laundering regulations.

Additionally, sectors like insurance and securities lack AML knowledge, resources, and facilities, resulting in considerably lower reporting volumes of large value and suspicious transactions. Consequently, the incentive for combating money laundering in these sectors is relatively low. The First Mutual Evaluation Report on AML statistics also indicate that insurance and securities companies are not legally obligated to detect money laundering activities. Furthermore, they are not required to pay attention to transactions involving natural or legal persons in countries that do not comply sufficiently with FATF recommendations. Therefore, there is no mechanism in place to implement anti-money laundering regulations in countries that fail to meet FATF standards.

Critiques of the existing anti money laundering regulations and theories

Criticism has been directed towards the anti-money laundering regulations applied to banking systems. The critiques center around whether the regulations effectively prevent money laundering, whether they are adequate for controlling laundering activities, and whether enforcement of the regulations is sufficiently robust. Coase (1960) and Stigler (1964) argue that laws enacted to curb money laundering may be irrelevant or counterproductive because they target money laundering itself, which is a manifestation of illegal activities rather than the cause. Masciandaro's (1998) model suggests that anti-money laundering regulations negatively impact banks' efficiency. This means that the more anti-money laundering regulations exist, the less efficient banks become, resulting in less efficient legislation. Rahn (2001) asserts that anti-money laundering legislation is ineffective and may even stimulate offenses since honest individuals find it difficult to prevent their assets from being exposed to offenders. He argues that the police create an increased demand for their services by inventing new crimes, which, in turn, creates a new criminal industry to evade the new laws.

An alternative argument suggests that the basic legal framework is insufficient in controlling money laundering activities due to the high incentives for engaging in such activities, as the long-term benefits exist, and the unpredictability of prosecution and high costs of deterrence (Djankov et al., 2002). It is unlikely that appropriate legal tools used in making legislation of money laundering can react and achieve their objectives as assumed in the simplest framework that evaluates the impact of regulations. This is due to imperfections in enforcing the judicial system itself (Djankov et al., 2002; La Porta et al., 2004), as well as the fact that not all relevant laws provide a proper set of legal tools to inhibit crimes.

The theories presented in this research fail to address the significance of international cooperation in the fight against money laundering. Buchanan (2004) argues that globalization benefits not only the legal economy but also the illegal economy, as it provides greater ease to launderers to move illicit funds across borders, evade national controls and set up and shut down laundering systems with greater ease. The availability of new financial instruments and trading opportunities and improved liquidity of financial markets have made it easier for launderers to allocate dirty money all over the world. The globalization has made it more difficult for investigators to track launderers, as they can transact among a greater number of jurisdictions, leading to an increase in the volume of legal obstacles. Empirical evidence from Mundlak's (1978) estimation on the economics of crime suggests that international cooperation enhances anti-money laundering regulations and reduces the scale of criminal activities in a country. Therefore, countries should promote and develop international cooperation in the fight against money laundering to decrease the amount of money laundering and crime worldwide (Ferwerda, 2009).

Conclusions

In the context of China, the society and economy have undergone dramatic changes in the past few decades, leading to an increase in modern crimes, such as profit-driven crime. However, the development speed of political and legitimate institutions did not keep pace with that of the economic and social circumstances, which modern crime relied on. Chinese society and economy developed more rapidly than the political and legitimate institutions that were meant to regulate them. Currently, Chinese political and legitimate institutions are too rigid to adapt to the vibrant economy and society, despite significant changes during the economic reform (Fu, 2002). This has resulted in a rise in a series of social problems, including crimes such as money laundering predicate offences, drawing China's attention to seek effective anti-crime approaches to tackle these issues. In China, criminal proceeds can be laundered through financial institutions such as banks, as well as underground banking. These laundering techniques reflect China's unique political and economic environment and highlight issues within the anti-money laundering system. The most common approach to launder money is by using businesses as fronts and underground banking. Money launderers have taken advantage of the economic reform that lifted restrictions on private enterprises. The external policies of China and its money laundering control policies have been significantly impacted by global superpowers, such as the USA. The political obligation of the Chinese government has enabled the adoption of anti-money laundering legislation and regulations to meet international standards in a brief period. However, imperfections have been detected in the rapid adoption of China's anti-money laundering system.

In terms of prevention in anti-money laundering work, there were ineffectiveness issues with the existing AML regulations. Firstly, administrative and regulatory sanctions were not elaborated upon, and limited information was available about administrative sanctions for responsible financial institutions such as banks. Secondly, the deficient coverage of the AML system in non-financial institutions, such as lawyers and precious metal dealers, weakened the performance of anti-money laundering management and supervision. Thirdly, financial institutions such as banks, who were obligated to report large-value and suspicious transactions, appeared to be inactive in monitoring financial transactions due to unclear responsibilities. Fourthly, the duty for banks to conduct incessant due diligence after the opening of a bank account lacked specific legitimate requirements, and customer due diligence checks were not powerful enough (Wang and Yang, 2007).

The assessment and the effectiveness of anti-money laundering regulations is challenging since little empirical work has been done to accurately reveal the extent of money laundering and its reduction in scale in China. Some critiques have been made toward the existing anti-money laundering regulations. Implementing money laundering countermeasures can be costly, and its expenses may exceed the benefits generated from the reduction of money laundering. There are problems that suggest that anti-money laundering regulations on banks are not working efficiently at the current stage. Firstly, the quantity of staff working in the financial institution unit is not adequate when considering China's population, economy, and large volume of financial activities, although the optimal percentage of the FIU remains unsolved. Secondly, customer due diligence is not a powerful deterrent for money launderers, especially for high-ranking officials, to take advantage of banks. Thirdly, according to empirical research, the quality of banks' reporting is doubtful, even though the quantity of suspicious activity reports has increased. Moreover, the ability and willingness of staff associated with anti-money laundering to detect large and suspicious transactions are questionable. Although it is challenging for the world to combat money laundering efficiently, further efforts should be made by the Chinese government to improve the implementation of anti-money laundering regulations in the future (Li, 2009).

Additionally, there are some areas that Chinese anti-money laundering regulations can be further improved. Firstly, more emphasis could be placed on the cooperation between regulatory authorities and financial institutions to ensure a more efficient anti-money laundering system. Secondly, there could be more explicit requirements for financial institutions to implement risk-based approaches in their anti-money laundering efforts. Thirdly, there could be more rigorous supervision and penalties for non-compliance with anti-money laundering regulations, particularly for non-financial institutions. Lastly, the development of technology can be utilized to enhance the effectiveness of anti-money laundering measures, such as the use of artificial intelligence and big data analysis in detecting suspicious transactions. The implementation of anti-money laundering regulations in China has progressed significantly over the past decade. However, there are still areas that need improvement, such as the coverage of non-financial institutions, the effectiveness of customer due diligence, and the quality of reporting. With the unique role of financial institutions in combating money laundering, their capacity to monitor fund transactions should also be improved. Learning from the experiences of other regions, such as Hong Kong, Singapore, and South Korea, can also provide valuable insights to further strengthen China's anti-money laundering framework.

China, which has the world's largest population, also has the largest number of bank users. Therefore, the pressure of anti-money laundering regulations on financial institutions, such as banks, is immense. The ability of staff in the AML system to work conscientiously, confidently, and actively is crucial to implementing these regulations. Therefore, a systematic training program is urgently needed, especially in remote and small branches of banks. Online training would be a good choice to lower expenses and ensure the widest coverage. It is also important to provide sufficient protection to staff when investigating suspected money laundering cases by detailing how to obtain evidence, freeze, seize and confiscate criminal proceeds. Additionally, promulgating provisions of sharing seized assets would improve the performance of money laundering countermeasures.

To tackle multinational money laundering activities, it is crucial to expand bilateral cooperation and mutual assistance agreements internationally to promote investigation efforts. This will require a reform of the legal system. The punishment of criminals who flee to other countries must be in accordance with the requirements of international conventions, even though it can be challenging to punish those who have been extradited. To combat money laundering activities in the region, it is crucial for Mainland China to establish an anti-money laundering working mechanism with the three Special Administrative Regions of China (i.e. Taiwan, Hong Kong, and Macao). Money launderers often prefer these regions due to their different money laundering legislation and regulations. To achieve a win-win situation, financial institutions and law enforcement agencies in Mainland China should collaborate closely with their counterparts in these Special Administrative Regions.

It is imperative to enhance the financial institution unit and require all financial institutions to establish internal anti-money laundering policies to improve the prevention of anti-money laundering in China. Regular training for staff and efforts to convert underground banking into legal business with sufficient supervision will aid in combating money laundering. Explicit requirements for conducting customer due diligence when opening bank accounts should be announced. Financial institutions should also undertake special customer due diligence when customers use first-generation identification cards, and enhance the inspection of the authenticity of their ID (Li, 2009). It is essential to establish anti-corruption mechanisms to combat money laundering. Many officials in the Chinese government have been reported to stimulate predicate offenses by laundering their bribes and embezzled state assets, rather than controlling money laundering. Given their political position, they can easily provide assistance to criminals to launder illegal proceeds, making it difficult to detect money laundering activities.

References

Allingham, M.G., & Sandmo, A., 1972. Income tax evasion: A theoretical analysis. *Journal of Public Economics*, 1(3–4), pp. 328–338.

Barone, R., & Masciandaro, D., 2011. Organized crime, money laundering and legal economy: Theory and simulations. *European Journal of Law and Economics*, 32(1), pp. 115–142.

Buchanan, B., 2004. Money laundering—A global obstacle. *Research in International Business and Finance*, 18(1), pp. 115–127.

Cassella, S.D., 2004. Money laundering, terrorism, regulation, laws and legislation. *Journal of Money Laundering Control*, 7(1), pp. 92–94.

Chan, A.L., 2001. *Mao's Crusade: Politics and Policy Implementation in China's Great Leap Forward.* Oxford: Oxford University Press.

Chinaculture, 2006. Ancient China's Merchant Groups and Merchant Culture. Available at: URL: http://www.chinaculture.org/gb/en_madeinchina/2006-02/20/content_79481.htm.

China News Agency, 2002, April 27. Bank of China hosted the international conference on anti-money laundering. *China's Financial Daily*, p. 4.

Chinese Anti-Money Laundering Bureau, 2007. China Anti-Money Laundering Report 2006. *The People's Bank of China Financial Service Report*, vol. 2. Beijing: Chinese Finance Publication.

Clement, P., 2001. The Basel Committee on Banking Supervision report on customer due diligence, October 2001. *Journal of Banking Regulation*, 3(3), pp. 206–207.

Crane, S., 2001. Dirty money. *Magazine for Financial Directors and Treasures*, p. 220.

Coase, R., 1960. The nature of the firm. *Economica*, 6, pp. 386–405.

Cowell, F.A., 1990. Cheating the government: The economics of evasion. *MIT Press Books*, 1.

Djankov, S., La Porta, R., Lopez-de-Silanes, F., & Shleifer, A., 2002. The regulation of entry. *The Quarterly Journal of Economics*, 117(1), pp. 1–37.

Entorf, H., & Hannes, S., 2002. *Crime in Europe: Causes and Consequences*. Berlin: Springer Science & Business Media.

FATF, 1990. The forty recommendations of financial action task force on money laundering. *Paris, www.fatf-gafi.org*, 22(11), p. 2010.

FATF, 2007a. *Guidance on the Risk Based Approach*. Paris: FATF.

FATF, 2007b. Anti-Money Laundering and Combating the Financing of Terrorism-People's Republic of China. Available at: URL: http://www.fatf-gafi.Org/dataoecd/33/ll/39148196.pdf.

FATF, 2009. Money Laundering FAQ. Available at: URL: http://www.fatf-gafi.Org/document/29/0,3343,en_32250379_32235720_33659613_1_1_1_1,00.html#howmuchmoneyislaunderedperyear.

FATF, 2012, February. *The FATF Recommendations*. Paris: FATF.

FATF, 2013a. *FATF Annual Report 2012–2013*. Paris: FATF.

FATF, 2013b. What Do We Do. http://www.fatf-gafi.org/pages/aboutus/whatwedo.

Favarel-Garrigues, G., Godefroy, T., & Lascoumes, P., 2011. Reluctant partners? Banks in the fight against money laundering and terrorism financing in France. *Security Dialogue*, 42(2), pp. 179–196.

Ferwerda, J., 2009. The economics of crime and money laundering: Does anti-money laundering policy reduce crime? *Review of Law & Economics*, 5(2), pp. 903–929.

FESR, 1999. *Foreign Exchange Statistics Report of People's Republic of China*. Beijing: Chinese Statistic Press.

Financial News, 2001. September 29. *Security Time*, p. 6.

Fu, H., 2002. Comparative criminal law and enforcement: China. In *Encyclopaedia of Crime & Justice* (2nd edition). Cheltenham: Edward Elgar.

Geiger, H., & Wuensch, O., 2007. The fight against money laundering: An economic analysis of a cost-benefit paradoxon. *Journal of Money Laundering Control*, 10(1), pp. 91–105.

Guo, J.A., 2004. Situation of and countermeasures against money laundering crime in China. In Broadhurst, R.G. (Ed.) *Crime and Its Control in the People's Republic of China: Proceedings of the University of Hong Kong Annual Symposium 2000–2002.* Centre for Criminology, The University of Hong Kong, People's Republic of China, Hong Kong, pp. 40–46.

Harvey, J., 2008. Just how effective is money laundering legislation? *Security Journal*, 21(3), pp. 189–211.

Harvey, J., 2009. The search for crime money-debunking the myth: Facts versus imagery. *Journal of Money Laundering Control*, 12(2), pp. 97–100.

He, B.S., 2002. *The Research on Organised Crime-Mainland China Black Society Crime*. Beijing: China Legal Publishing House, p. 102.

He, Z., 2009. 60 Years of New China, the Financial History and Brilliant Achievements of the Hardships. Available at: URL: http://www.sourcejuice.eom/1270147/2009/10/28/60-years-New-China-financial-history-brilliant-achievements-hardships/.

Huang, W., 2002. New corruption types in China. Paper presented at the conference of China Anti-Corruption Strategies in 21th Century in Beijing.

IMF Survey, 2001. *IMF Publications*. Washington, DC: IMF Survey.

La Porta, R., López-de-Silanes, F., Pop-Eleches, C., & Shleifer, A., 2004. Judicial checks and balances. *Journal of Political Economy*, 112(2), pp. 445–470. https://doi.org/10.1086/381480.

Levi, M., 2002. Money laundering and its regulation. *The Annals of the American Academy of Political and Social Science*, 582(1), pp. 181–194.

Levi, M., & Reuter, P., 2006. Money laundering. In Tonry, M., ed., *Crime and Justice: A Review of Research*. Chicago, IL: Chicago University Press, vol. 34, pp. 289–375.

Li, X.B., 2009. *Money Laundering and Its Regulation in China*. Cardiff: Cardiff University.

Liang, W., 2002. Study on banking legislation of China since 1990s. *Journal of Social Science*, 1, p. 129.

Liu, N., 2000. Crackdown on money laundering. *Economic Review*, 2, p. 78.

Masciandaro, D., 1999. Money laundering: The economics of regulation. *European Journal of Law and Economics*, 7(3), pp. 225–240.

Masciandaro, D., & Barone, R., 2008. Worldwide anti-money laundering regulation: Estimating the costs and benefits. *Global Business & Economics Review*, 10(3), pp. 243–264.

Matthews, K., & Thompson, J., 2014. *The Economics of Banking*. Wiley, pp. 229–245.

Mundlak, Y., 1978. On the pooling of time series and cross section data. *Econometrica: Journal of the Econometric Society*, 46(1), pp. 69–85. https://doi.org/10.2307/1913646

People's Bank of China, 2011. *China Anti-Money Laundering Report 2010*. Beijing: China Financial Publishing House, pp. 2–7.

Phpwind, 2008. *How Many Schools of Tomb Raiders Were There in China?* Available at: URL: http://www.7758521.org/simple/index.php7t377.html.

Rahn, R.W., 2001, January. Why the war on money laundering should be aborted. In: Syverson, P., eds., *Financial Cryptography. FC 2001. Lecture Notes in Computer Science*, vol 2339. Berlin, Heidelberg: Springer. https://doi.org/10.1007/3-540-46088-8_14.

Rahn, R.W., 2001, January. Why the war on money laundering is counterproductive? In *AML Conference Paper, vol. 30. Conference: Financial Cryptography, 5th International Conference*, FC 2001, Grand Cayman, British West Indies.

Reuter, P., & Truman, E.M., 2004. *Chasing Dirty Money: The Fight against Money Laundering*. Washington, DC: Peterson Institute.

Ryder, N., 2008. The financial services authority and money laundering a game of cat and mouse. *The Cambridge Law Journal*, 67(3), pp. 635–653.

Schneider, F., & Windischbauer, U., 2008. Money laundering: Some facts. *European Journal of Law and Economics*, 26(3), pp. 387–404.

Schroeder, W.R., 2001. Money laundering: A global threat and the international community's response. *FBI Law Enforcement Bulletin*, 70, p. 1.

Schulte-Kulkmann, N., 2006. The architecture of anti-money laundering regulation in the People's Republic of China-shortfalls and requirements for reform. *European Journal of Crime, Criminal Law and Criminal Justice*, 14, p. 408.

Spence, J.D., 1991. *The Search for Modern China.* New York: WW Norton & Company Publishing.

Shehu, A.Y., 2005. International initiatives against corruption and money laundering: An overview. *Journal of Financial Crime*, 12(3), pp. 221–245.

Stessens, G., 2000. *Money Laundering: A New International Law Enforcement Model*. Cambridge: Cambridge University Press.

Stigler, G., 1964. Public regulation of securities markets. *Journal of Business*, 37, pp. 117–142.

Takats, E., 2011. A theory of 'crying wolf': The economics of money laundering enforcement. *Journal of Law, Economics & Organization*, 27(1), pp. 32–78.

Tanzi, V., 1996. *Money Laundering and the International Financial System*. The IMF Working Papers, IMF, Washington, DC.

Unger, B., 2013a. The history of money laundering. In B. Unger & D. Van der Linde, eds., *Research Handbook on Money Laundering*. Cheltenham: Edward Elgar Publishing, pp. 19–34.

Unger, B., & van der Linde, D., 2013. *Research Handbook on Money Laundering*. Cheltenham: Edward Elgar Publishing, Incorporated.

UNODC, 2013a. GPML Mandate. Available at: http://www.unodc.org/documents/money-laundering/GPML-Mandate.pdf.

UNODC, 2013b. UN Instruments and Other Relevant International Standards on Money-Laundering and Terrorist Financing. Available at: http://www.unodc.org/unodc/en/money-laundering/Instruments-Standards.html?ref=menuside.

van den Broek, M., 2011. The EU's preventive AML/CFT policy: Asymmetrical harmonisation. *Journal of Money Laundering Control*, 14(2), pp. 170–182.

Walker, J., 1998. Modeling Global Money Laundering Flows. Retrieved from http://members.ozemail.com.au.

Walker, J., & Unger, B., 2009. Measuring global money laundering: 'The walker gravity model'. *Review of Law & Economics*, 5(2), pp. 1418–1418.

Walter, I., 1993. The economics of international money laundering. *Papers on Latin America*. Columbia University: The Institute of Latin American and Iberian Studies, September.

Wang, X., 2013. The UK Anti-money Laundering Legislation Can Be Used for Reference in China [Online]. Available: http://www.chinacourt.org/article/detail/2013/01/id/889019.shtml.

Wang, S.N., & Yang, J.G., 2007, August. A money laundering risk evaluation method based on decision tree. In *2007 International Conference on Machine Learning and Cybernetics*. IEEE, pp. 283–286.

William, A.J., Wong, W., & Zweig, D., eds., 1991. *New Perspectives on the Cultural Revolution*. Cambridge: Harvard University Press.

World Financial Report, 2006. Reveal How to Launder Money in Different Sectors. Available at: URL: http://finance.icxo.com/htmlnews/2006/04/26/844055_1.htm.

Yang, S., 1997. On the reform measures of foreign exchange law in China. *Journal of Liaoning University*, 5, p. 94.

Yang, S., 2002. Money laundering in China: A policy analysis. *Journal of Contemporary Criminal Justice*, 18(4), pp. 370–380.

Yang, S., & Wei, L., 2010. Detecting money laundering using filtering techniques: a multiple-criteria index. *Journal of Economic Policy Reform*, 13(2), pp. 159–178.

Ye, J., et al., 2011. Government plays a leading role in the campaign of anti-money laundering. *Journal of Xia Men University*, pp. 2–4. Available at: URL: http://dspace.xmu.edu.cn/handle/2288/150.

Zhong, T., 2006. China anti-money laundering report. *The PBC Financial Service Report*. Beijing: Financial Publishing House.

Index

Note: **Bold** page numbers refer to tables and *italic* page numbers refer to figures.

Abbott, L.J. 29
Abhishek 66
Aerts, W. 88
agricultural household 16
Alareeni, B.A. 85
alternative 1–3, 84, 93, 122, 137
Amel-Zadeh, A. 85
Anbumozhi, V. 89
anti-crime strategies 131
anti-money laundering (AML) laws 121, 133–139
Aristei, D. 31

Bai, Y. 32
banks 1, 26, 27, 89; Chinese 3; gender bias 37, 38; loans 30–35, 41–45; money laundering regulations 117–140; women entrepreneurs 41; World 28
Bear, S. 29
Becker, G.S. 26, 30, 124
Bell, R. 6
Bellucci, A. 31, 35–36
Benevolence Pharmaceuticals 67
Bialek 64
Blanchflower, D.G. 26, 31
Blau, F. D. 7–8
Blinder, A. S. 6, 7, 12, 14
Blinder-Oaxaca decomposition 11–15, 21
Bowen, Howard 57, 59
Brammer, S. 88, 90
Broadstock, D.C. 91, 92
Brooks, C. 90
Brown 54
Buchanan, B. 119, 137
Bui, A.T. 31, 35–36
Burgess, Z. 29

Cai, D. 36
Camilleri, M.A. 85
Campbell 54
Cao, Lingyan 64
Carroll 57–60
Carter, D.A. 29
Cassella, S.D. 118
CED *see* corporate environmental disclosure (CED)
CFP *see* corporate financial performance (CFP)
challenges 2–3, 26, 79, 86, 93, 119
Chang, Wei 63
Chaudhuri, K. 32, 36
Chen, Lisi 63
Chen, R. 61
Chen, X. 27, 32
Cheng, X. 91
China 1–3; CSR information disclosure 53–82; ESG 83–93; gender wage, rural migrant workers 5–22; money laundering regulations 117–140; regional economic development 97–115; women's entrepreneurship 26–45
China Banking and Insurance Regulatory Commission (CBIRC) 86
China Micro and Small Enterprise Survey (CMES) 33, 34, 37, 38, 44
China Migrants Dynamic Survey (CMDS) 12, 16, 21
China Resources SANJIU: business stability 68; content analysis 72, **73–75**; CSR information disclosure mode 68; CSR reports 67, **69,** 70; features of 77–78; *vs.* FOSUN PHARMA 72, **76,** 76–77, **77**;

medical accidents, incidence of 67; report appearance and analysis **71,** 70–71; report review and continuity analysis 70, **71**
China Securities Regulatory Commission (CSRC) 86
Chinese 1–3, 37, 53, 55–57, 132–136, 138–140; Criminal Law 121, 127; economic reform 8, 18–20, 22; ESG 83–93; 'hot' money 117, 120; labor market 18; rural migrant workers 15–17; SANJIU 67, 78; state-owned enterprises 65; tradition and gender discrimination 9–10; women entrepreneurs 29, 30, 32
Chinese Anti-Money Laundering Bureau 134
Chinese Communist Party (CCP) 1, 9
Chinese economic reform 8, 9, 19, 20, 22
Chinese Financial Institution Anti-Money Laundering Regulation (CFIAMLR) 133, 135, 136
Clement, P. 133
Coase, R. 122, 137
Cobb, C. W. 100
Colaço 54
Coleman, S. 33
collective enterprises 6
Combes, P.-P. 10
Comfort, Daphne 54
Commercial Bank Law 134
Communist Party of China 8, 53
Cong, Feng 65
Cooke 64
corporate 12; financial performance, ESG 83–92; *see also* corporate social responsibility (CSR)
corporate environmental disclosure (CED) 62
corporate financial performance (CFP) 66, 83–84, 87–90, 93
corporate social responsibility (CSR) 29, 87; China Resources SANJIU (*see* China Resources SANJIU); disadvantages of, China Resources Group 78–80; disclosure 53–54, 63–64; economic consequences 64–65; external drivers 61; financial performance and evaluation theory 58–59; firm's value 61–63; growth of 55–57; Integrated Report 54; internal drivers 61; irrelevance 66; negative correlation 65–66; positive correlation 65; praxis of 57–58; pyramid model 54; shareholder value 60; social impact hypothesis 60; stakeholder theory 59–60
Cotton, J. 15
Cowling, M. 35
Cramer, N. 88
Crane, S. 120
credit constraints, women's entrepreneurship 26–28; age and 37–38; in Beijing and Guangdong Province 40–45; economic growth 31; education and 38; entrepreneurial process 30; financial institutions 30; industry and 38–39; lending process, gender discrimination 32; methods and methodological debates 33–36; region and 39–40; risk aversion 29, 33
Creswell, J.W. 36
CSRC *see* China Securities Regulatory Commission (CSRC)
Cunningham, J.A. 29

data envelopment analysis (DEA) 98–99
Davis 57
De Paola, M. 6
Demers, E. 91
Démurger, S. 10
Deng, X. 91
development 1–3, **73–75**, **76**, 83, 128, 132, 138, 139; China Resources SANJIU 68, 78; corporate 57; CSR theory 60; economic 16, 28, 29, 33, 34, 39, 53, 97–115; ESG 84–87, 93; trade 130–131
disequilibrium theory 100, 102
disparity 1–2, 39
Douglas, P. H. 100
Du, Jian 64
Du, Yuesheng 129–130
Duncan, C. 7

Economic Freedom Index 8
economic growth 1, 97, 103, 107; endogenous 99, 101; production function model of 100; science and technology contribution to 97; theory of 99–102
economic policy 3, 90, 101, 104–105, 127, 138

Edmans 65
education 1–2, 5–7, 10, 17–21, 30, 35, 101, 105–107, 131; credit constraints 38–40; MSE entrepreneurs 41–45
endogenous economic growth 99, 101
enterprises 10, 13, 53, 65, 86, 87, 102–107, 114–115; China 55–57; collective 6; CSR 59, 61–63; environmental information disclosure 61; food industry 54; pharmaceutical 65, 67–68, 78, 80; private 6, 8, 138; risk 65; state-owned 6, 9, 65, 90; MSEs, women's entrepreneurship 26–45
environment 2–3, 29, 39, 53–64, **73–77**, 79, 80, 103, 107; economic 138; ESG 83–93; resources 111–112, *113*, **113**
environmental and social governance (ESG): CFP 84, 87–90, 93; challenges 93; corporate performance 83–86; development process 84; EID 92–93; FP 83–84; growth of 86–87; impact of 84; investment 83–84; market performance 84, 90–92; UNPRI 83; Valdez Principles 83
Environmental Information Disclosure (EID) 92–93
Esteban-Sanchez, P. 89, 92
Etzkowitz, Henry 100

Farhadi, M. 6
Feng, J. 61, 91
Feng, Liyan 64
Ferrell, A. 53, 88
financial 3, 26–30, 36, 53–55; CSR disclosure 64–65; ESG 83–93; evaluation theory 58–59; institutions 26, 30, 86, 117, 118, 120–121, 131, 133–136, 138–140; irrelevance 66–67; money laundering regulations 117–121, 130–140; negative correlation 65–66; positive correlation 65–66
Financial Action Task Force (FATF) 119–120, 132, 135–137
firm performance (FP) 83
Freeman 59–60
Friedman, M. 59, 60
Friel, S. 6
Fu, Xiaoqian 56
FUSON PHARMAR 79

Galli, E. 26, 27, 31, 33, 36
Gallo, M. 31
Gao, Y. 27, 32
gender 3, 26, 27, 29–32; credit constraints 33–41, 43; entrepreneurship 28–29; inequality 5–10, 16, 18, 19, 21, 22; rural migrant workers 5–22
gender wage differential, rural migrant workers: Blinder-Oaxaca decomposition 12–15; gender discrimination 5, 6, 9–10; gender inequality 6–9; *hukou* system 5; methodological debates 11; OLS 12, 17–21; regional differences in 11, 15–17; sex determination 5
Goodell, J.W. 91
governance 54, 81, 85–86, 88–90, 92
Great Cultural Revolution 131
growth pole theory 102
Guenther, T. 89, 91
Gul, F.A. 29
Guo, Lan 63
Guo, X. 61
Guoyou, Q. 90

Hąbek 57
Haifeng, Wang 109
Haiping, Lv 98
Hamdan, A. 85
Han Dynasty 128
Han, J. 89
Haniffa 64
Hansen Pharmaceuticals 67
Hayashi, F. 36
He, Shen 128–129
Hillier, David 54
Houweling, T. A. J. 6
Hu, H. 27
Hu, Q. 29–30
Hu, Z. 32
Huang, Chao 63
Huang, J. 59
Huang, X. 29
Hui, Yang 97, 98, 104–105
Hung 65
Huse, M. 29

income disparities 1
inequality 1–3; gender 5–10, 16, 18, 19, 21, 22; income 10, 131
institutions 102–104, 112; financial 26, 30, 86, 117, 118, 120–121, 131, 133–136, 138–140; labor market 7–8;

peer 63; political and legitimate 138; third-party 79, 81
International Monetary Fund (IMF) 118–119
Ismail, R. 6

Jiang, Yanjun 66
Jingge, Guo 16, 17
Johansson, M. 6
Johnson, E. 1
Jones, Peter 54

Kahn, L. M. 7–8
Kang, Y. 58
Kangtai Pharmaceuticals 67
Karagozoglu, N. 88
Katz, K. 6
Kim, J. 88, 90, 92
Klapper, L.F. 30

Landi, G. 90–91
Lanli, Yi 98, 104–105
Le, L.H. 32, 36
Lee, C. 61
legitimacy theory 61
Leon, F. 36
Levi, M. 132, 133
Li Yuhong 98, 99, 103–106
Li, Changqing 63
Li, P. 91
Li, S. 10, 32
Li, W. 29
Li, Ying 56
Li, Zheng 58
Lian, Chunhui 63
Liang, H. 88
Lijuan, Liu 100, 106
Lin, B. 66
Linde, D. van der 118
Lindell, M. 88
Liu, N. 120
Liu, P.-W. 7, 8, 10
Liu, Shenghua 56
Liu, X. 30, 89
Liu, Y. 30
Locke, S. 26, 31
logit regression model 35, 36
Loretto, W. 7
Lu, Z. 8–9, 11
Luan, C. 89, 92
Lückerath-Rovers, M. 29
Luo, X. 7
Lys 64
Lyu, Y. 37–42

Ma, X. 32
macroeconomic perspectives, money laundering regulations 122–124
Magnani, E. 9, 11
Maignan, Isabelle 53, 54
Maloni 54
Malthus 101
Mandel, H. 8
Margolis, J.D. 87–88
Market Leninism 1
market performance 84, 90–92
Marlow, S. 29
Marmot, M. 6
Martinez Dy, A. 29
Marzuki Amiruddin, A. 87
Mascia, D.V. 27, 31, 36
Masciandro, D. 122, 137
Matthews, K. 124
McGregor, R. 1
McGuire 58
McKinsey 83
McWilliams 66
Mellahi 61
Meng, X. 7, 8, 10
micro and small enterprises (MSEs) *see* women's entrepreneurship
microeconomic perspectives, money laundering regulations 124–128
Ming dynasty 129
Mitter, R. 1
money laundering: administrative and regulatory sanctions 133–135; in ancient times 128–129; anti-money 119, 122; on banks 133; Chinese Criminal Law 121; critiques of 137–138; 'dirty' funds 118, 120–121; 'dirty' proceeds 117; economic reform 130–132; empirical evidence 119; history of 128; macroeconomic perspectives 122–124; microeconomic perspectives 124–128; report 135–137; tax evasion 117; triads 129–130
monopoly capitalism 2
Moro, A. 26, 31, 33, 36
Muhammad 54
multinational money laundering activities 140
Mundlak, Y. 119, 138
Muravyev, A. 31, 32, 45
Murillo Huertas, I. P. 8, 11
Mussida, C. 6

Naili, Jin 99, 110
National Bureau of Statistics of China 15
National Health Commission 15
Naughton 64
Neider, L. 26
Neumark, D. 14
Ni, Hengwang 63
Nielsen, S. 29
Nyman, H. 6

O'Connell, V. 88
Oaxaca, R. 6, 7, 12, 14
ordinary least squares (OLS) 12

Pan Yue 2–3
Paolone, F. 89, 92
Parker, S.C. 30
Pavelin, S. 88, 90
penalty rate 127
performance culture 77, 78
Pham, T. 27, 31
pharmaceutical industry 62
Piazzalunga, D. 6
Picchio, M. 6
planning 112, 115
Polo 54
private enterprises 6
Protsch, P. 6

Qing Bang 130–131
Qing dynasty 128
Qiu, Y. 89

Rahn, R.W. 122, 137
Ralston, David A. 54
Ramos, R. 8, 11
regional 3, 27, 33; economic development 39, 97–115; gender wage differential, rural migrant workers 5–22
regional balanced development theory 100–102
regional disequilibrium theory 100, 102
regional economic development: 19th CPC National Congress 97; colleges and universities role 103–107; cooperation pattern 114–115; correlation analysis 99; DEA 98–99; disequilibrium theory 100, 102; growth pole theory 102; modern innovation theory 100; intermediary service system 115; political factors 99; principal component analysis 98; surplus 100–101; triple helix theory 100, 102; Zhejiang Province 97; Zhejiang universities 107–114, *108–111,* **108–111, 113,** *113*
regional uneven development theory 100
regulations 104; CSR 53–66, 84, 85, 87, 88, 90, 93; market 115; money laundering 117–140
Renneboog, L. 88
resident household 16
responsibility 129, 134, 138; *see also* corporate social responsibility (CSR)
return on equity (ROE) 92
return on net assets 58
return on total assets 58
Reuter, P. 132, 133
Robb, A. 33
Rossi, S.P.S. 27, 31, 36
Rui, Xiang 58
Rupley 54
rural: microcredit recipients 32; migrant workers 5–22

Saleh, M. 88
Schäfer, D. 31
Schumpeter, Joseph 100, 102
Sciarelli, M. 90–91
Scoppa, V. 6
Semyonov, M. 8
Serafeim, G. 85
Shamsuddeen 54
Shanghai Stock Exchange (SSE) 33, 62, 86, 87
Shareholder Supremacy 59
Shelton, Oliver 57
Shen, D. 91
Shenzhen Stock Exchange (SZSE) 55, 56, 62, 67, 86
Siegel 66
Simão 54–55
Simon, H. 8, 11
small 11, 19, 103, 107; women's entrepreneurship 26–45
Smith, Adam 100–101
Smith, M. 87
social 2–3, 106, 115, 131, 132, 138; cultural gender bias 31; security 12; *see also* corporate social responsibility (CSR); environmental and social governance (ESG)
socialist system 18–19, 22
Solow, R. 100
Song, S. 8–9, 11
special economic zones (SEZ) 2
Srinidhi, B. 29

Stakeholder Doctrine 59
stakeholder theory 59–60
state 1–3, 10, 11, 31, 56, 98, 102, 140
state-owned enterprises 6, 9, 31, 65, 90
statistical discrimination 28
Stefańczyk, J.K. 32, 36
Stigler, G. 122, 137
sustainability 84, 86, 91–92

Talavera, O. 27, 31
Tang, M. 89, 92
taste-based discrimination 28
Taylor, S. 6
Tharenou, P. 29
Thompson, J. 124
'Three-anti campaigns' 132
Thrikawala, S. 32, 35–36
triple helix theory 100, 102
Trumpp, C. 89, 91
two-channel promotion system 77

Unger, B. 118

Walker, J. 119, 120
Walsh, J.P. 87–88
Wang 65
Wang, H. 32, 64
Wang, J. 10
Wang, Min 63
Wang, R. Y. 20
Wang, Shihui 65
Wang, Wencheng 65
Wang, Yuetang 63
Wei, Zhihua 63
Weichselbaumer, D. 8
Weiping, Wang 97, 98, 103
Wellalage, N.H. 26, 31, 32, 35–36
Wenxiang, Sun 99, 104
Western feminism 9–10
Winter-Ebmer, R. 8
women 5–9, 16, 19, 20, 129; entrepreneurship 26–45
women's entrepreneurship: age constraints 37–38; Beijing 40–44; in China 37; credit constraints 29–33; education constraints 38; gender and 28–29; Guangdong Province 27–28, 33, 40–44; industry constraint 38–39; methods and methodological debates 33–36; region constraint 39–40; risk levels 26, 27
women-led micro and small enterprises *see* women's entrepreneurship
World Bank 28–29
World Economic Forum 28
Wu 56
Wu, Chenlei 76
Wu, Danhong 63
Wu, Haixia 63
Wye, C.-K. 6

Xiang, Peng 105, 111–112
Xiang, Rui 58
Xiao, Xiang 64
Xiao, Z. 60
Xiaoqiu, Yao 97, 98
Xiaoyang, Fan 109
Xiaoyang, Zhang 107
Xie, J. 89
Xu 68–72
Xu, N. 98–100
Xu, Shangkun 59
Xu, Y. 99, 100, 104

Yafei, Luo 109
Yahya, K. 87
Yan, J. 27, 32
Yan, Liang 107
Yan, S. 61
Yang 132
Yang, Hanming 63
Yang, M. 20
Yang, Rudai 59
Yang, Song 120
Ye, J. 120
Yin, Kaiguo 65
Yingzhi, Xu 99, 110
Yujuan, Chen 97, 98

Zedong, Mao 29
Zhang, J. 7, 8, 10
Zhang, N. 29–30
Zhang, Xiaoling 130
Zhang, Y. 100
Zhang, Zhaoguo 66
Zhao, Tianjiao 64
Zhejiang universities, regional economic development 107–114, *108–111*, **108–111, 113,** *113*
Zheng, Jun 65
Zheng, Li 58
Zhou, D. 29–30
Zhou, Enlai 131–132
Zhu, J. 29
Zhu, R. 9, 11
Zhu, Tingxuan 56
Zhu, Wenli 56
Zweimüller, M. 8

For Product Safety Concerns and Information please contact our EU representative GPSR@taylorandfrancis.com
Taylor & Francis Verlag GmbH, Kaufingerstraße 24, 80331 München, Germany

www.ingramcontent.com/pod-product-compliance
Lightning Source LLC
LaVergne TN
LVHW010648300926
849161LV00005B/1061

* 9 7 8 1 0 3 2 5 6 8 1 7 1 *